SERGiO NEXT MAD BOOK

EDITED by NICK MEGLIN

A Time Warner Company

If you purchase this book without a cover you should be aware that this book may have been stolen property and reported as "unsold and destroyed" to the publisher. In such case neither the author nor the publisher has received any payment for this "stripped book."

WARNER BOOKS EDITION

Copyright © 1992 by Sergio Aragonés and E.C. Publications, Inc.
All rights reserved.
No part of this book may be reproduced without permission.
For information address:
E.C. Publications, Inc.
485 Madison Avenue
New York, N.Y. 10022

Title "MAD" used with permission of its owner,
E.C. Publications, Inc.

This Warner Books Edition is published by
arrangement with E.C. Publications, Inc.

Warner Books, Inc.
1271 Avenue of the Americas
New York, N.Y. 10020

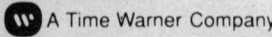 A Time Warner Company

Printed in the United States of America

First Printing: August, 1992

10 9 8 7 6 5 4 3 2 1

ATTENTION SCHOOLS

WARNER books are available at quantity discounts with bulk purchase for educational use. For information, please write to: SPECIAL SALES DEPARTMENT, WARNER BOOKS, 1271 AVENUE OF THE AMERICAS, NEW YORK, N.Y. 10020.

TO
MARK EVANIER !

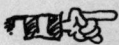

(2)

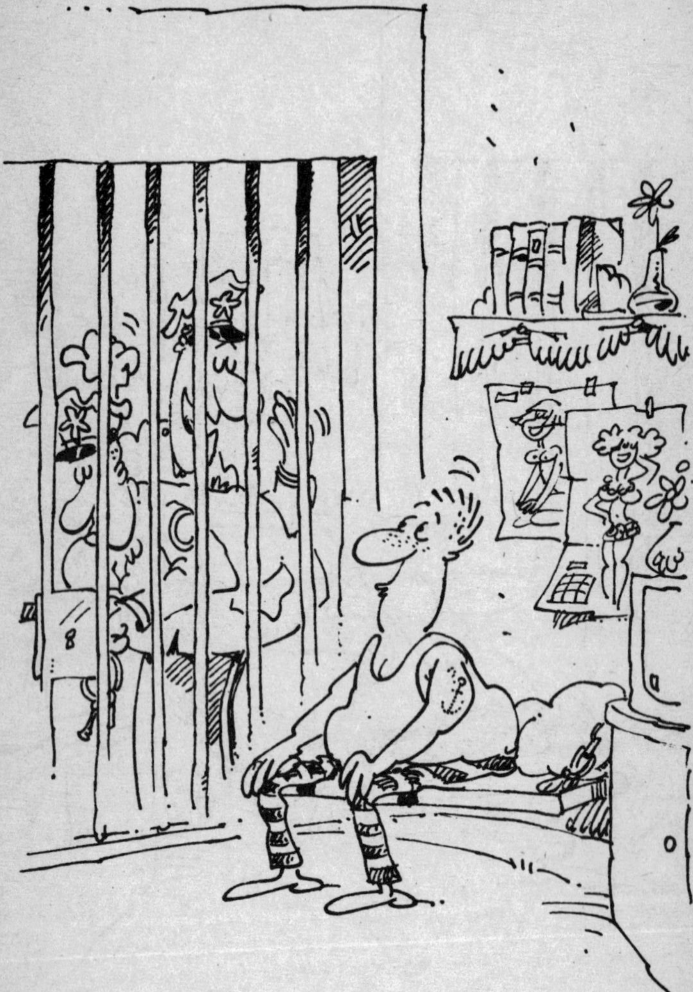

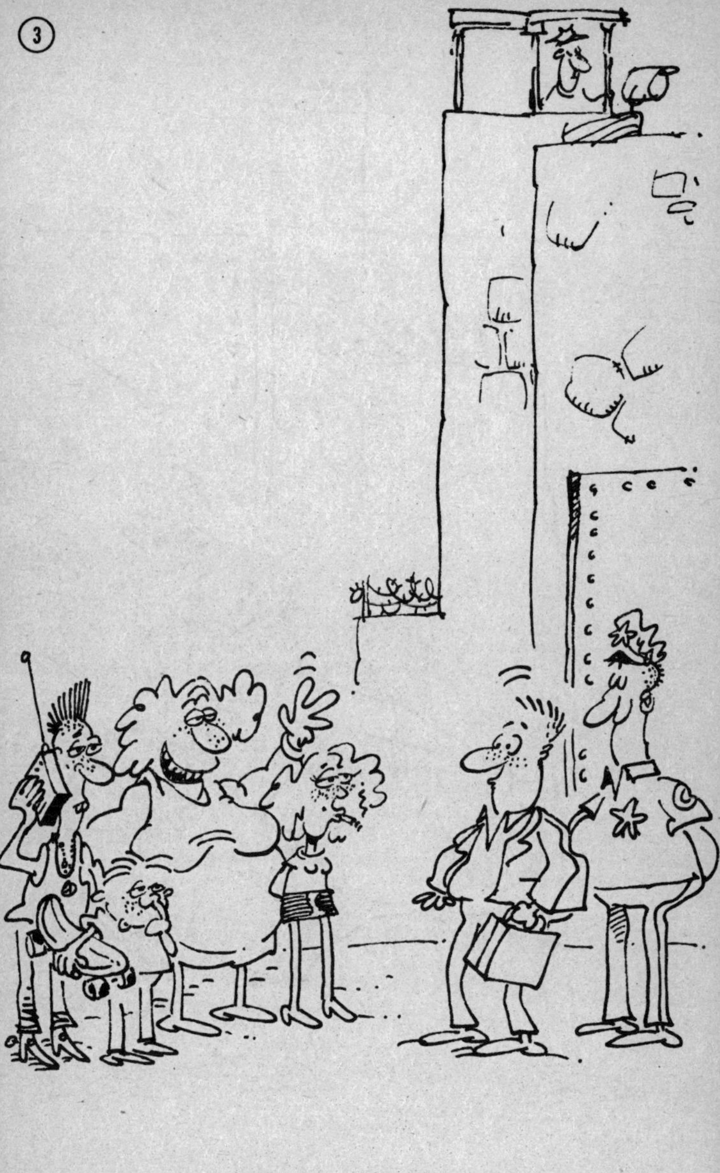

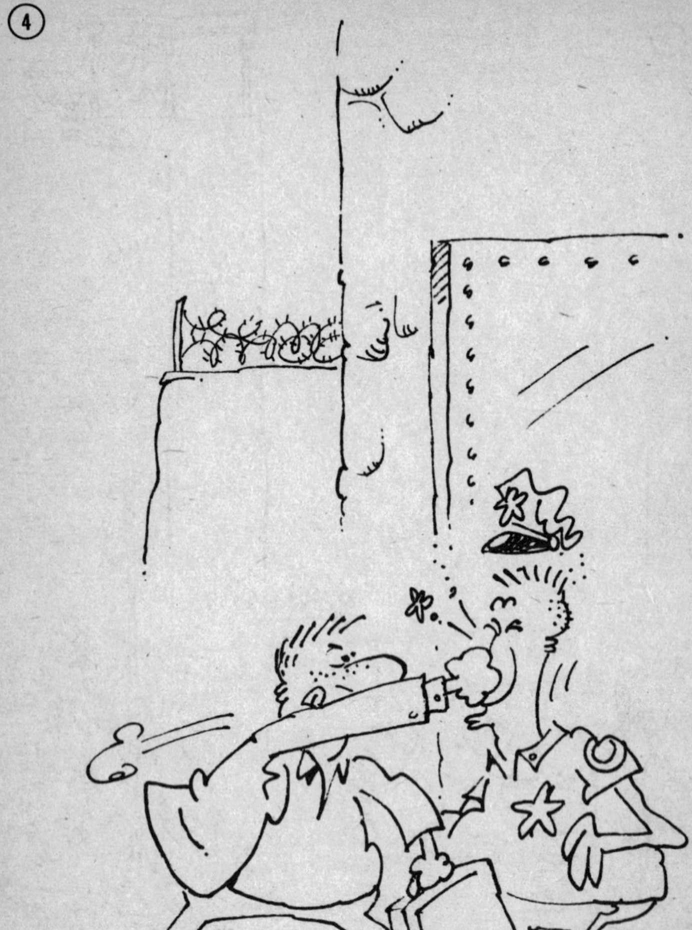
4

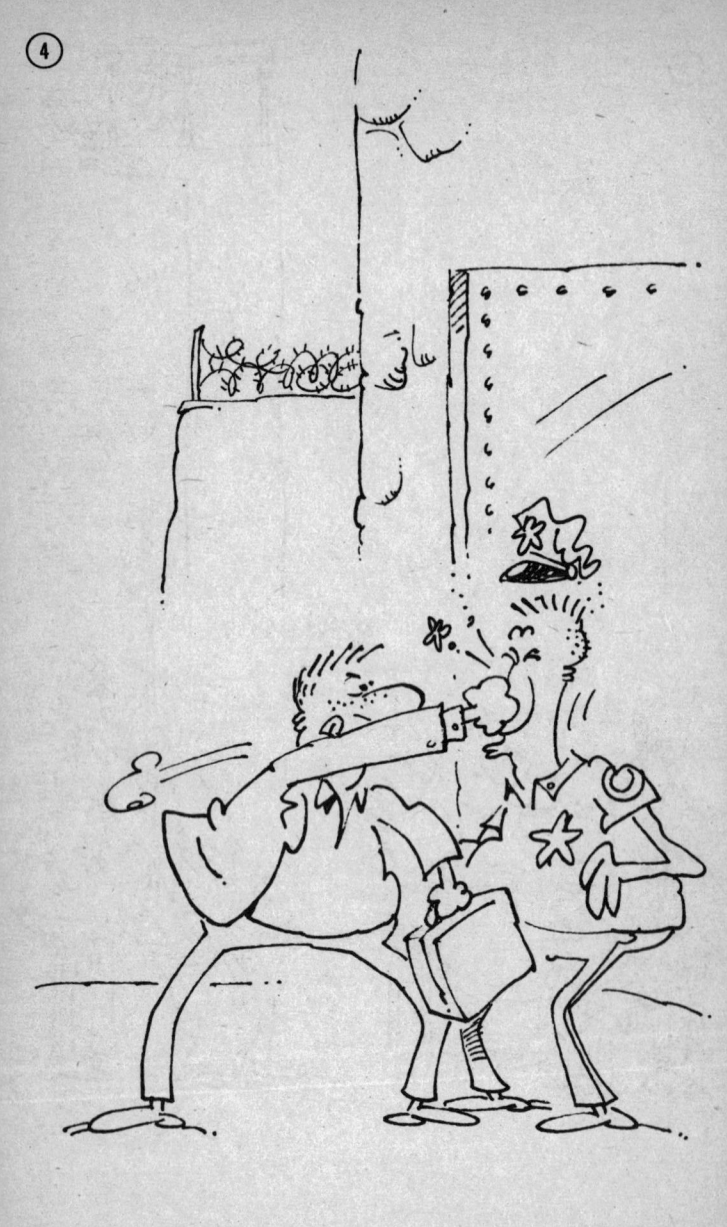

5

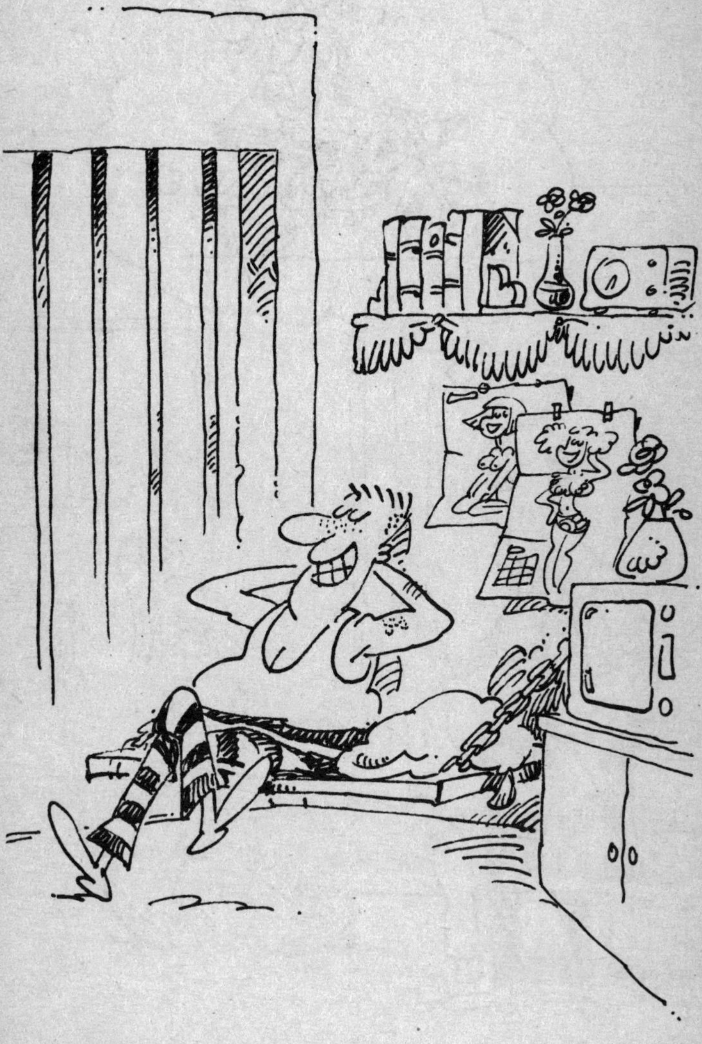

(1)

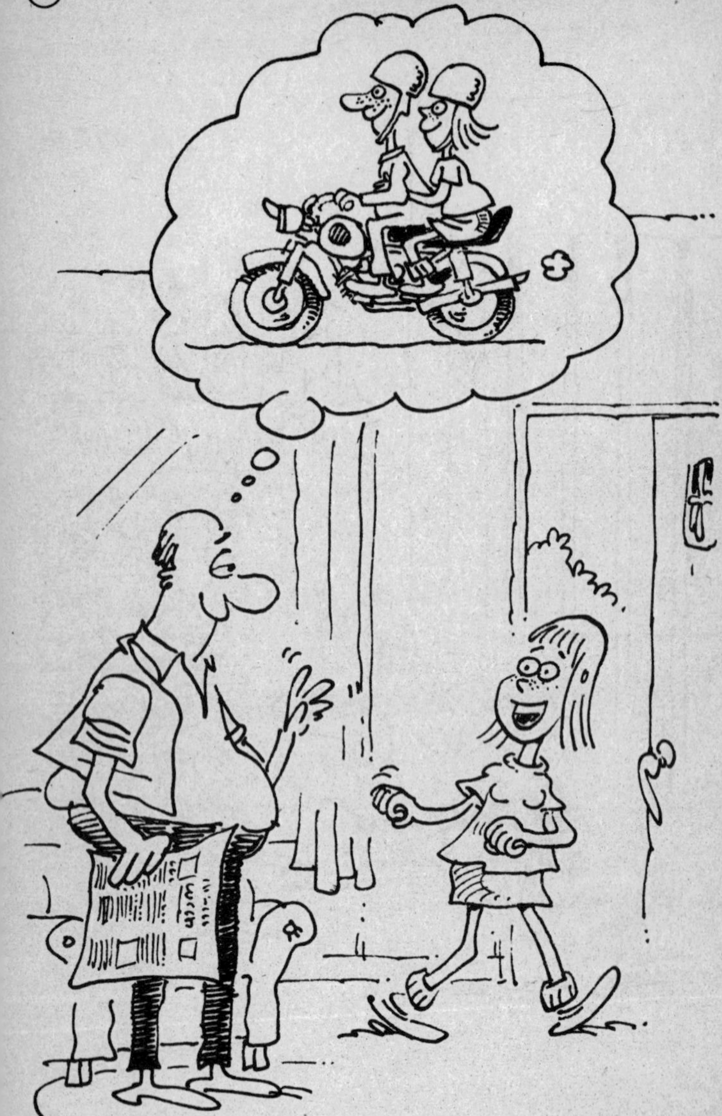

2

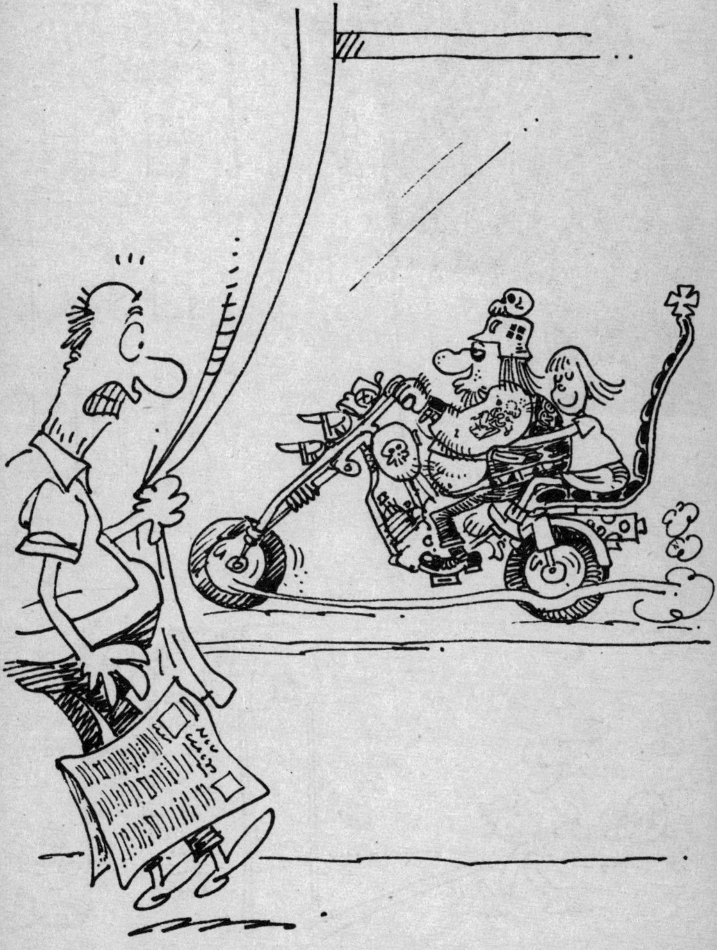

1

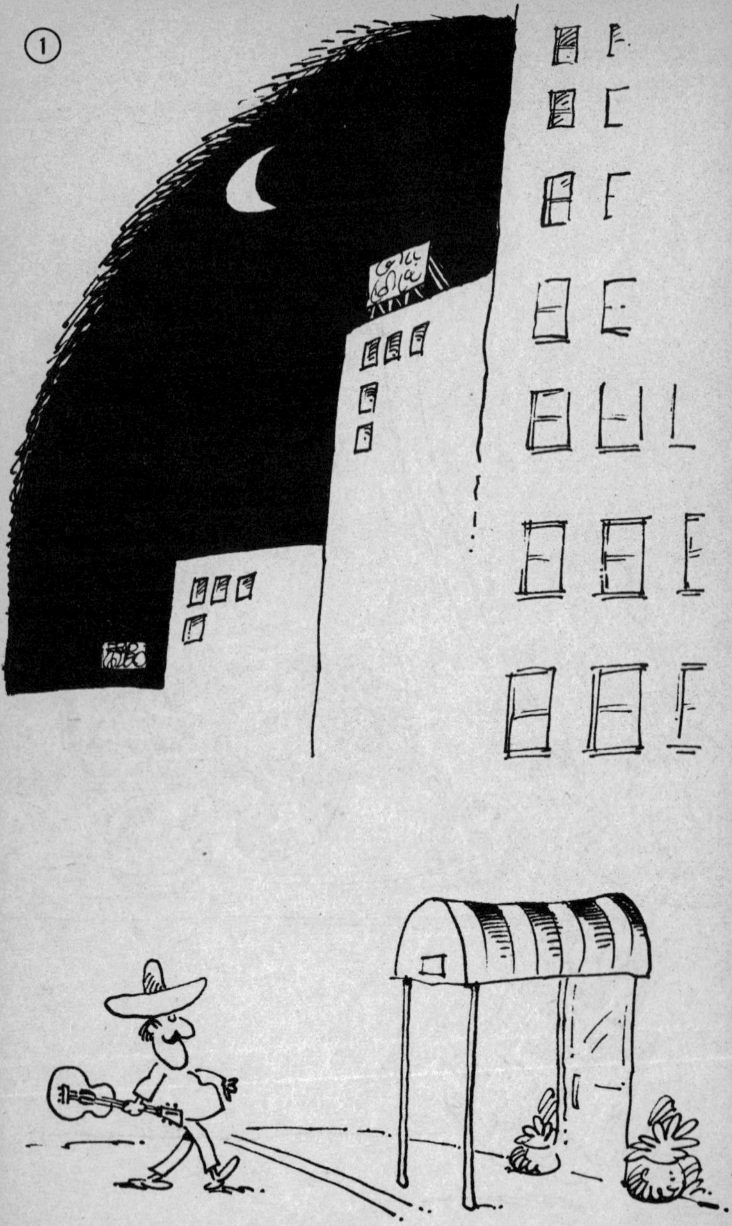

2

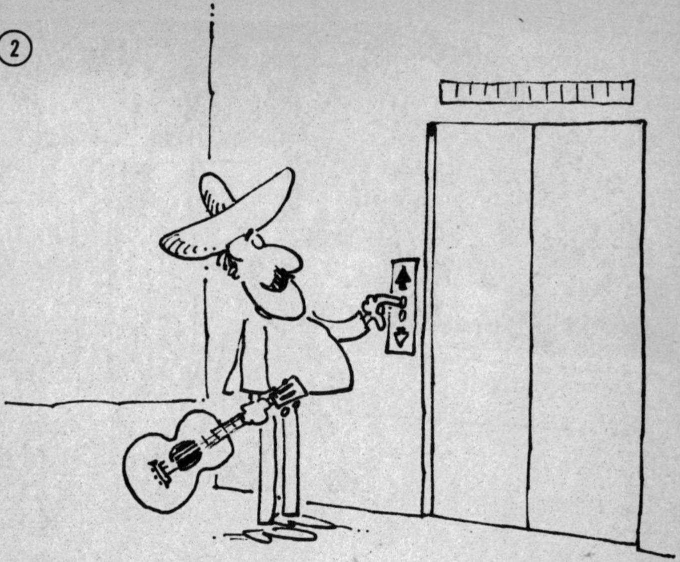

3

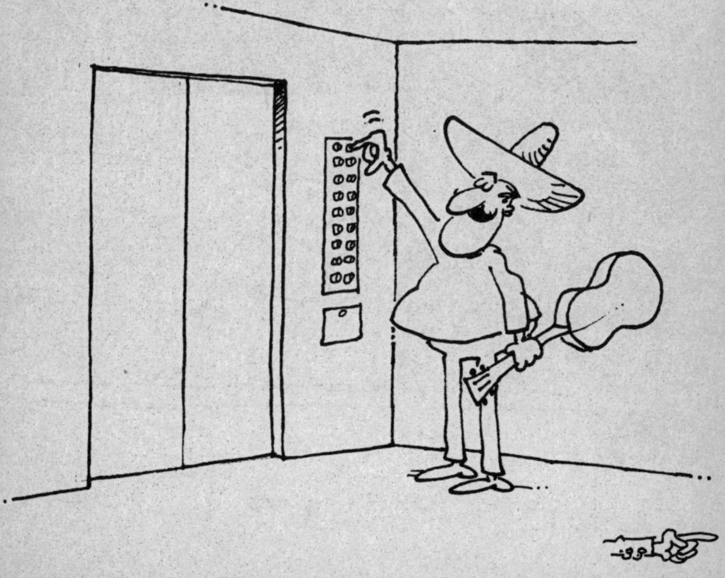

4

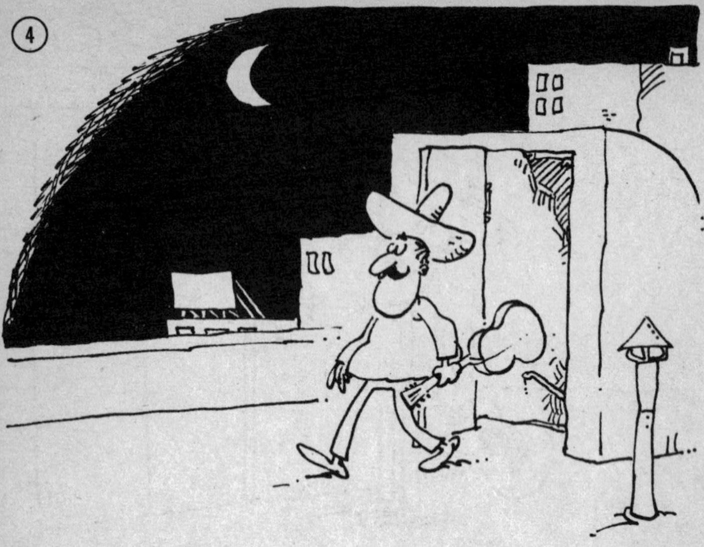

5

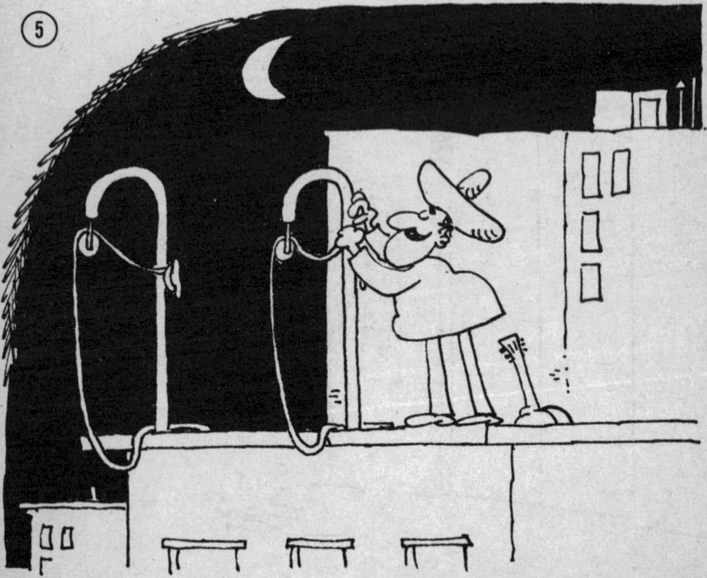

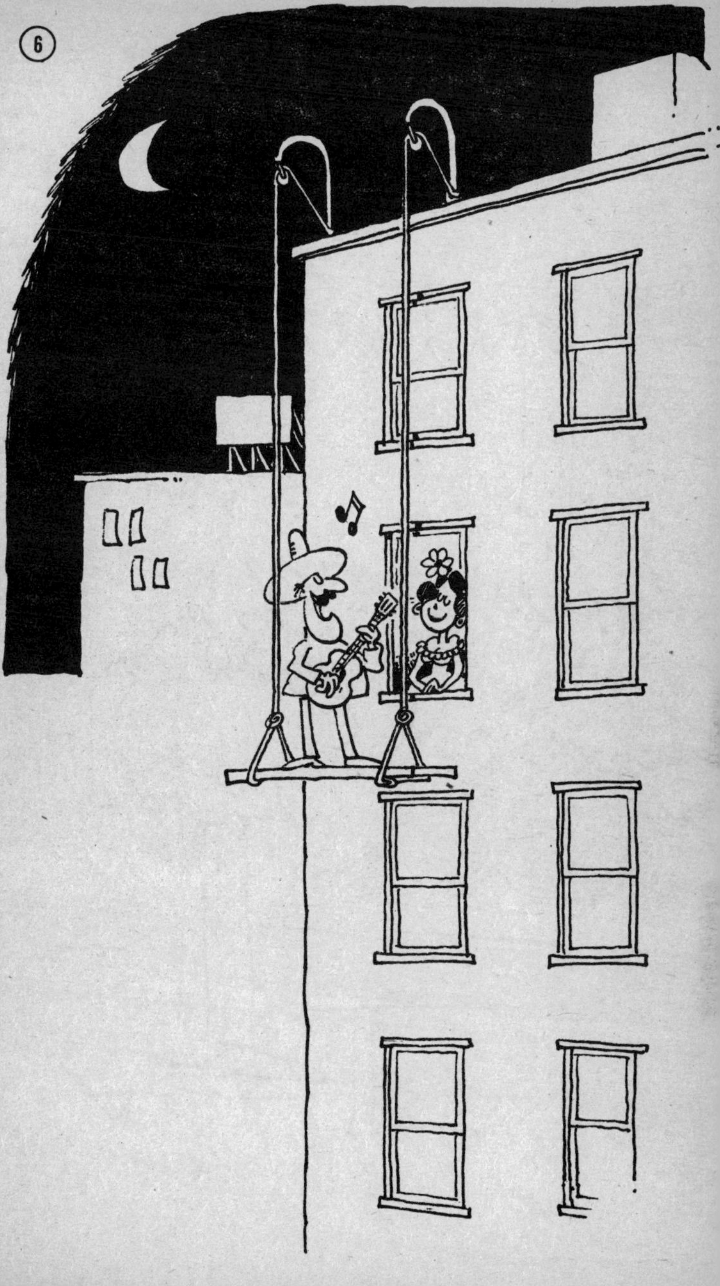
6

①

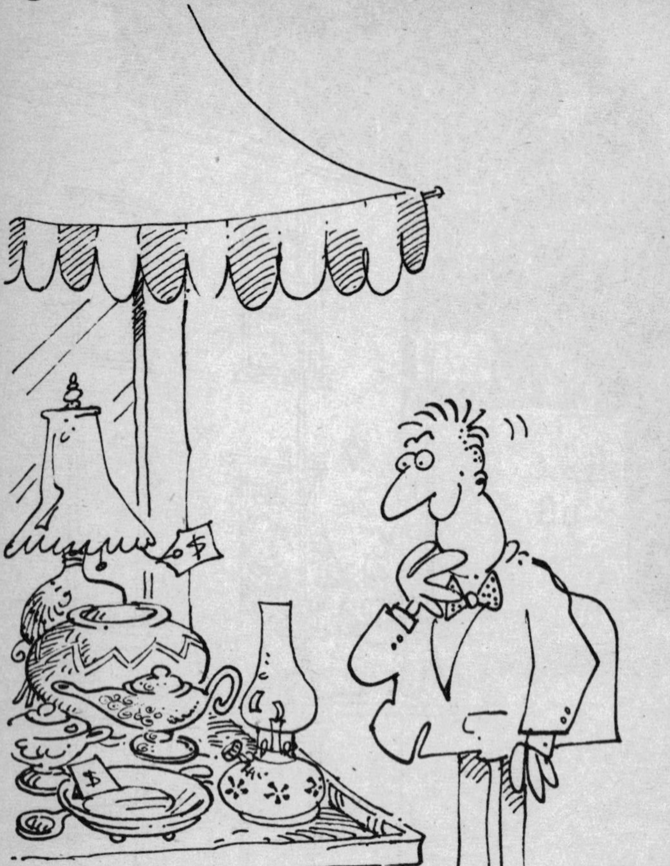
$
$

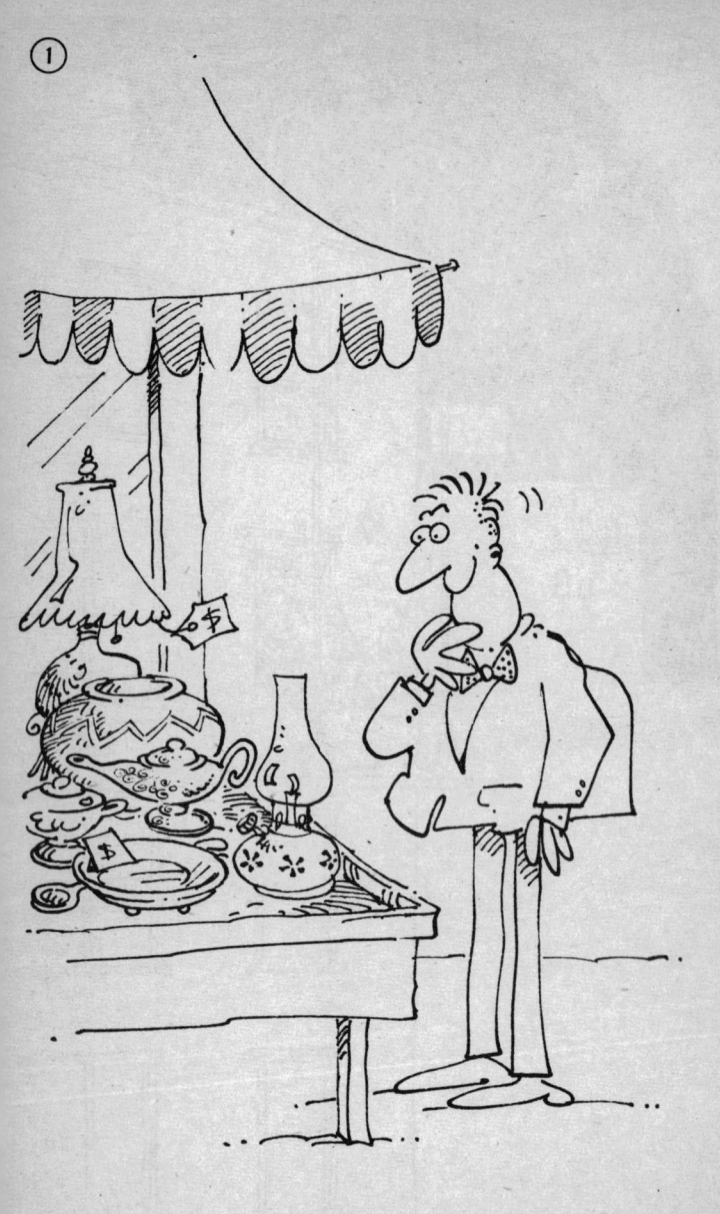

2

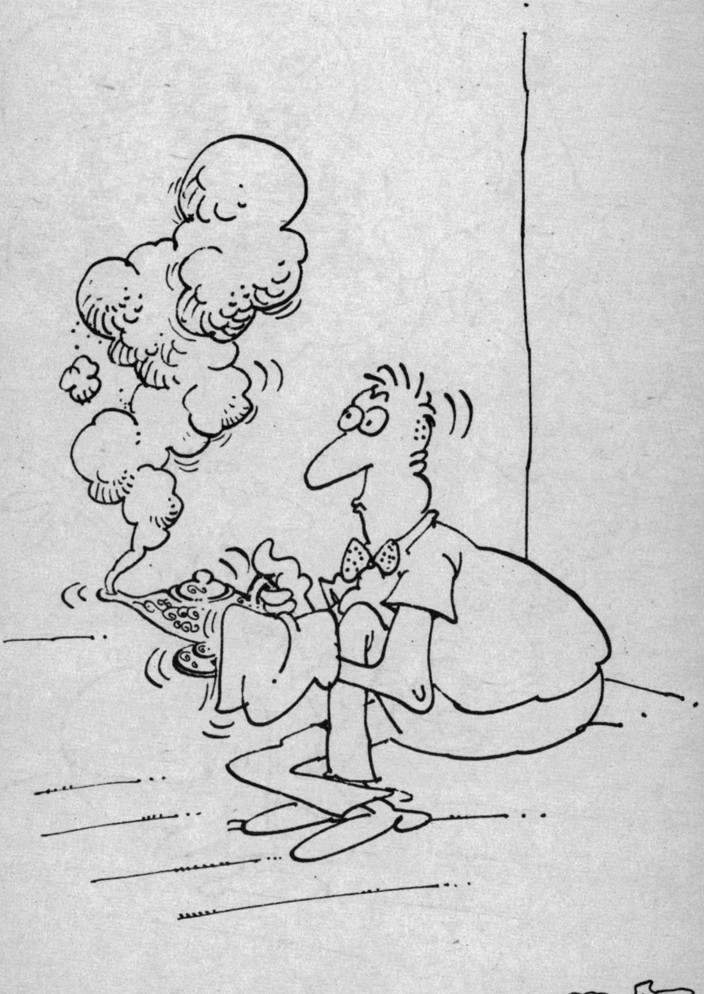

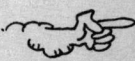

3

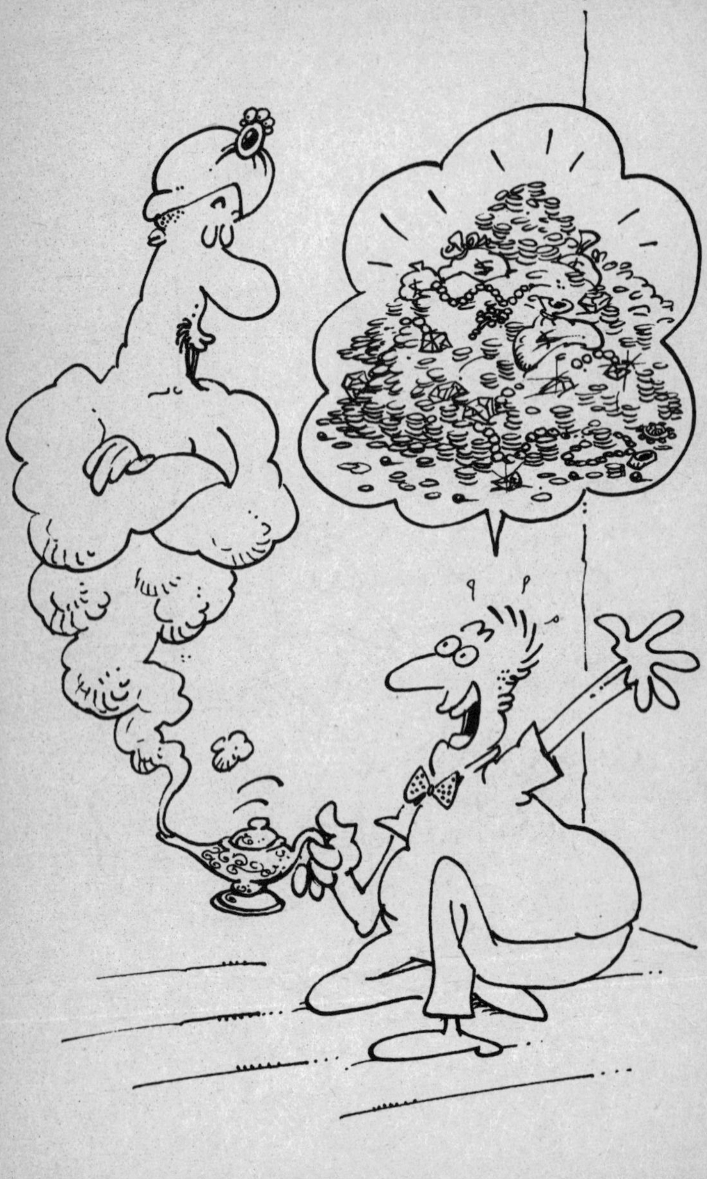

4

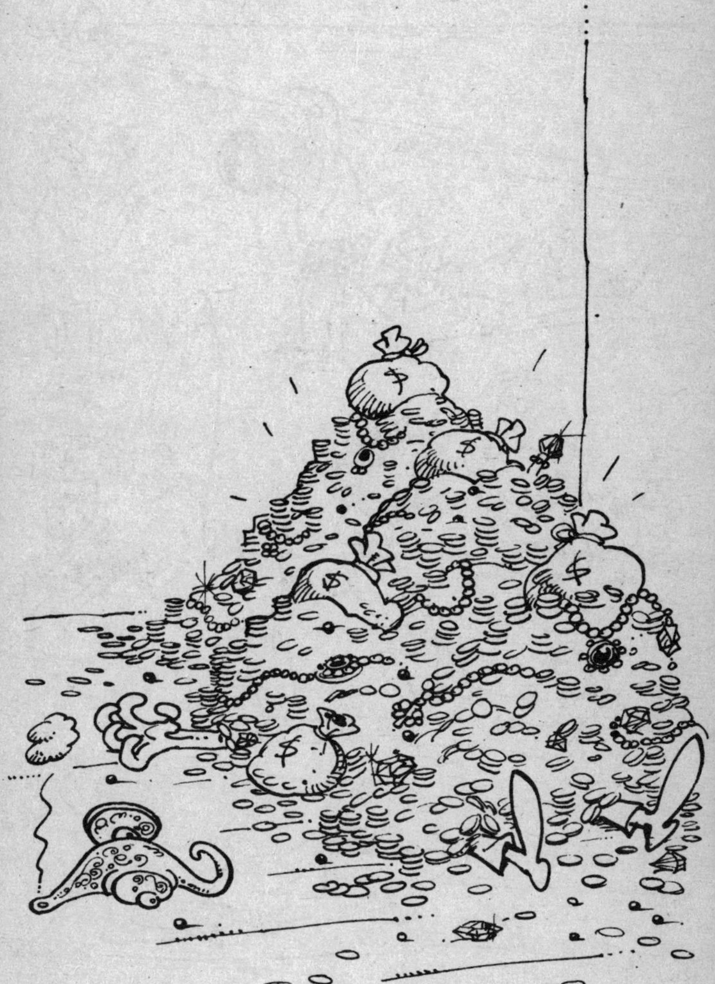

①

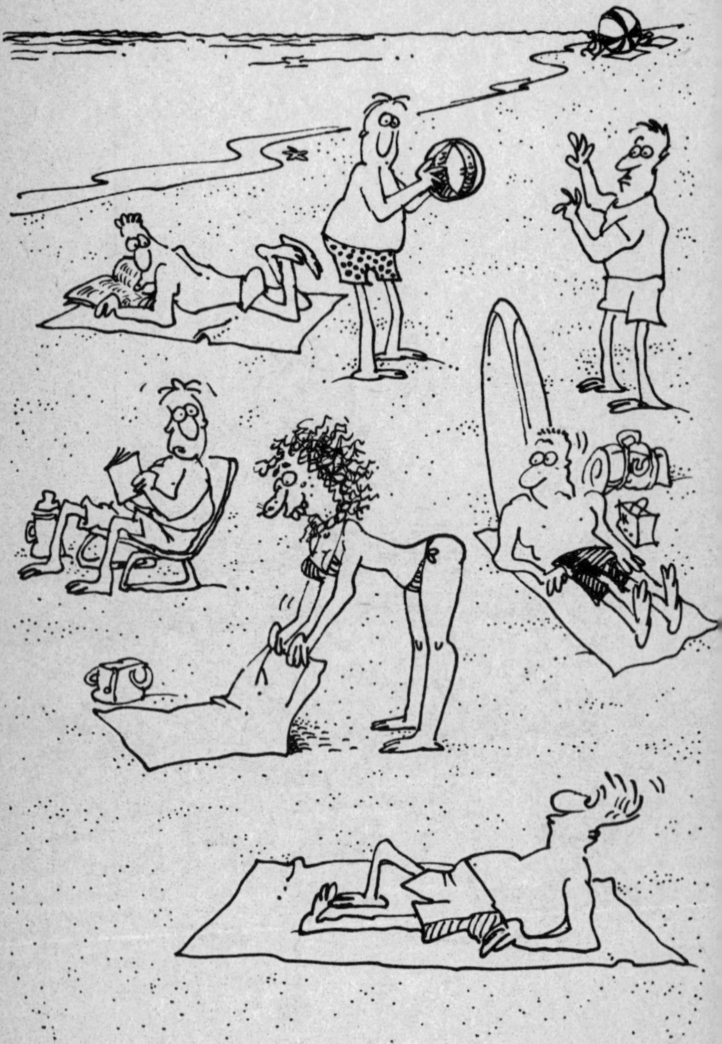

2

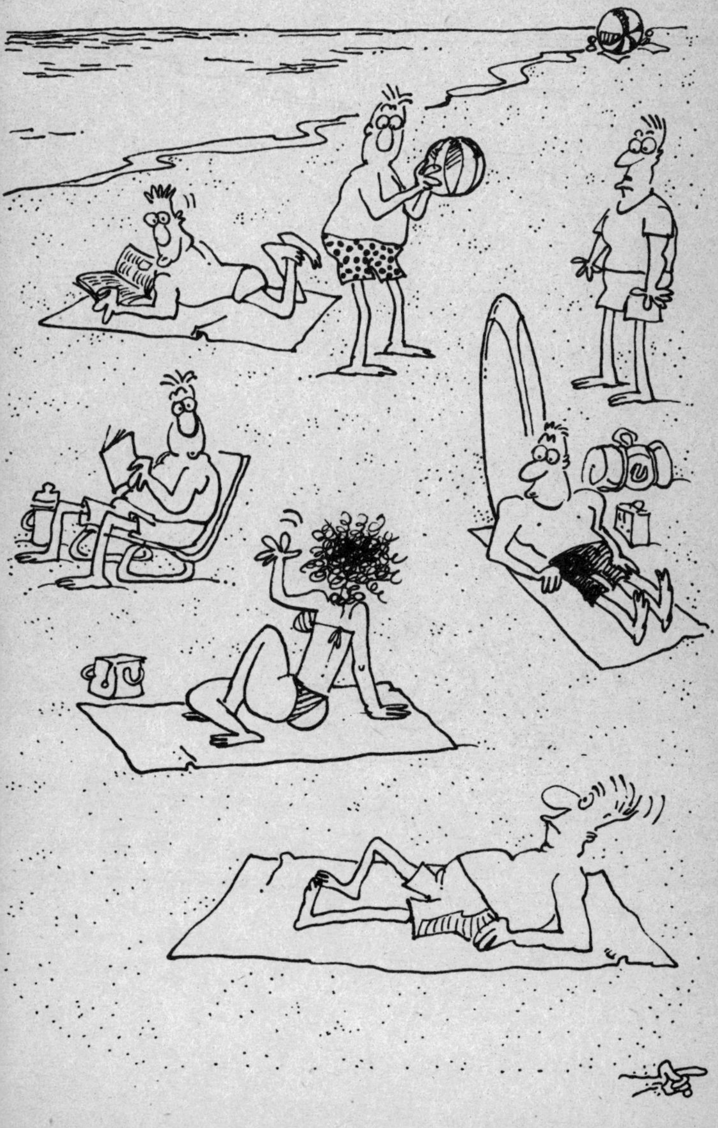

3

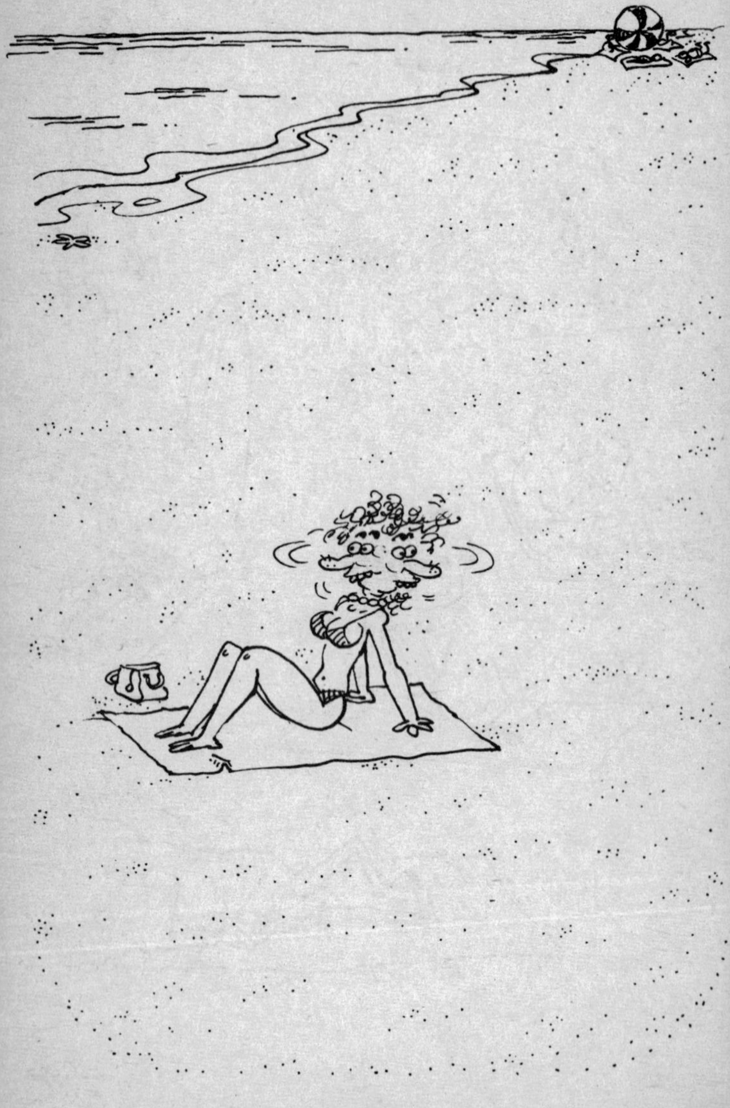

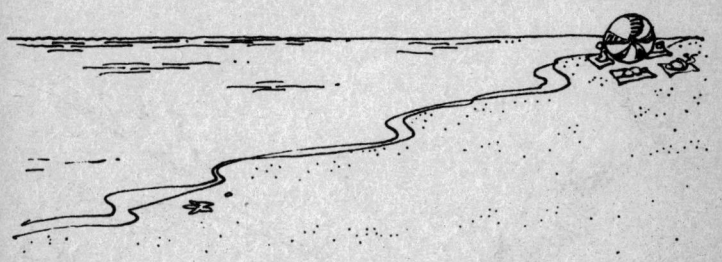

1

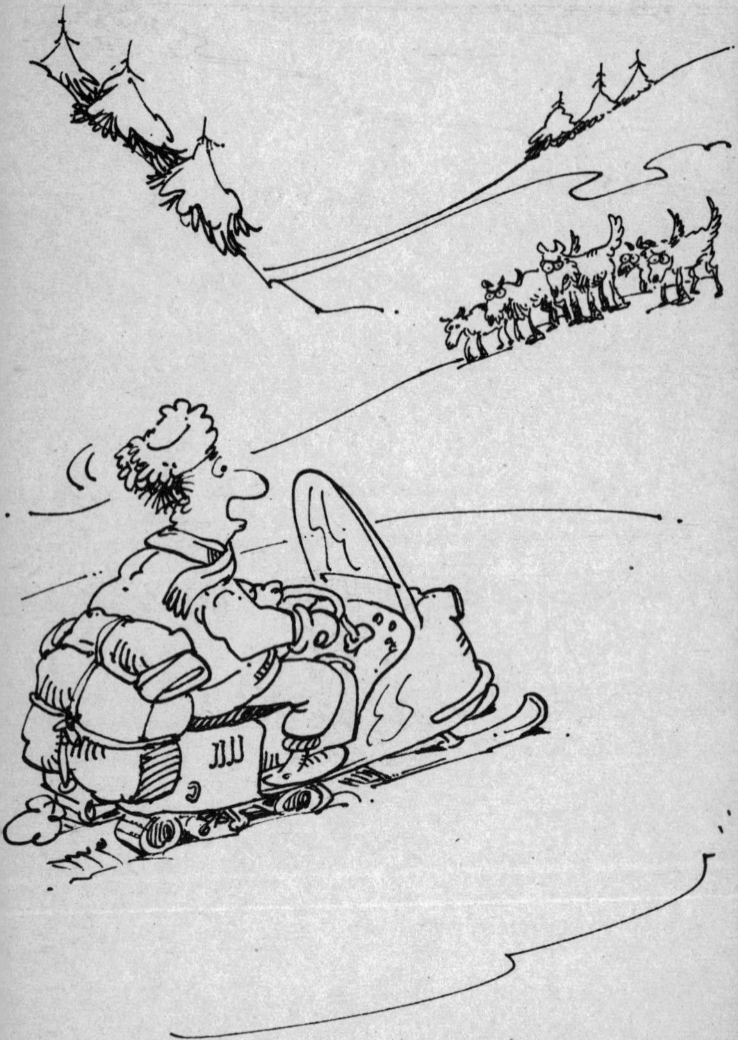

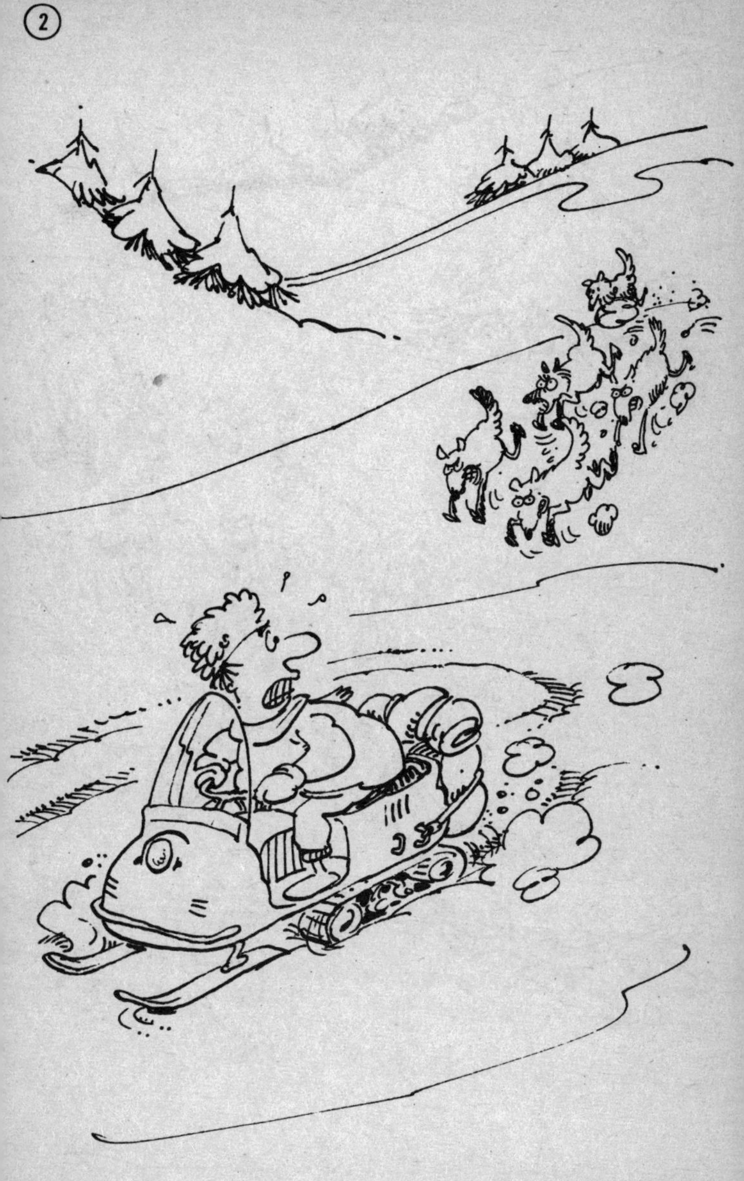
2

3

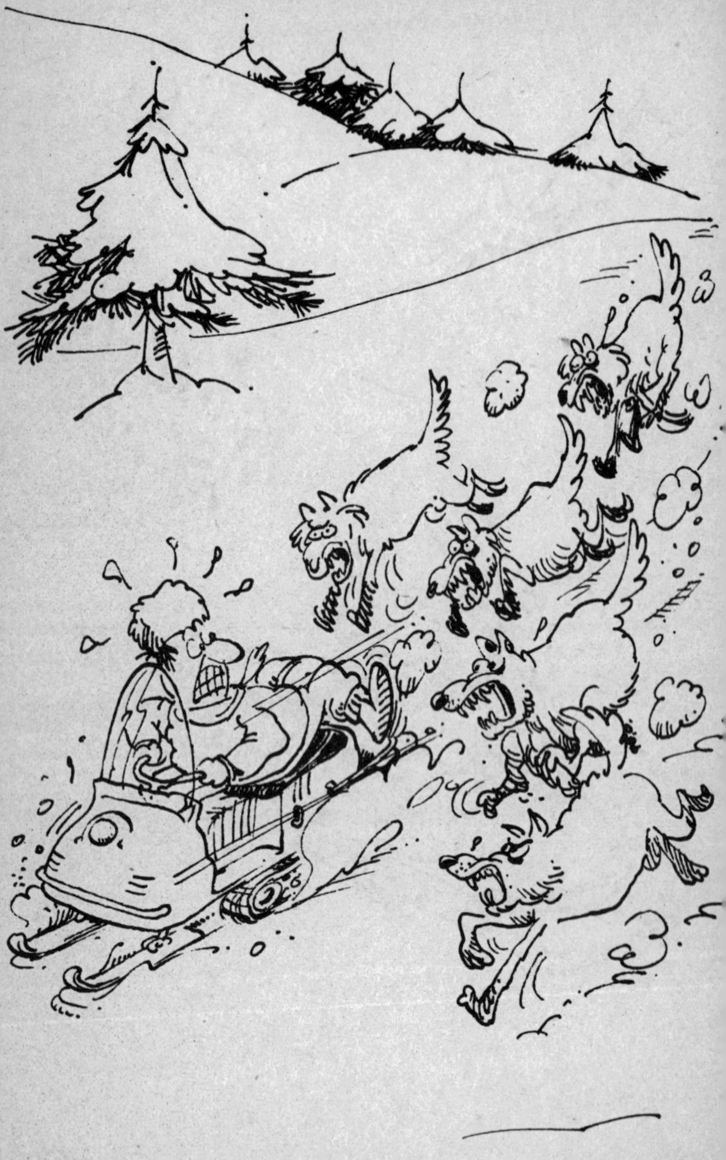

4

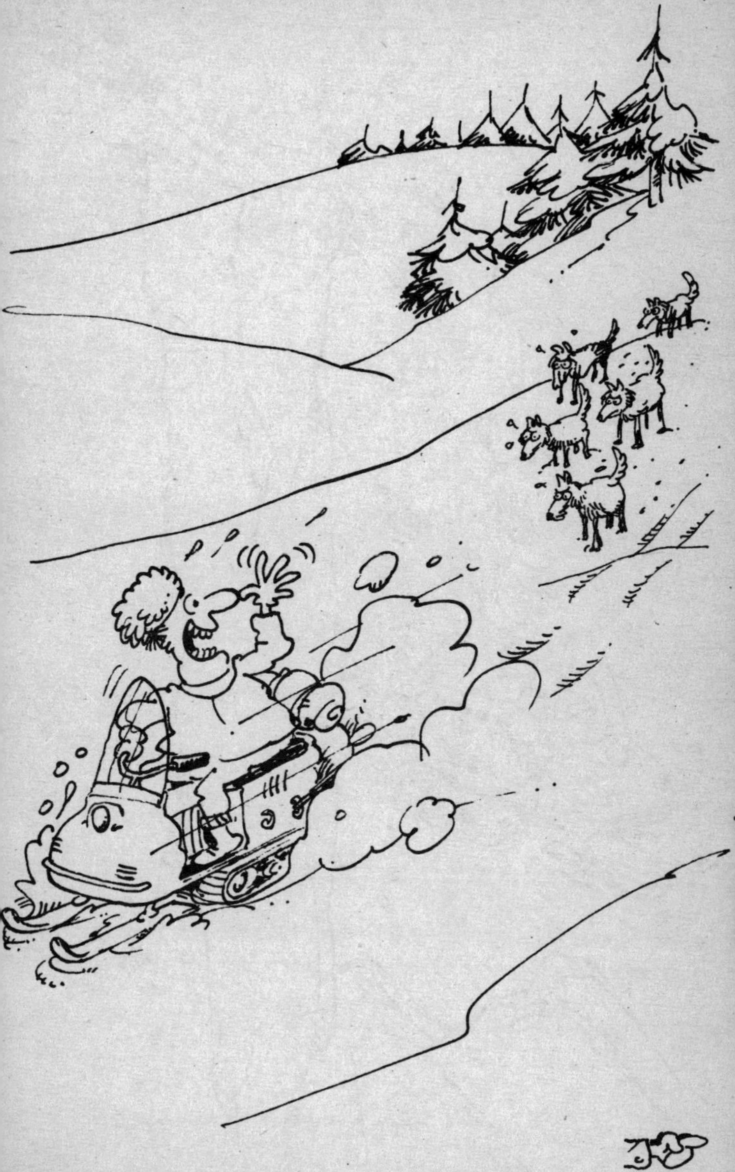

5

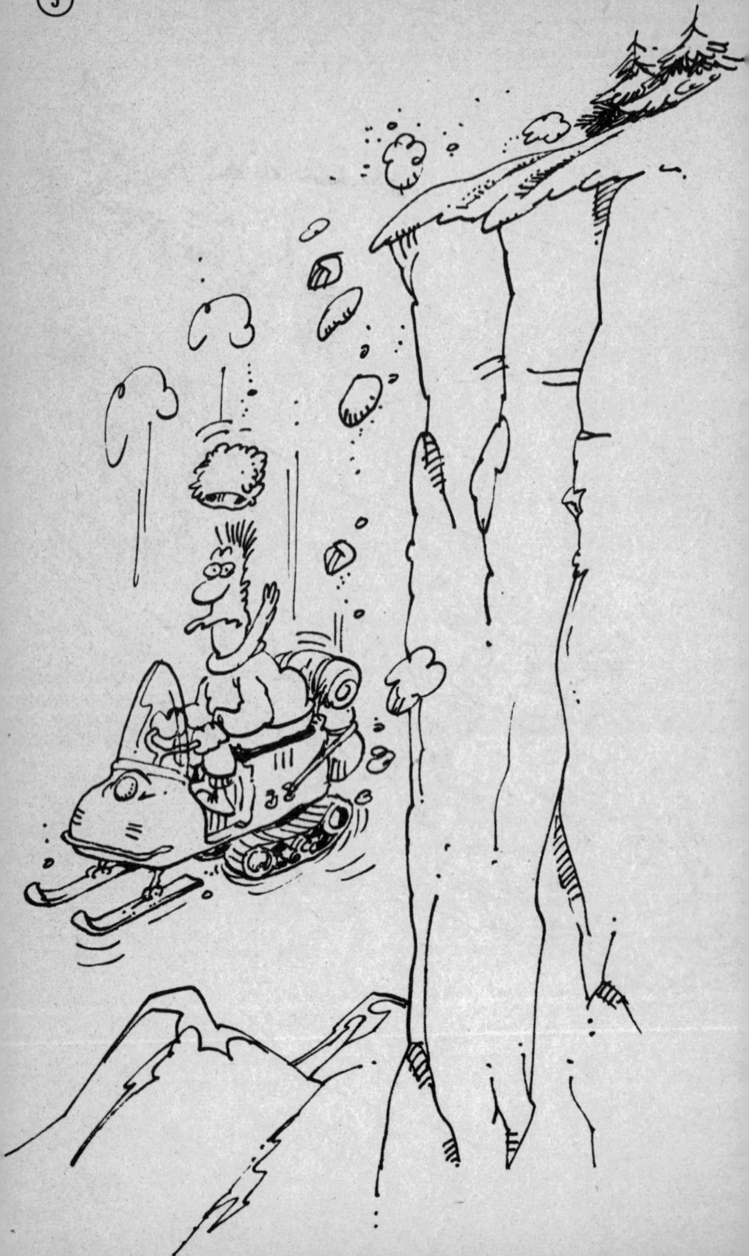

1

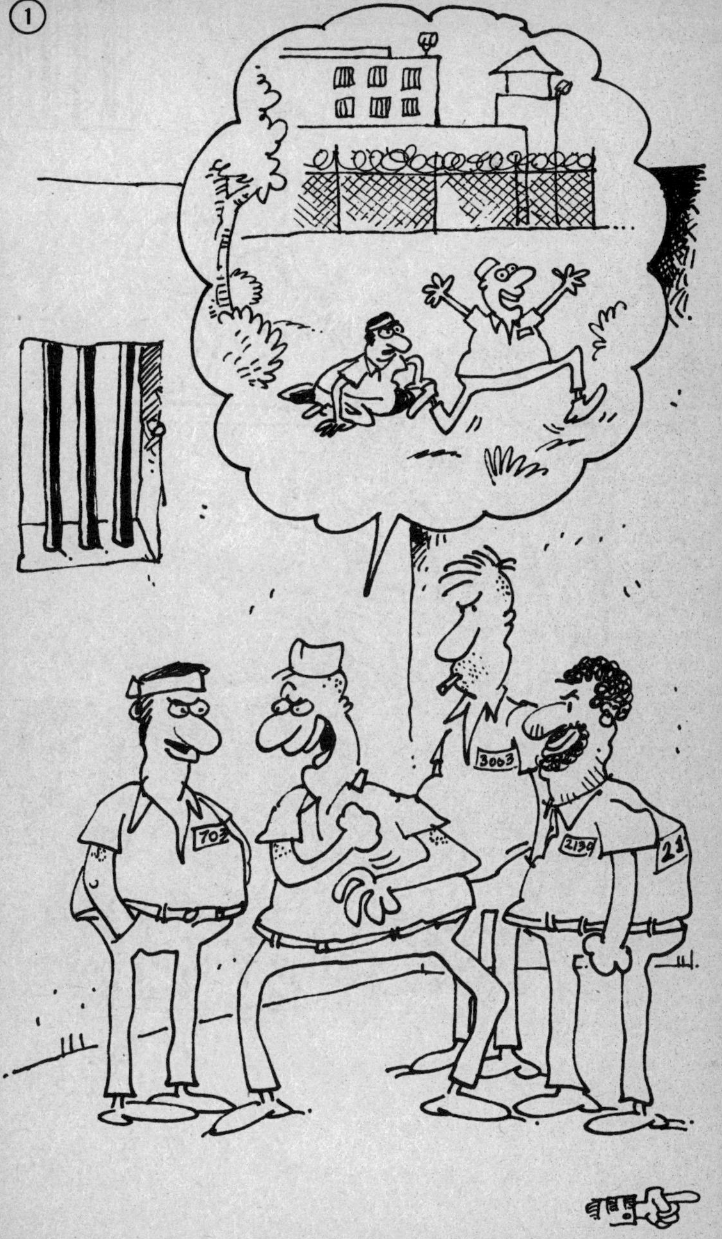

2

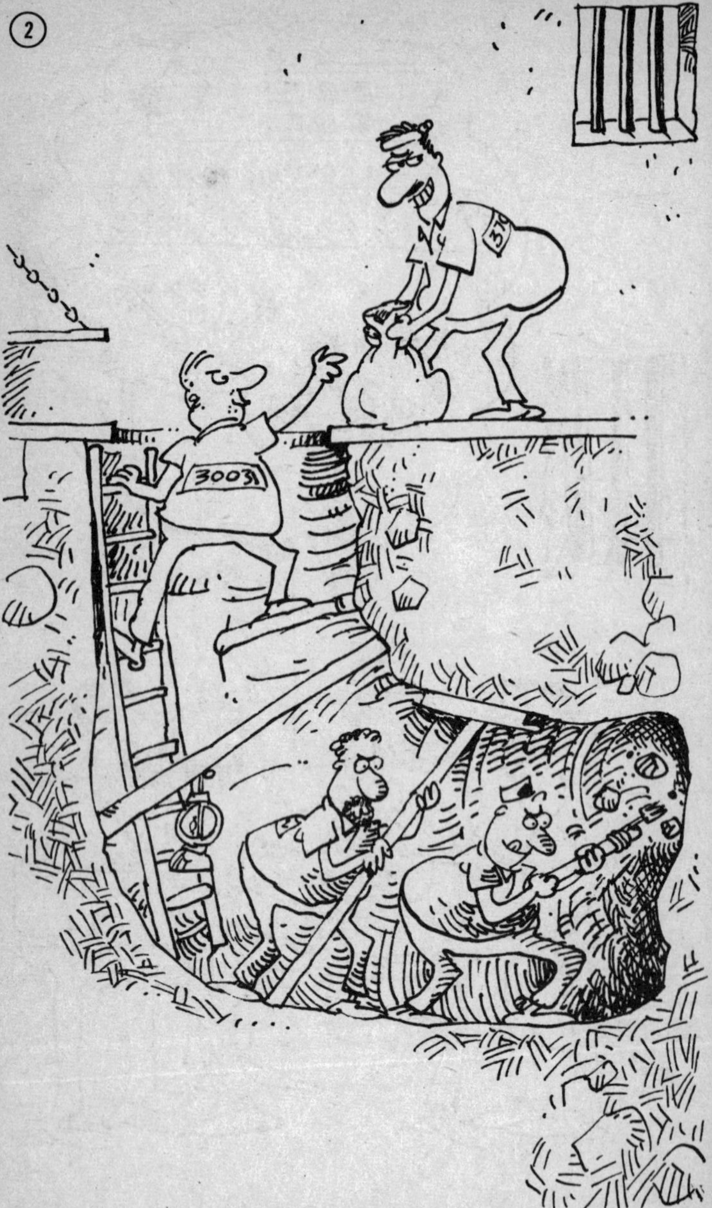

3003

③

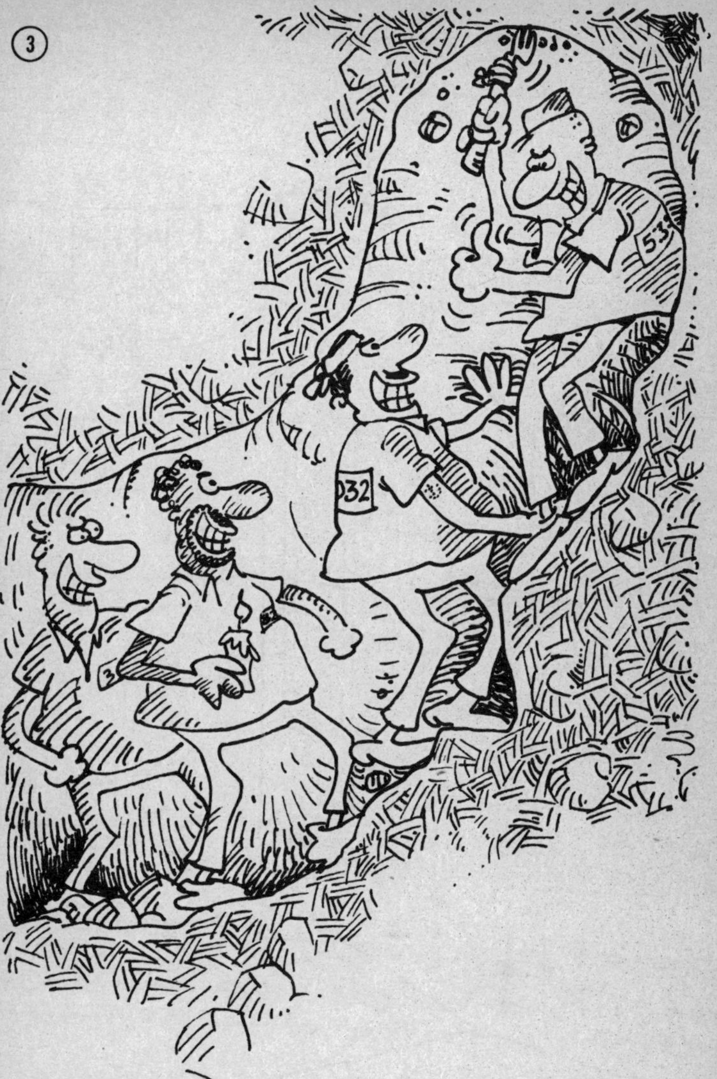
53
032

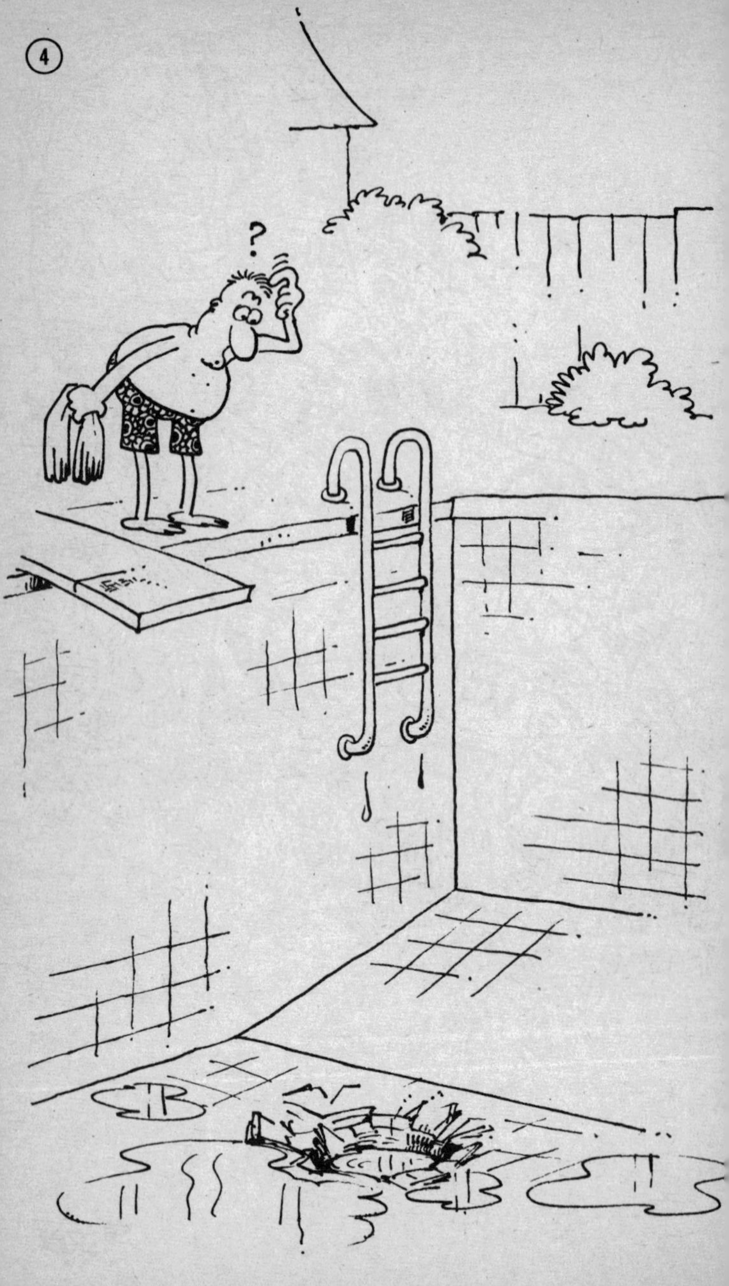
4

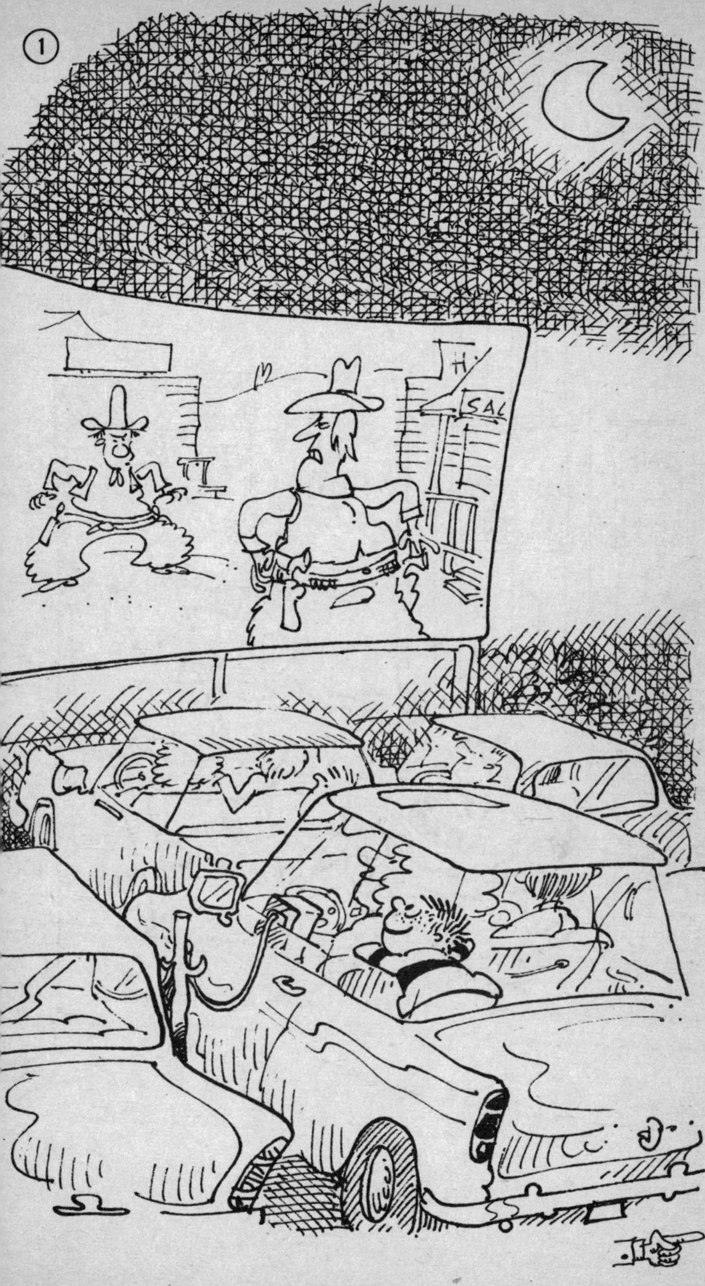
1
SAL

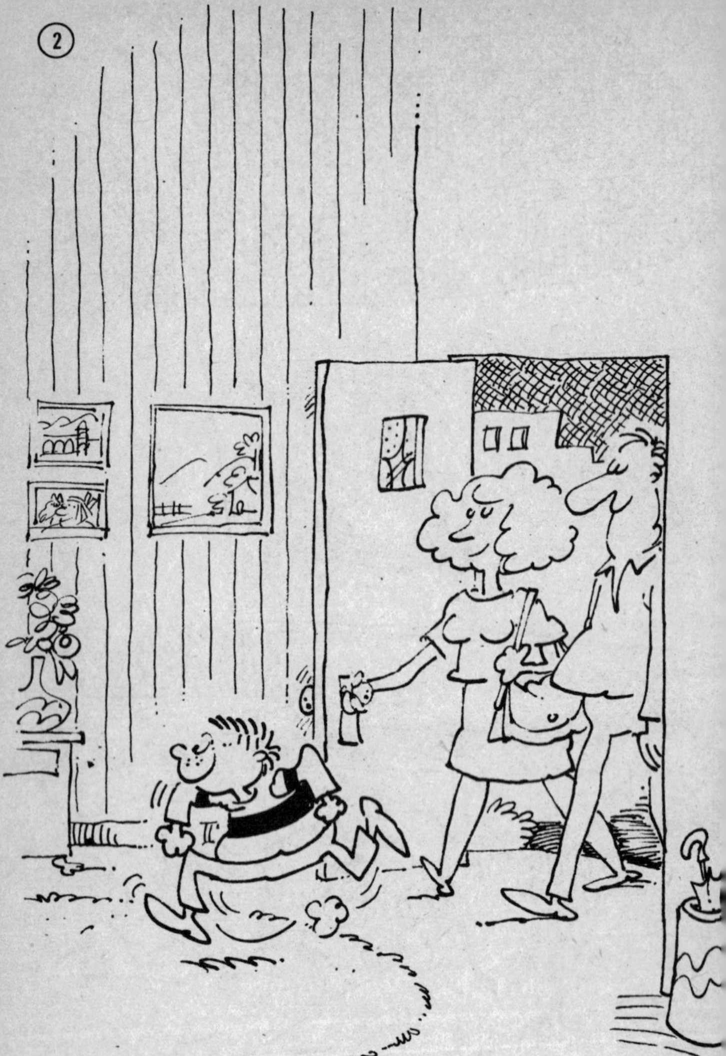
2

3

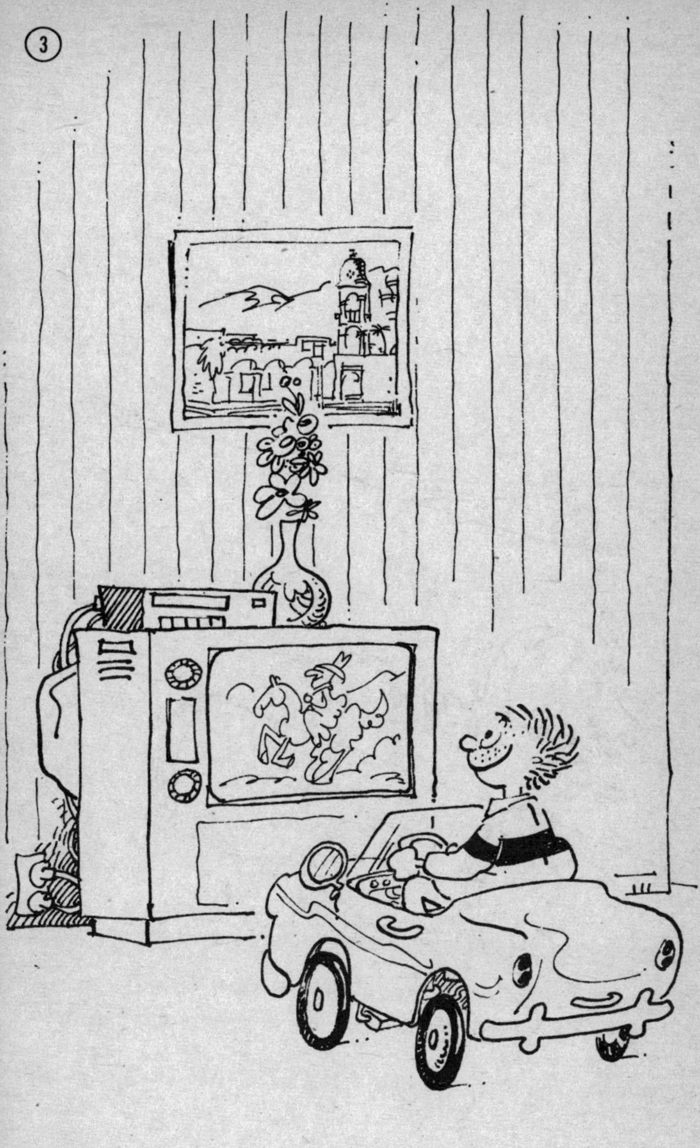

①

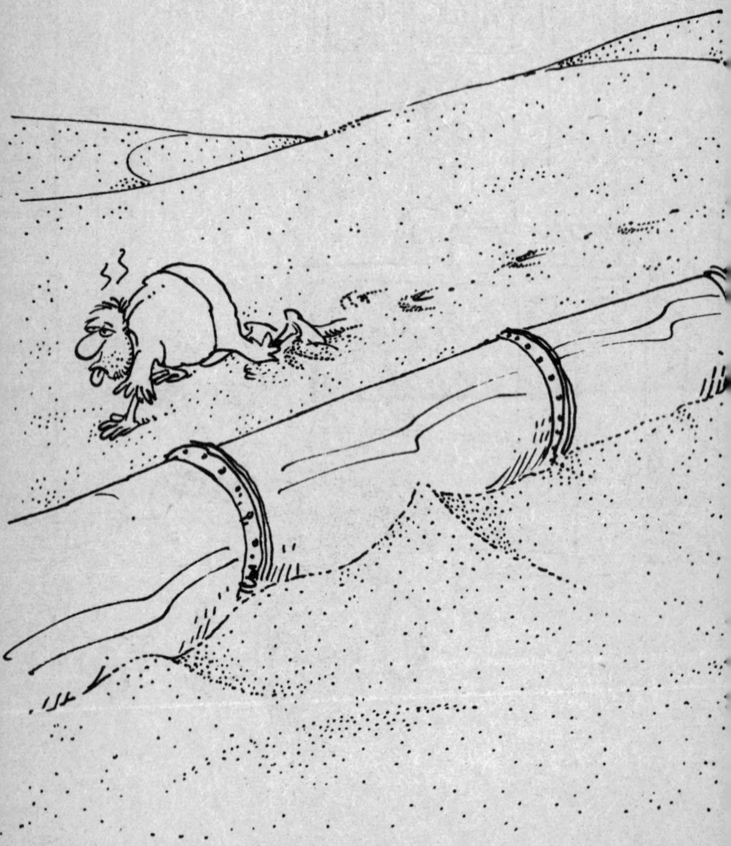

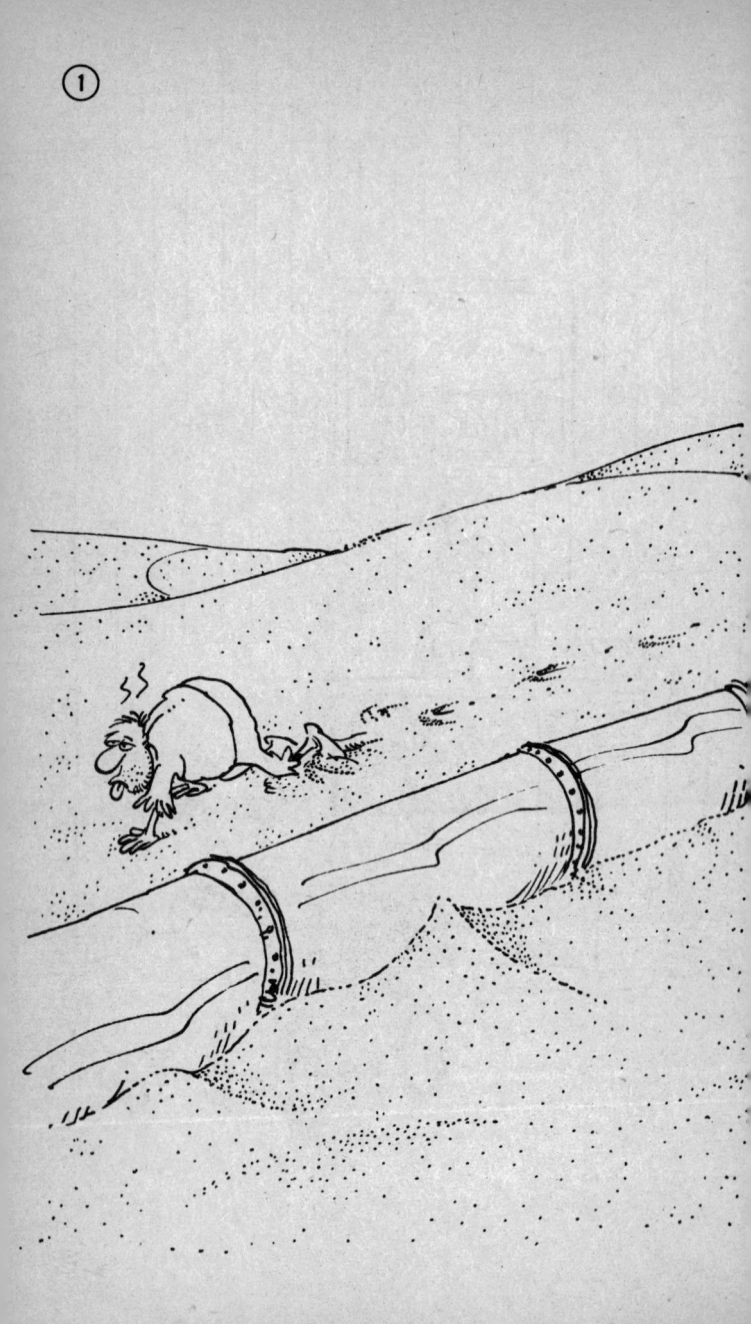

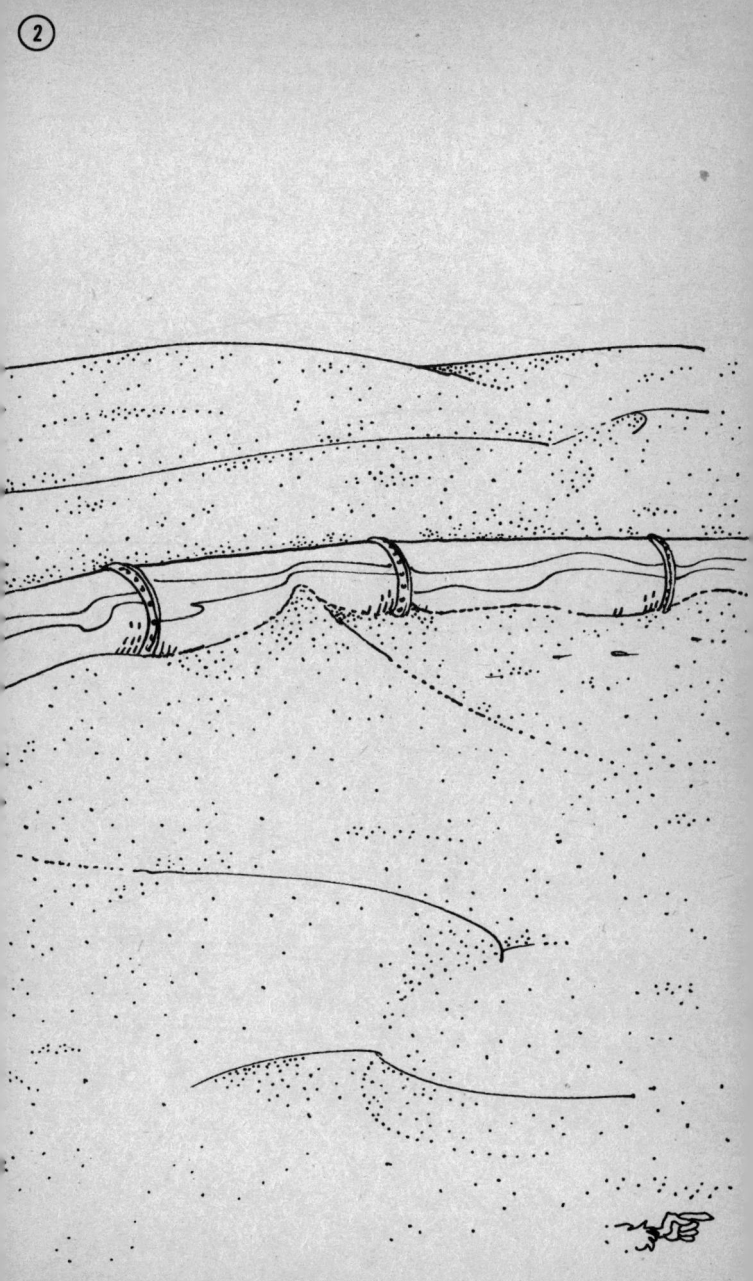

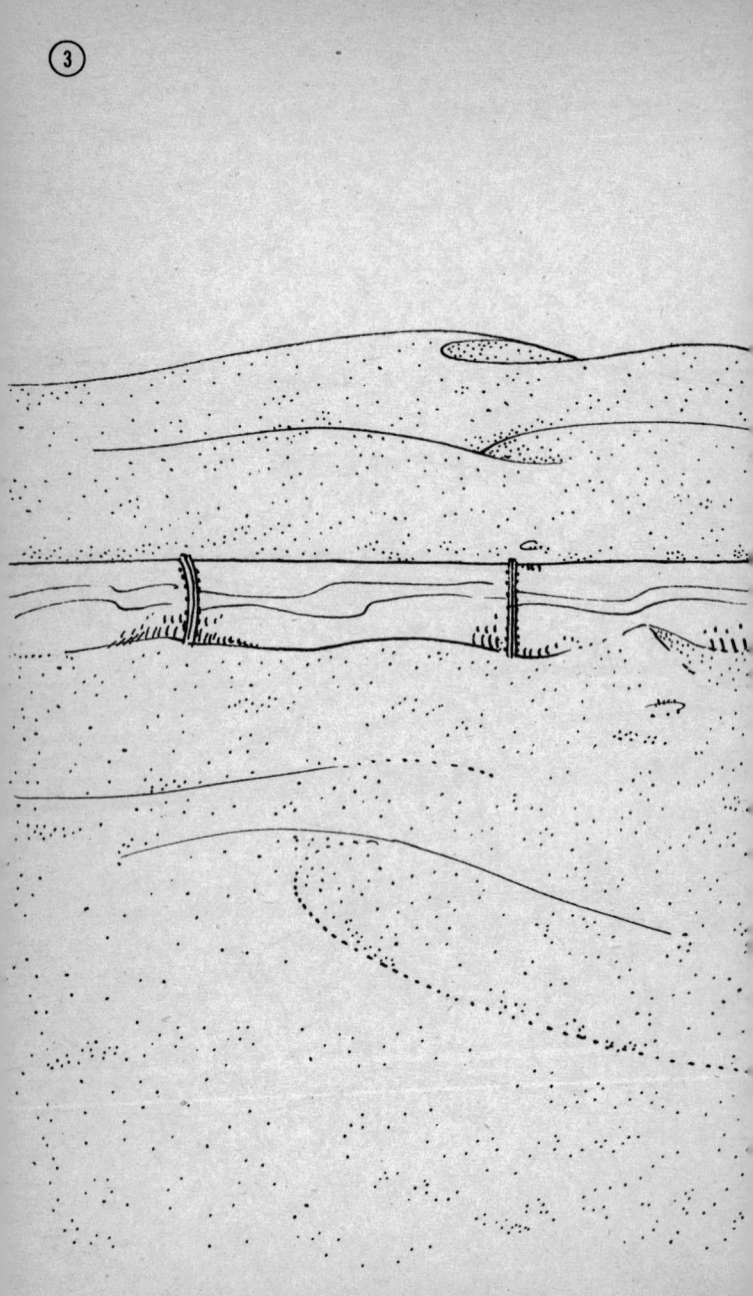

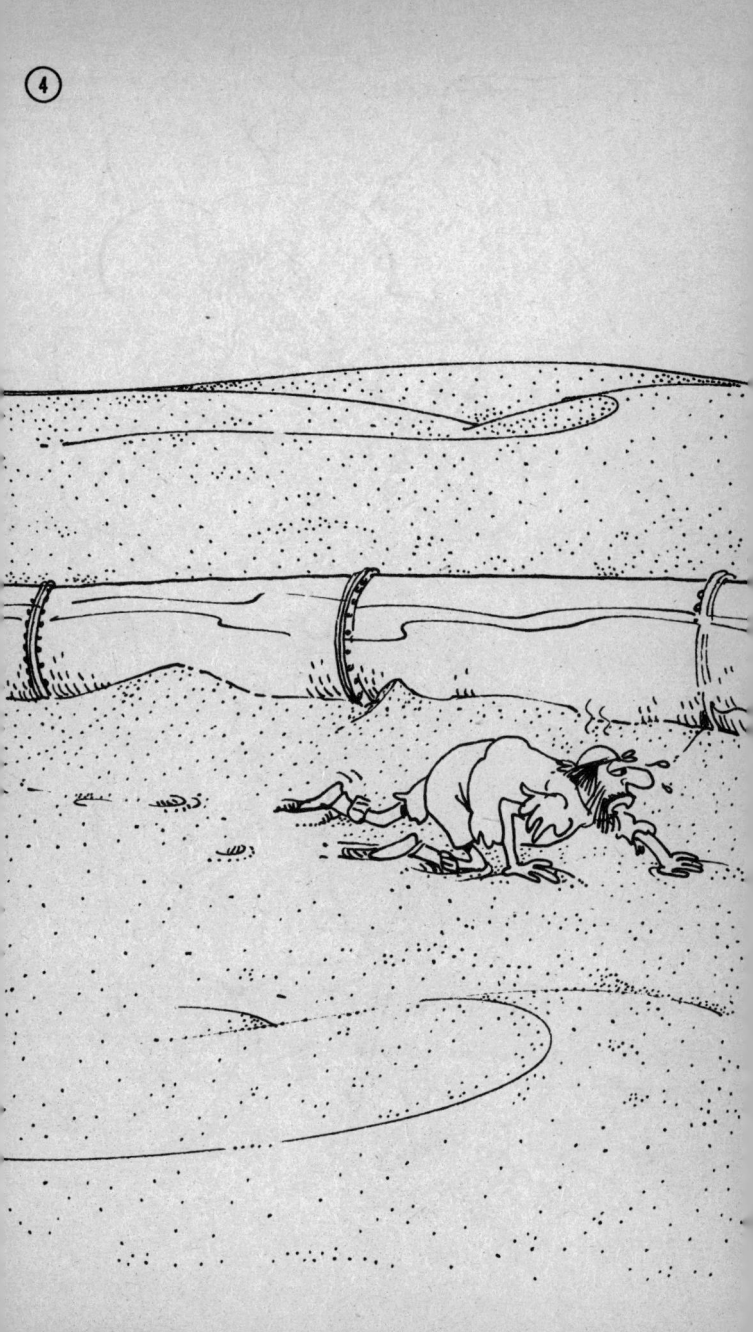

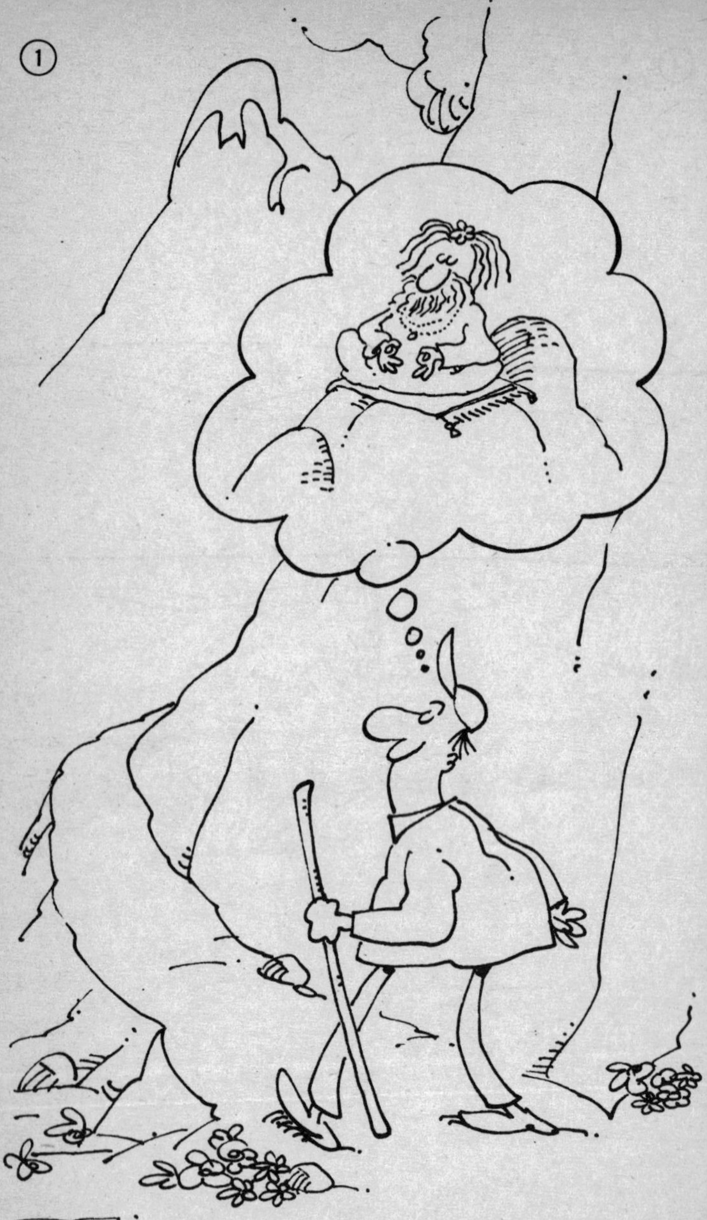
1

②

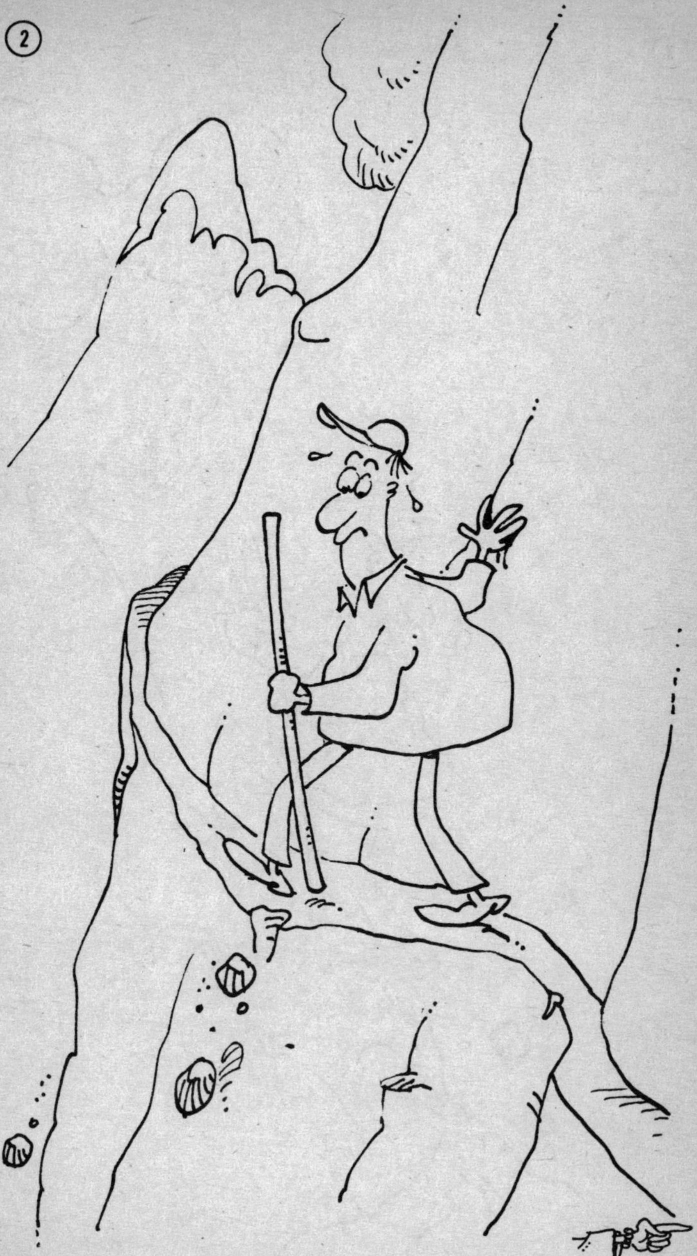

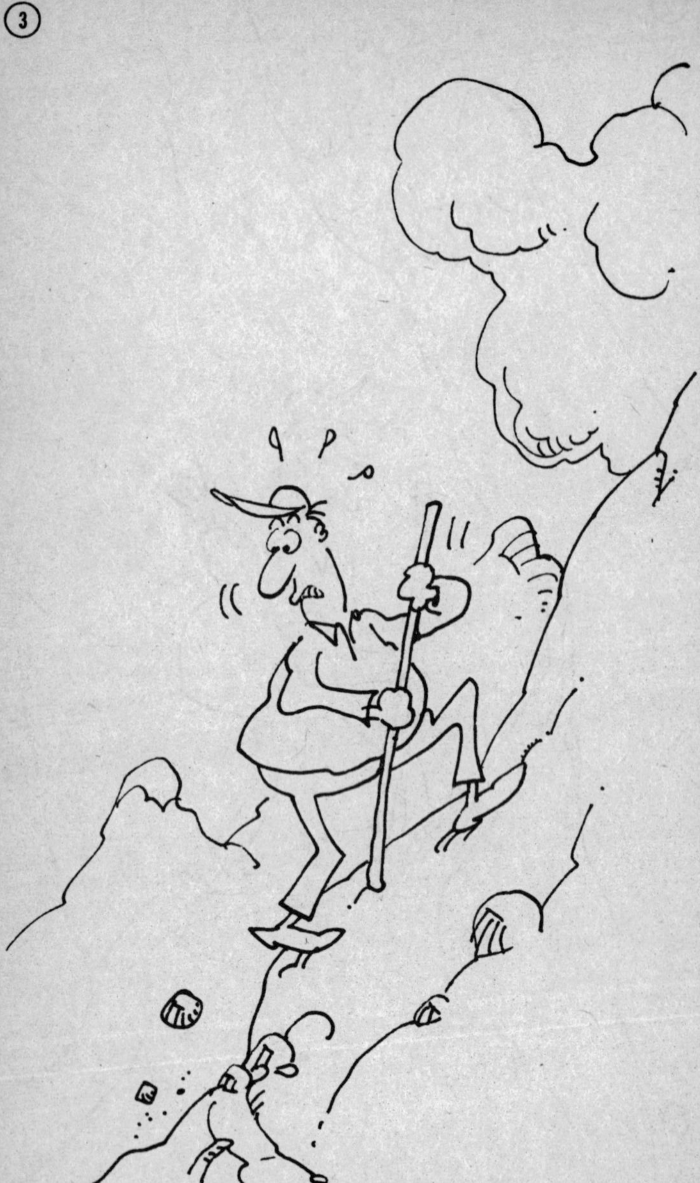

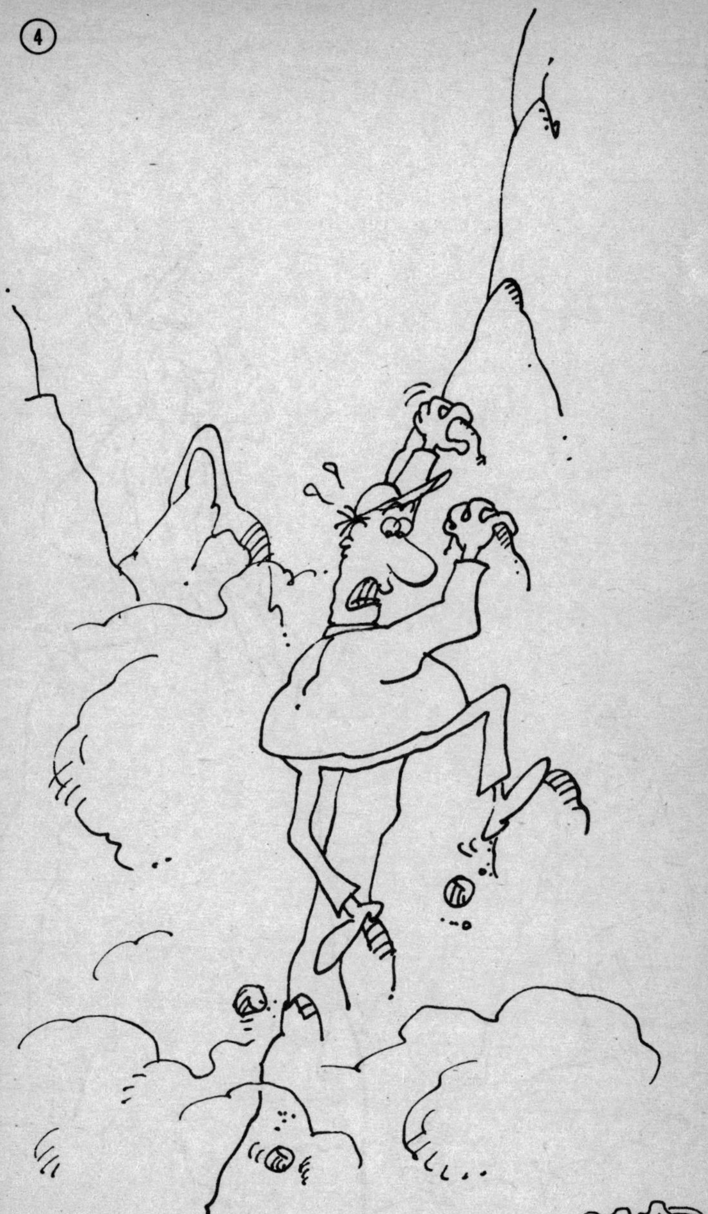
4

5

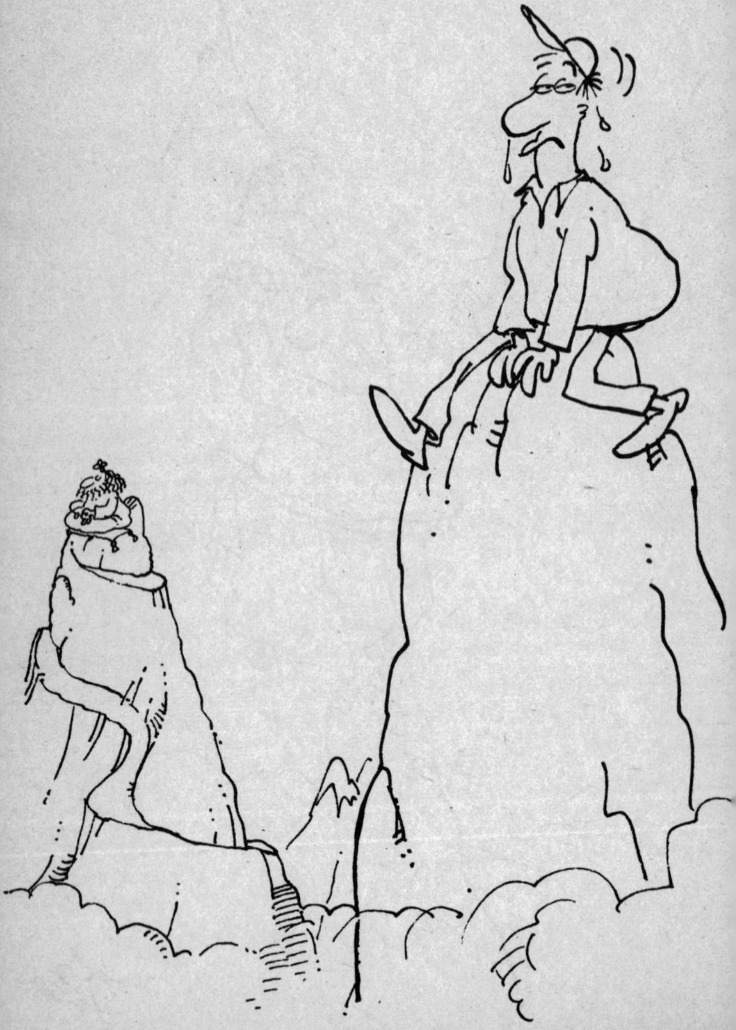

1

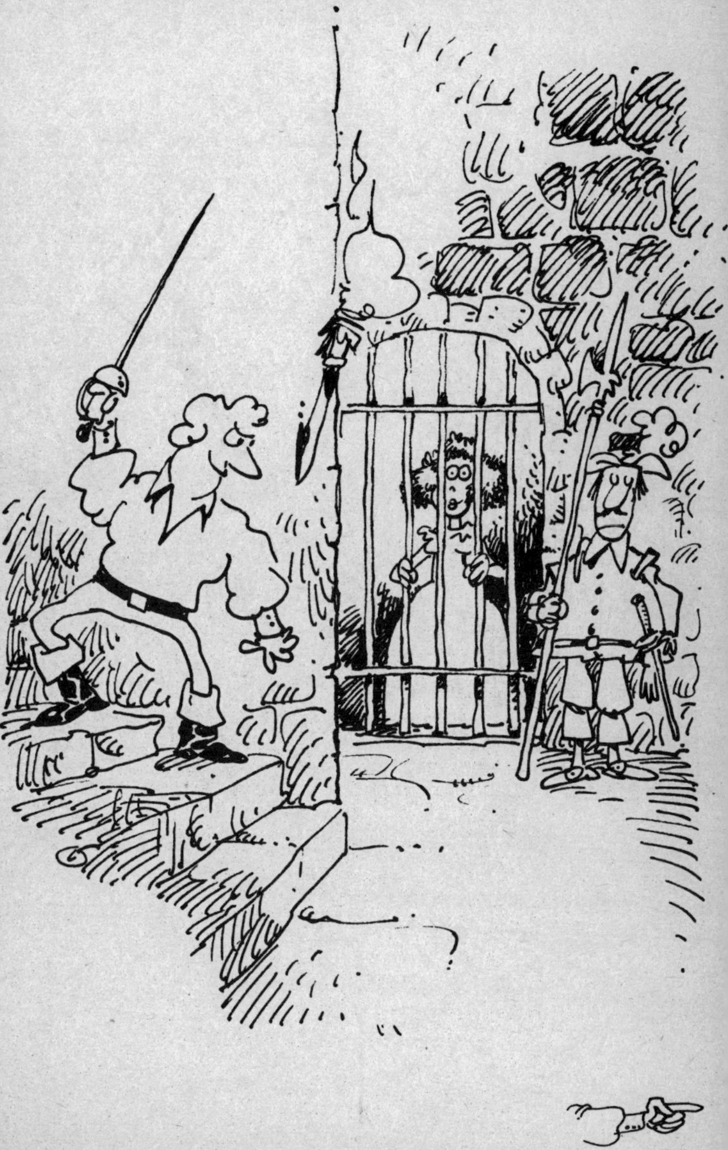

2

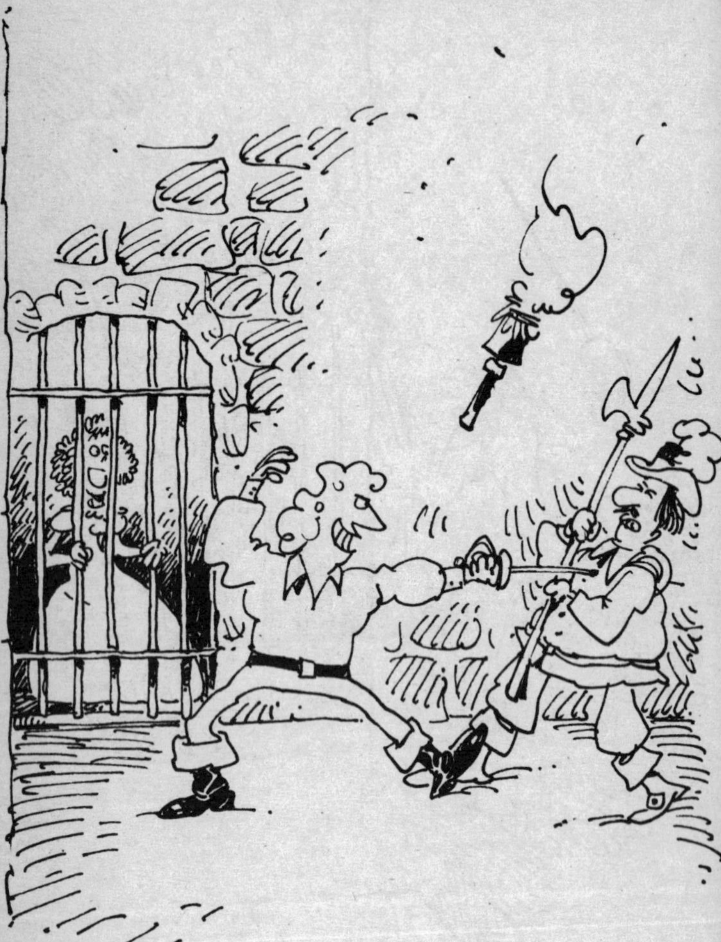

3

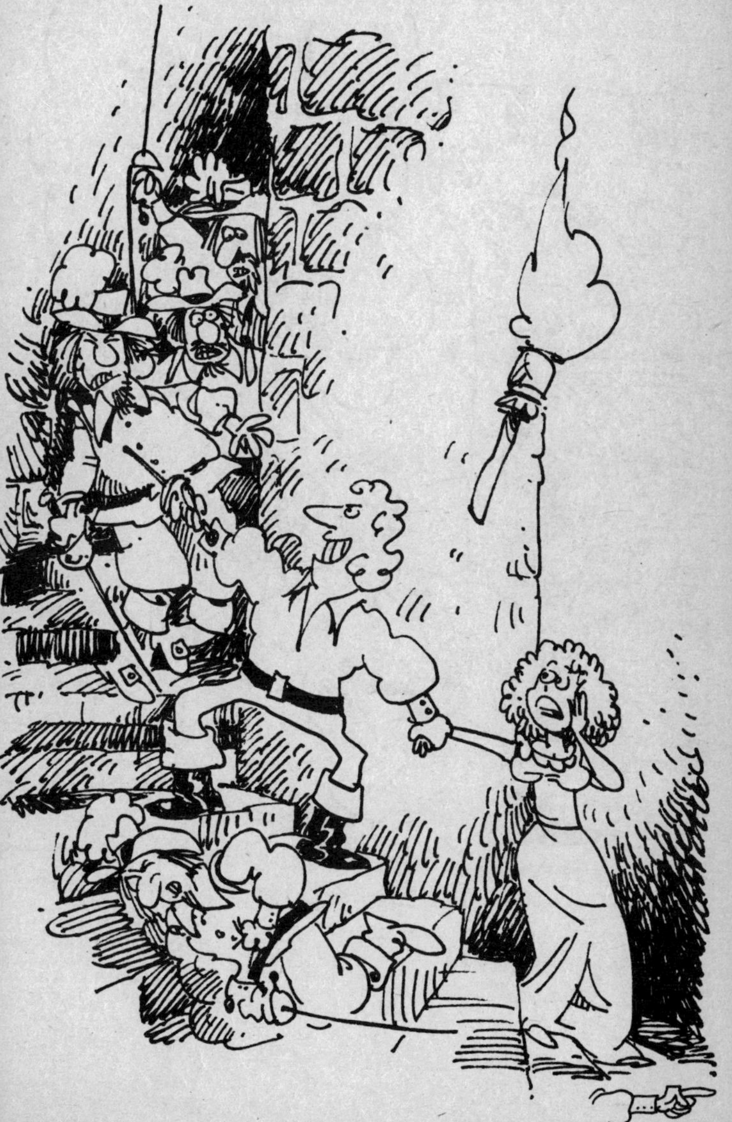

4

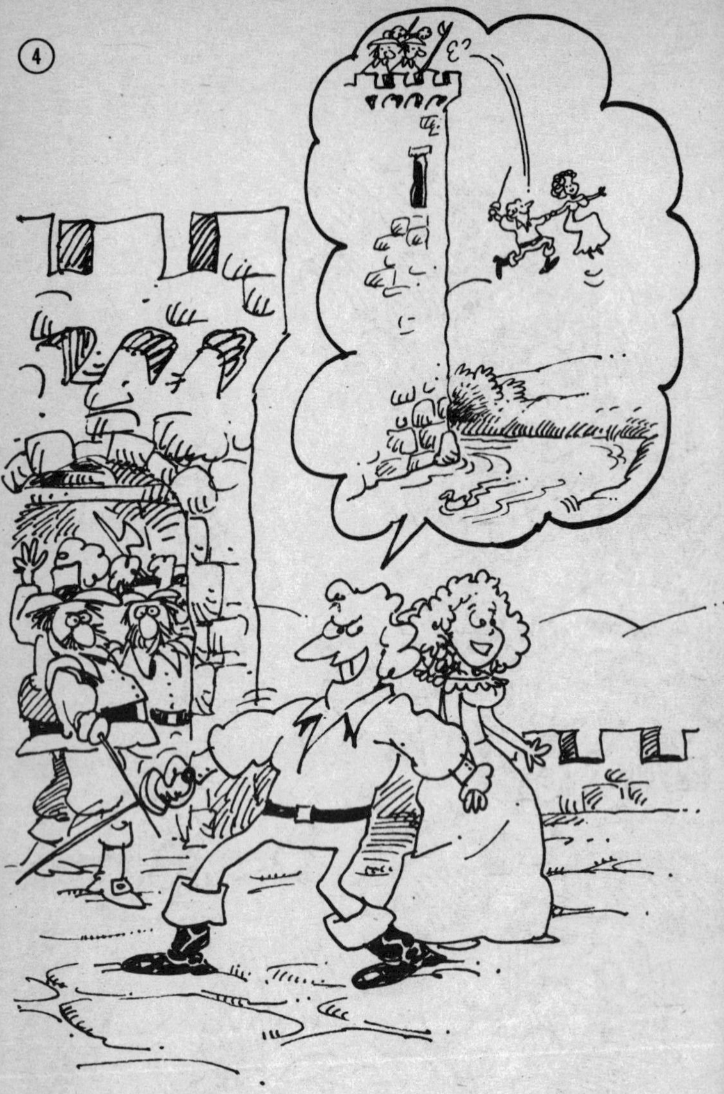

5

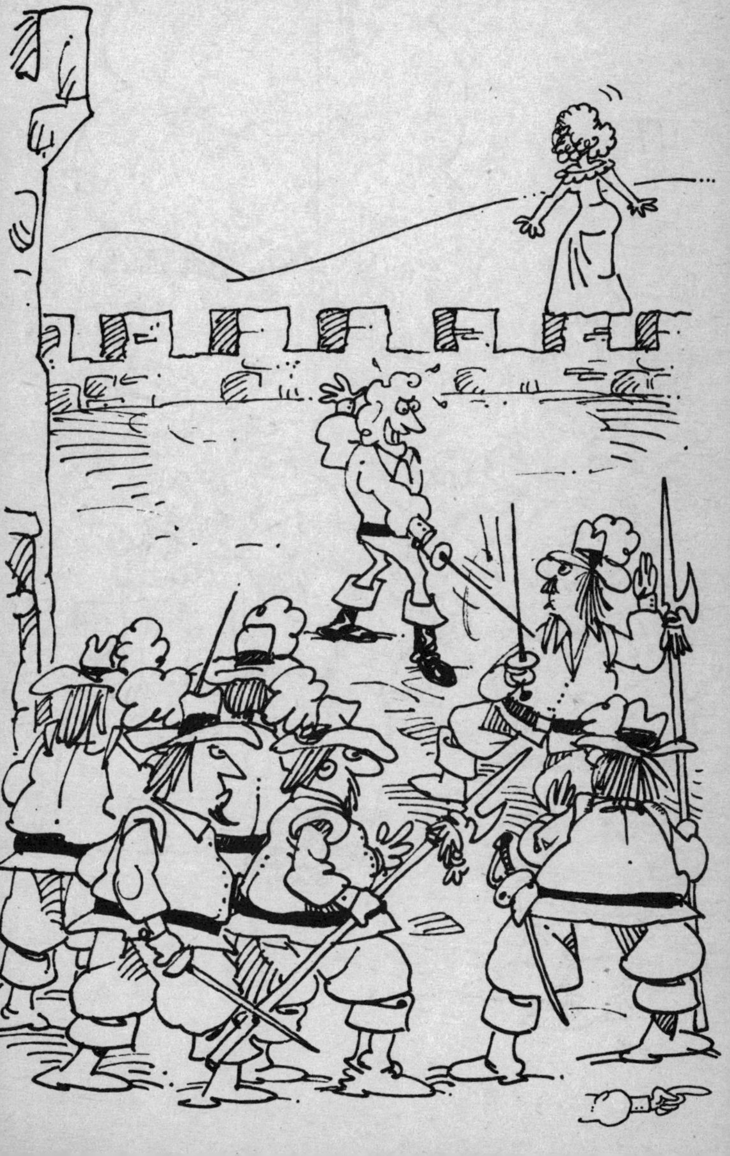

6

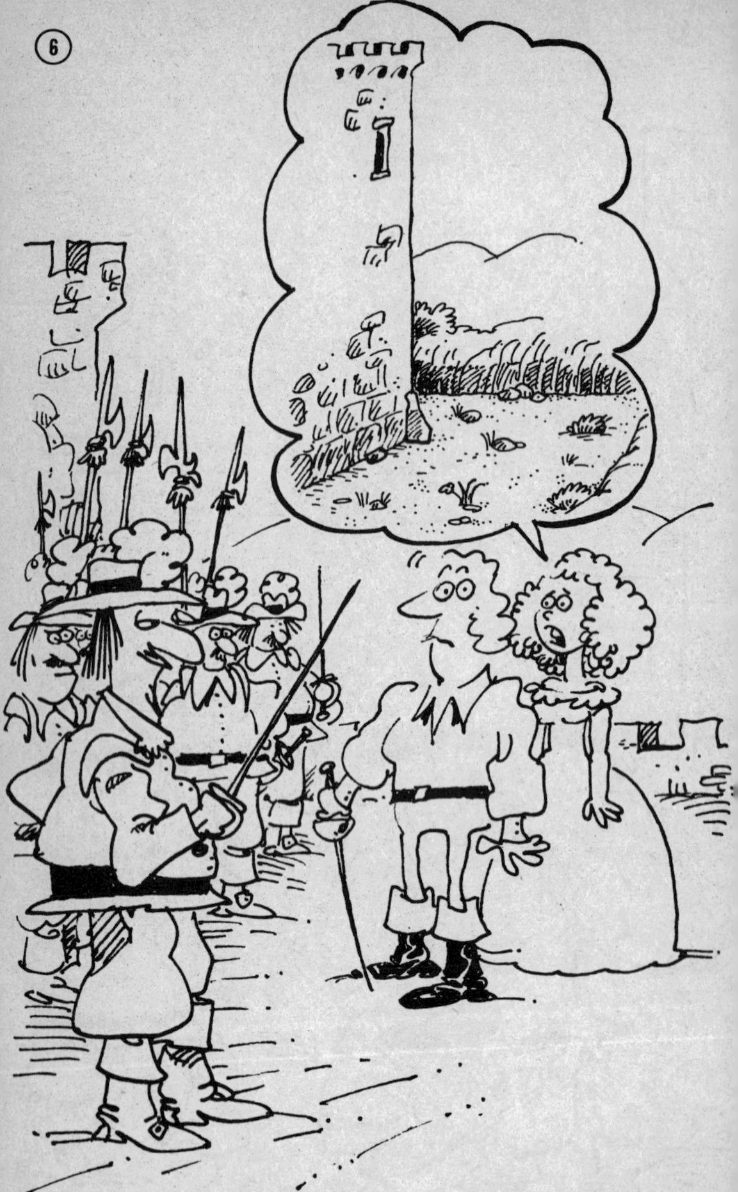

①

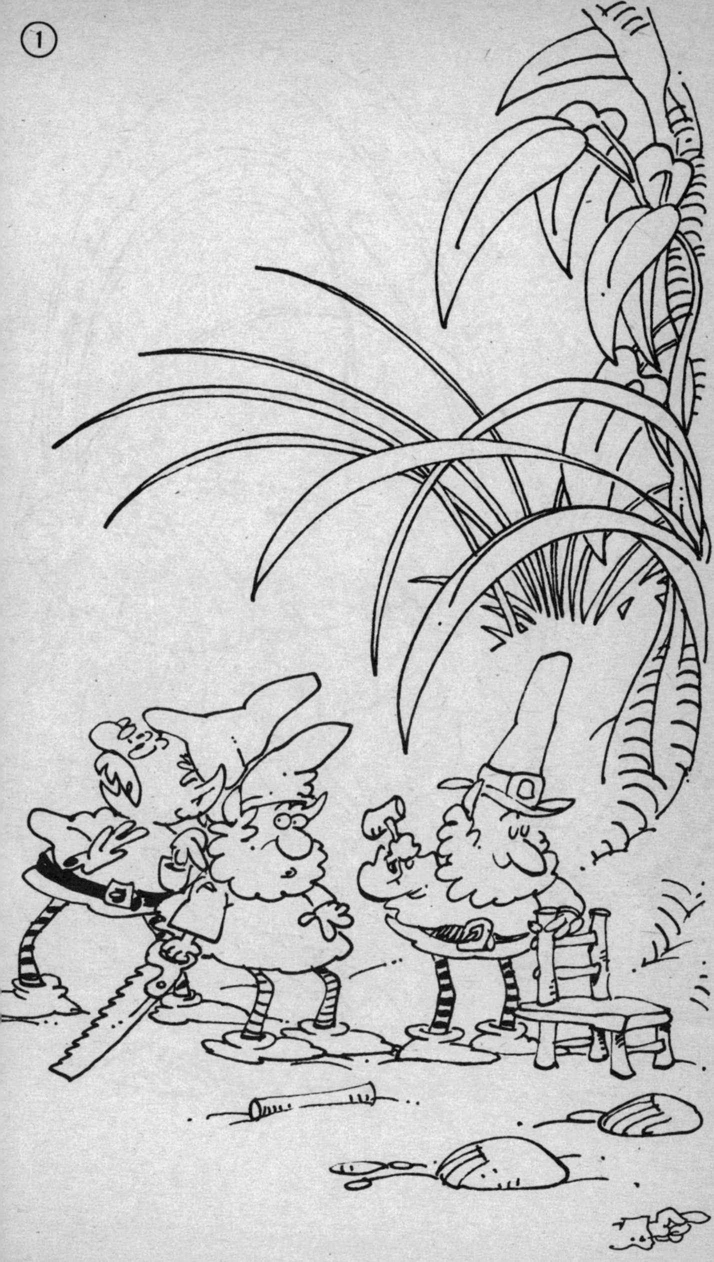

2

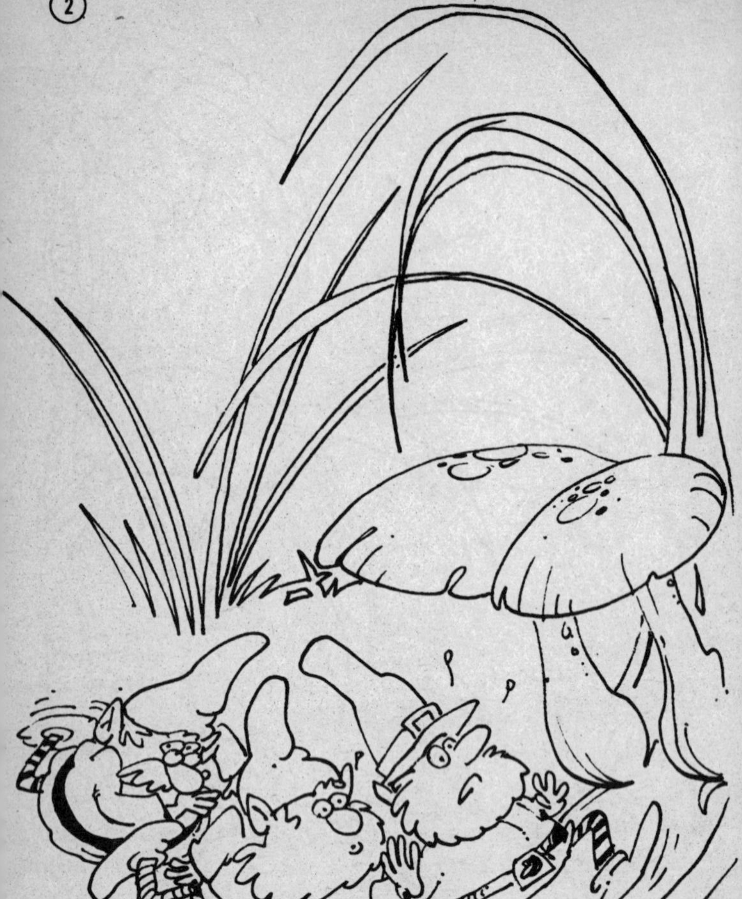

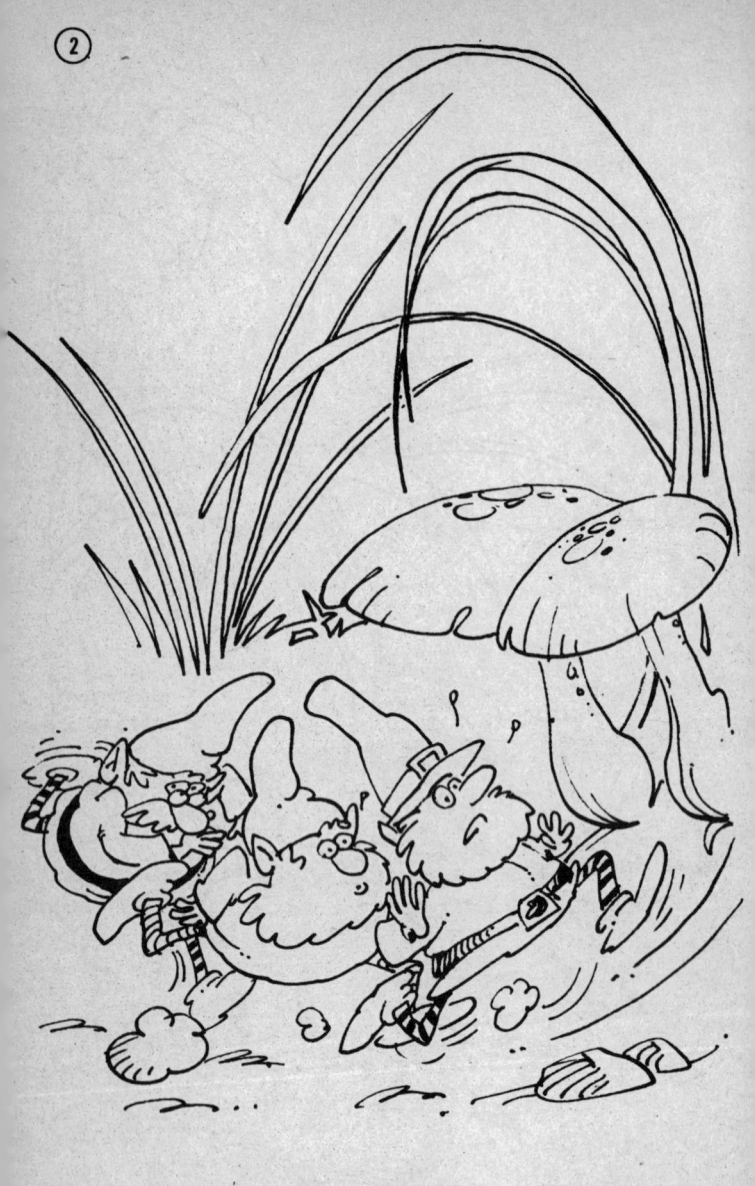

3

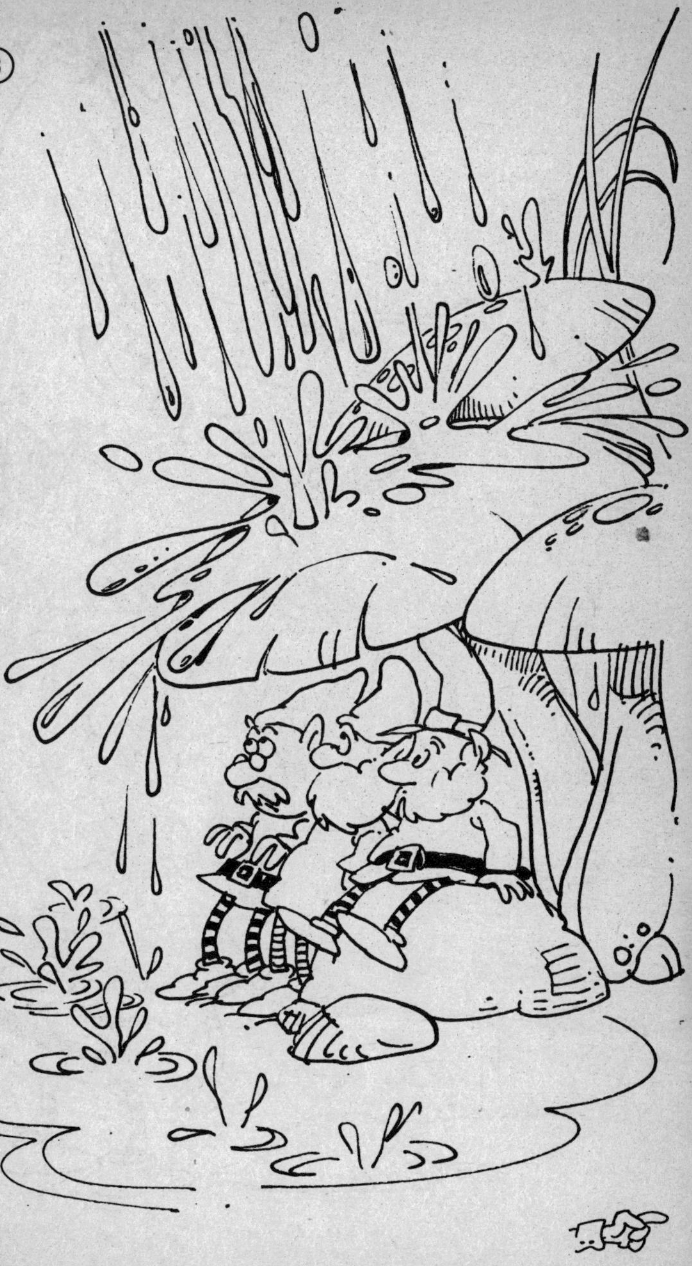

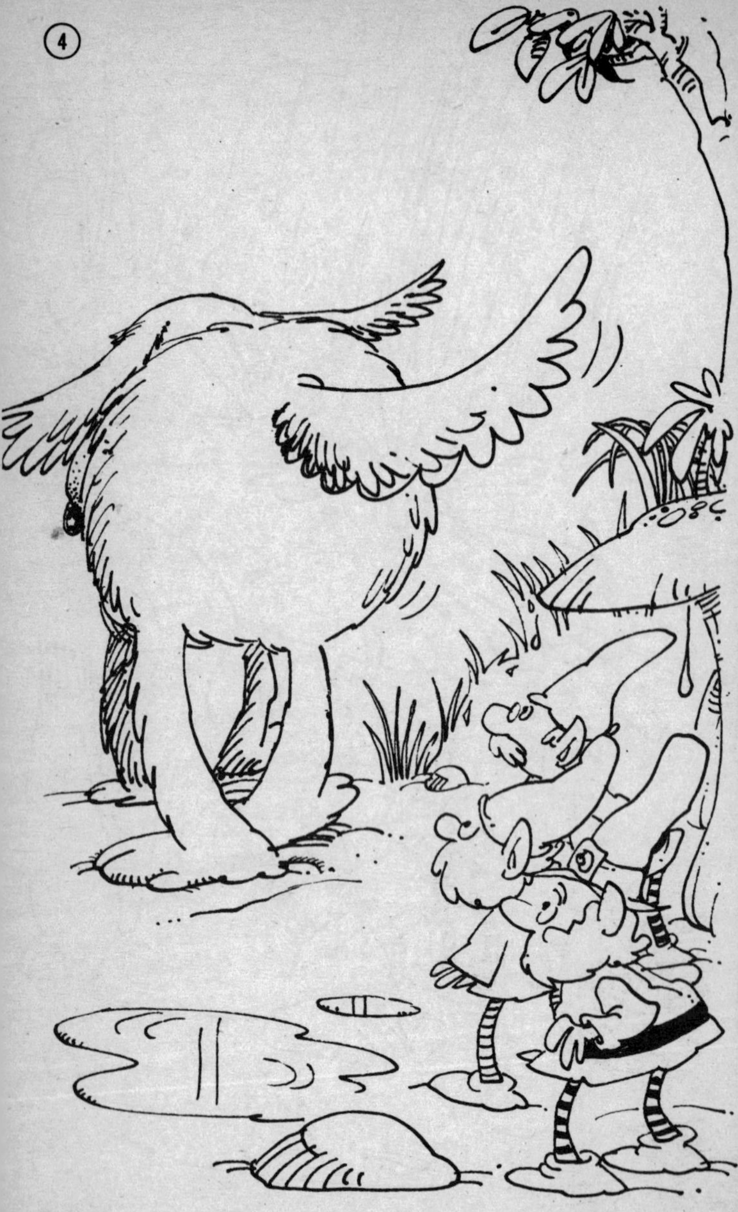
4

1

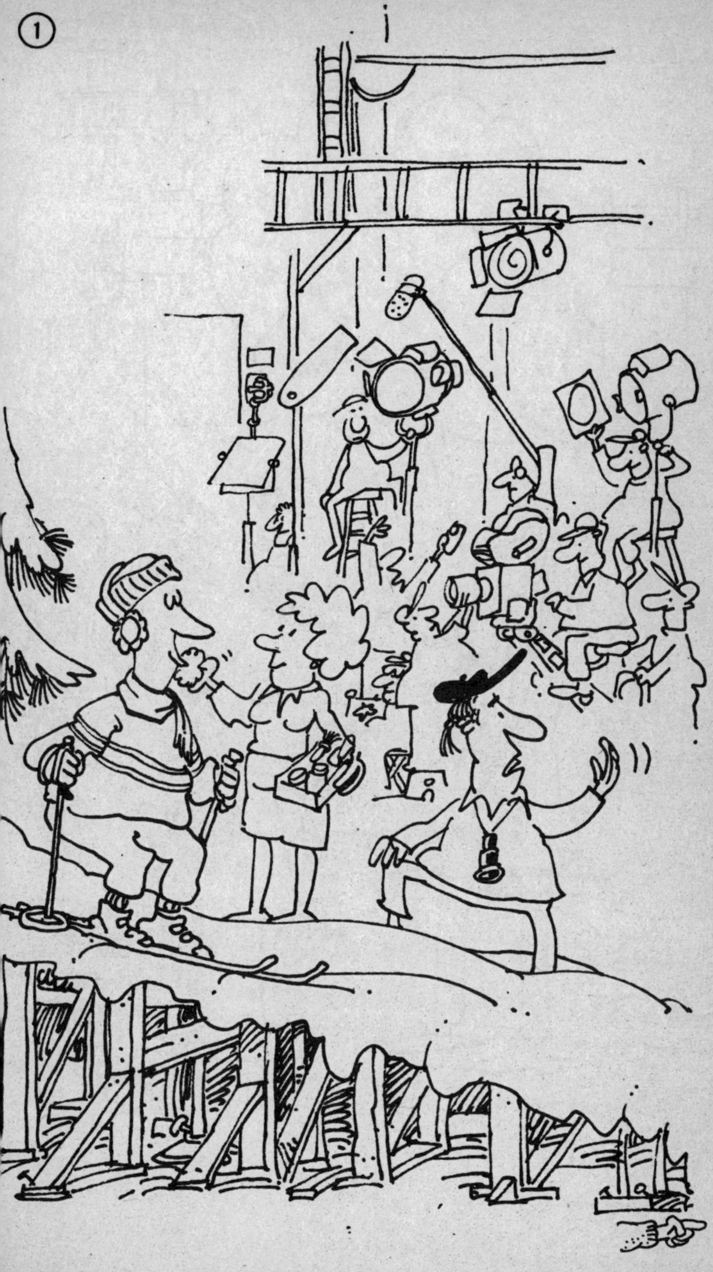

(2)

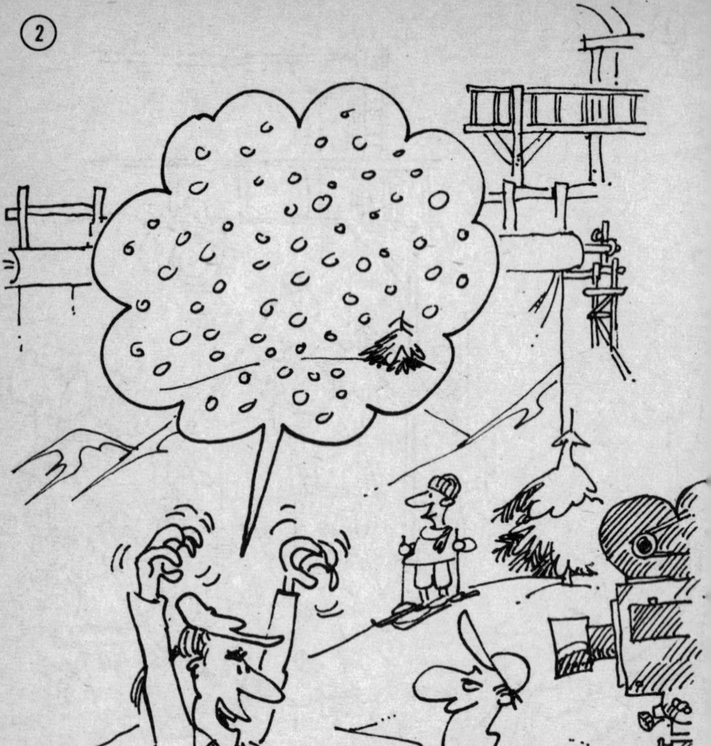
FX

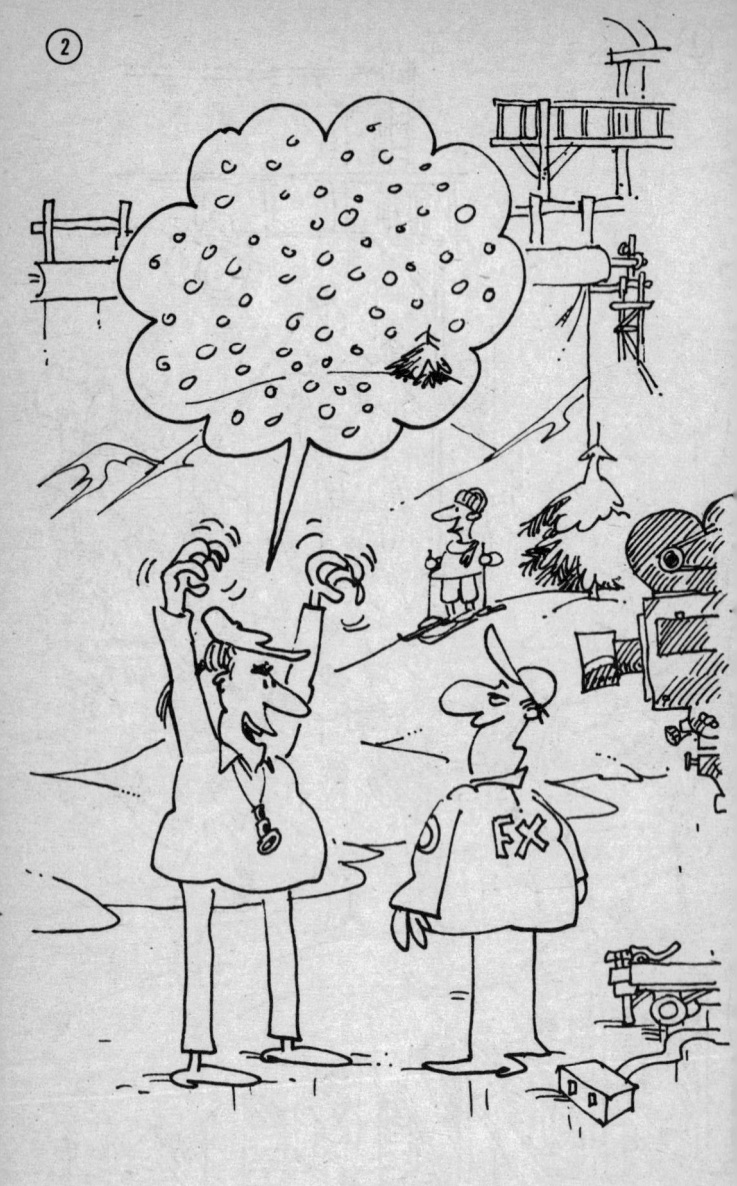

3

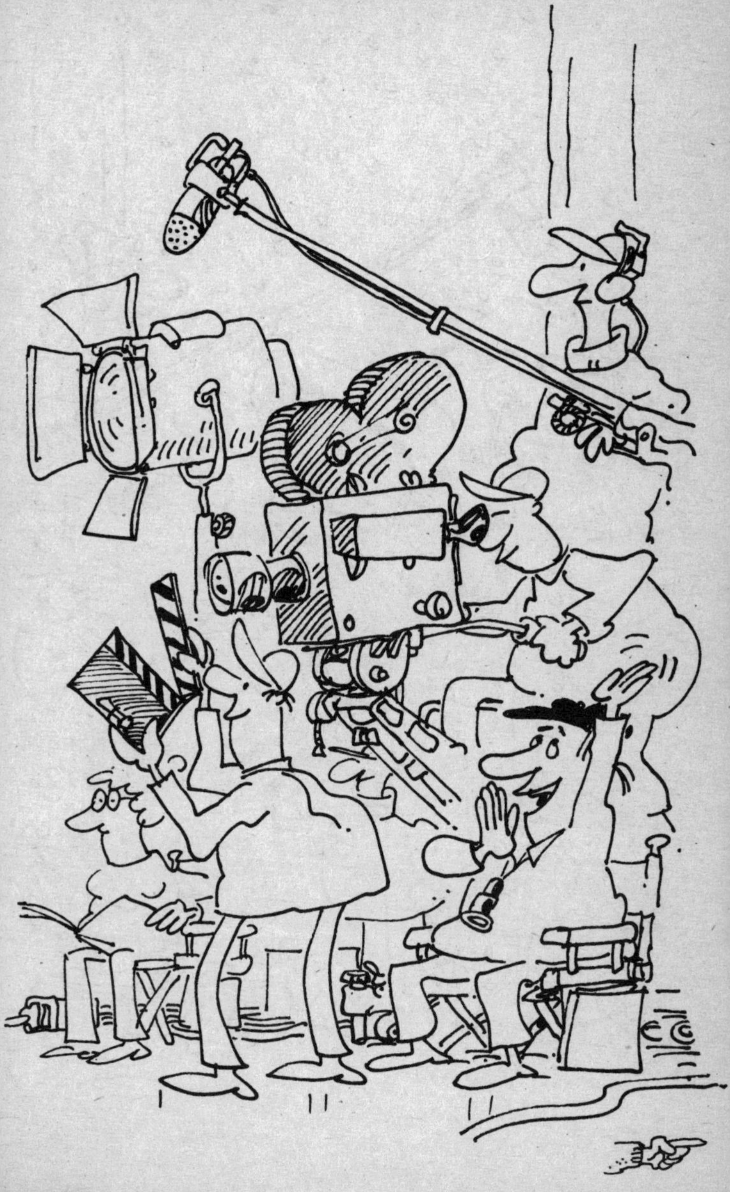

4

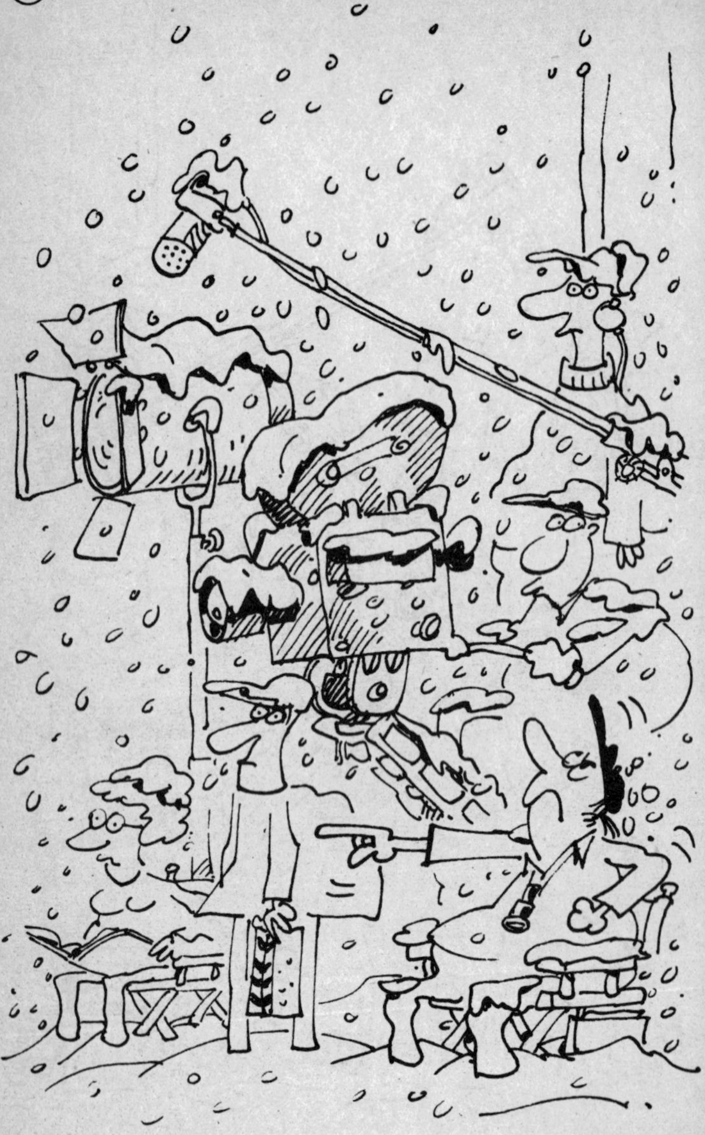

(1)

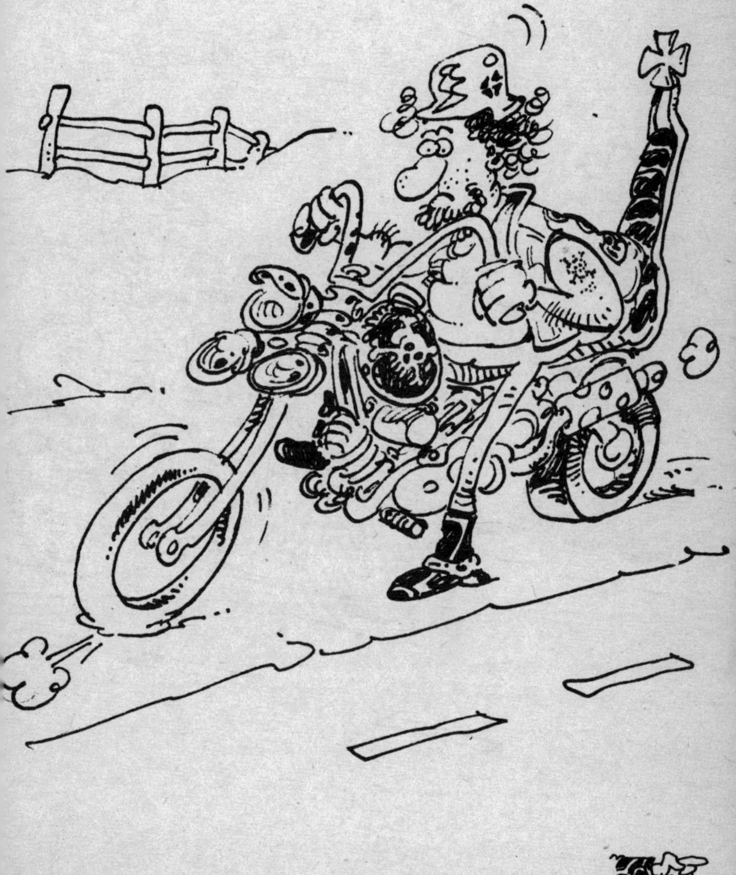

2

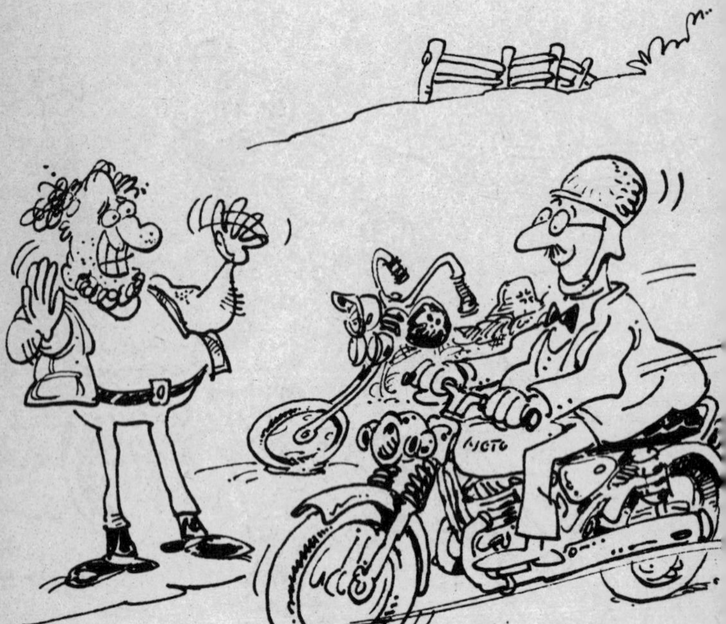
MOTO

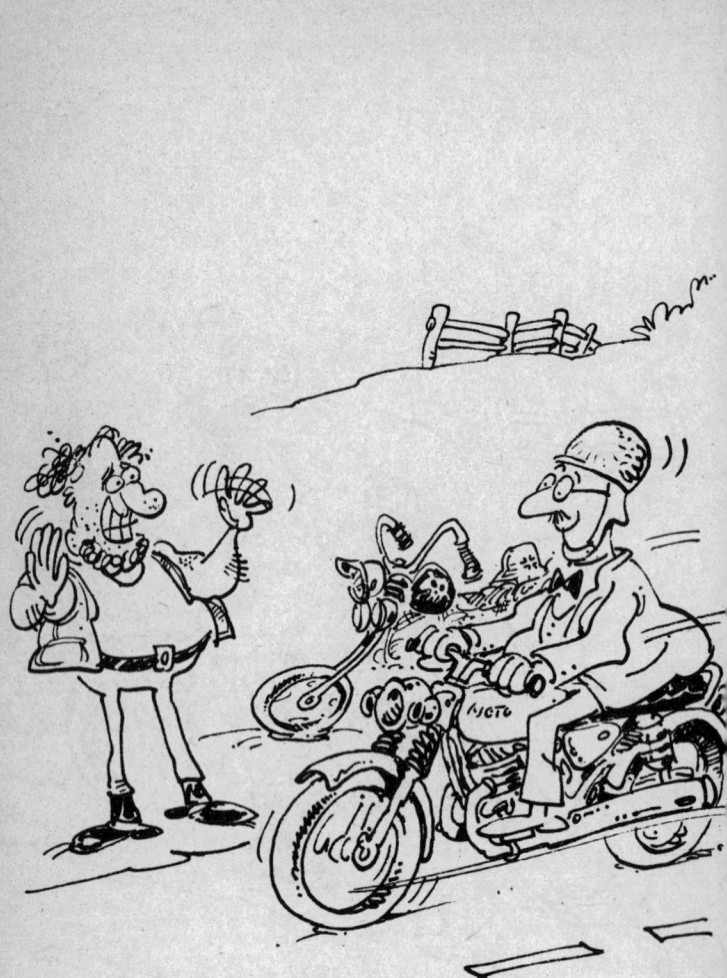

(3)

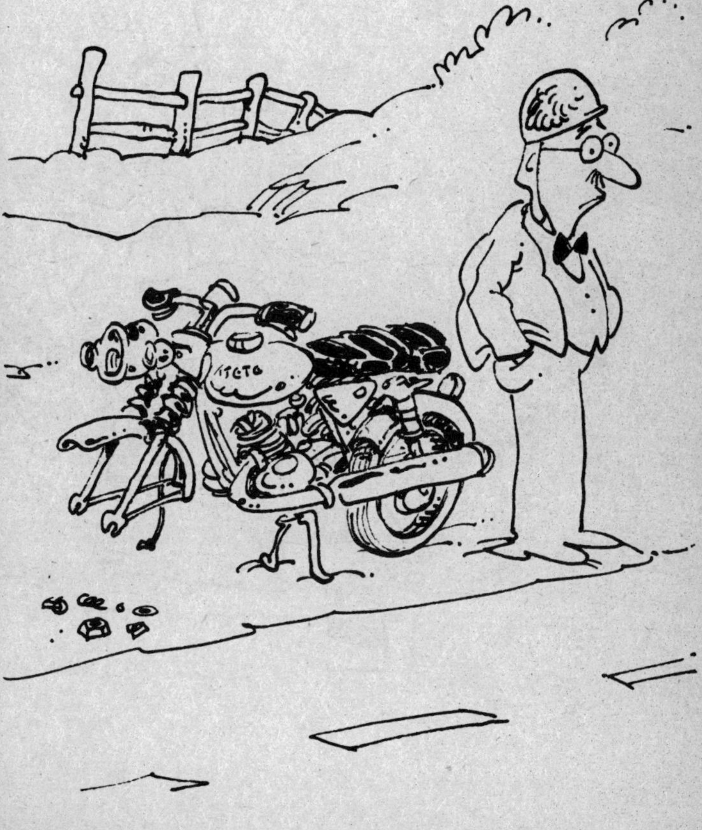

1

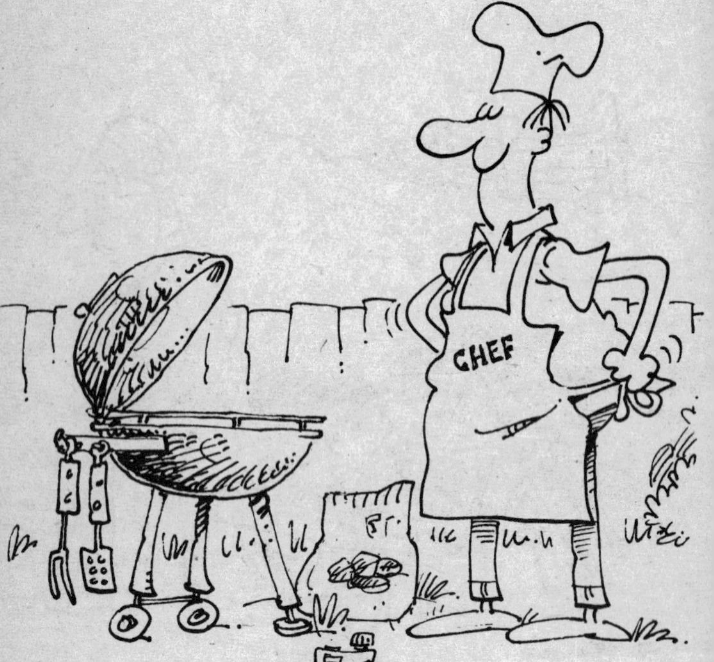
CHEF

(2)

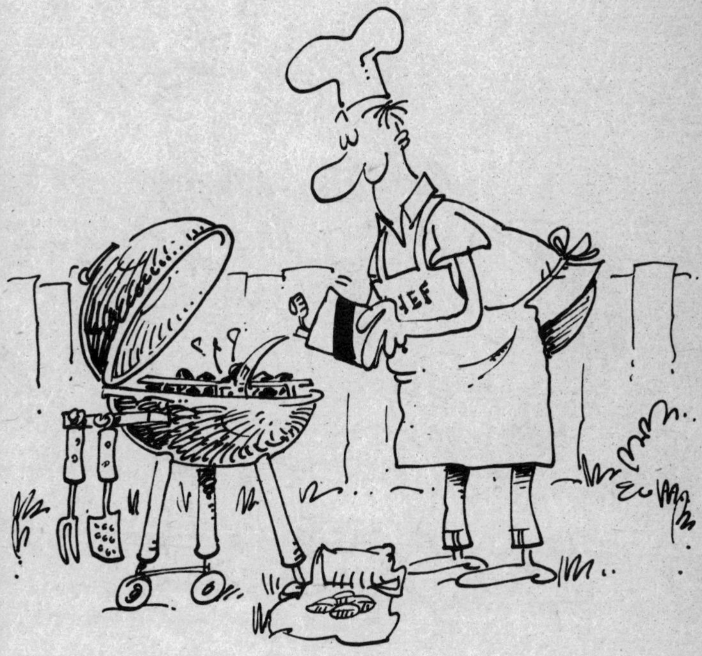
HEF

③

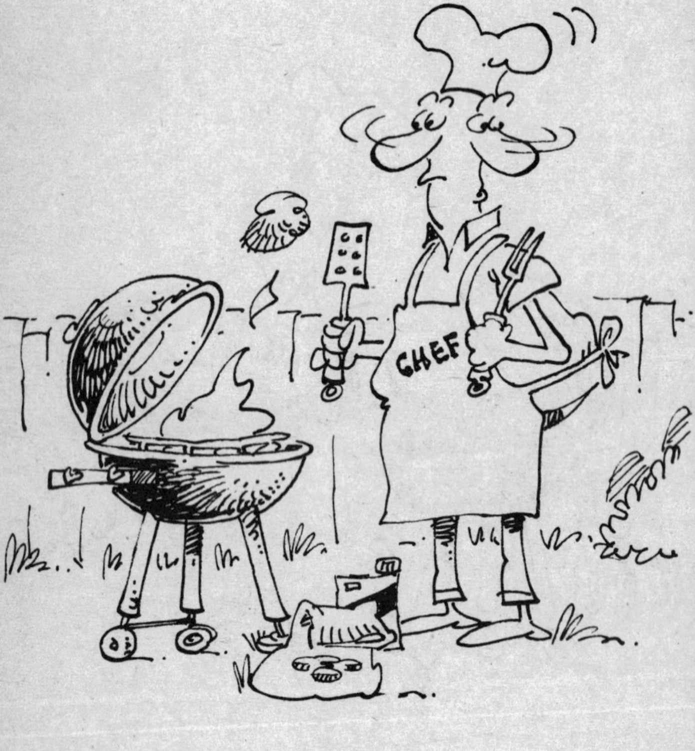
CHEF

4

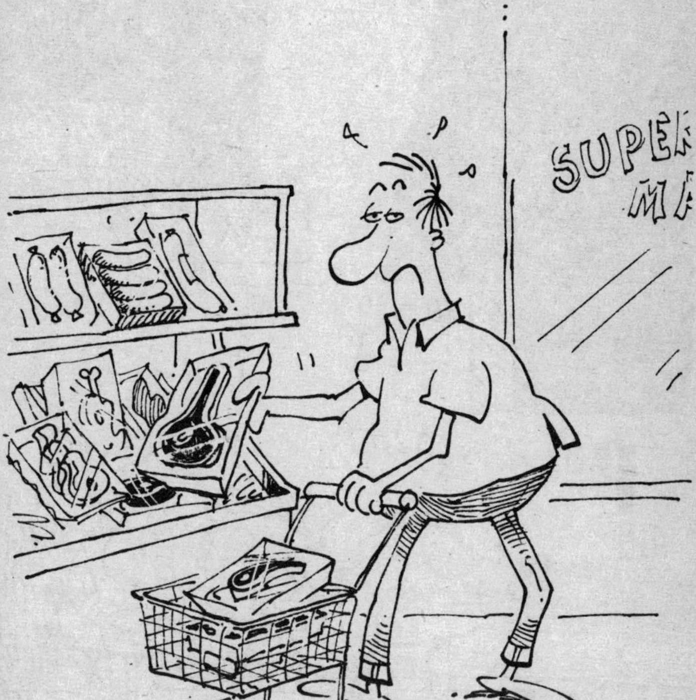
SUPE

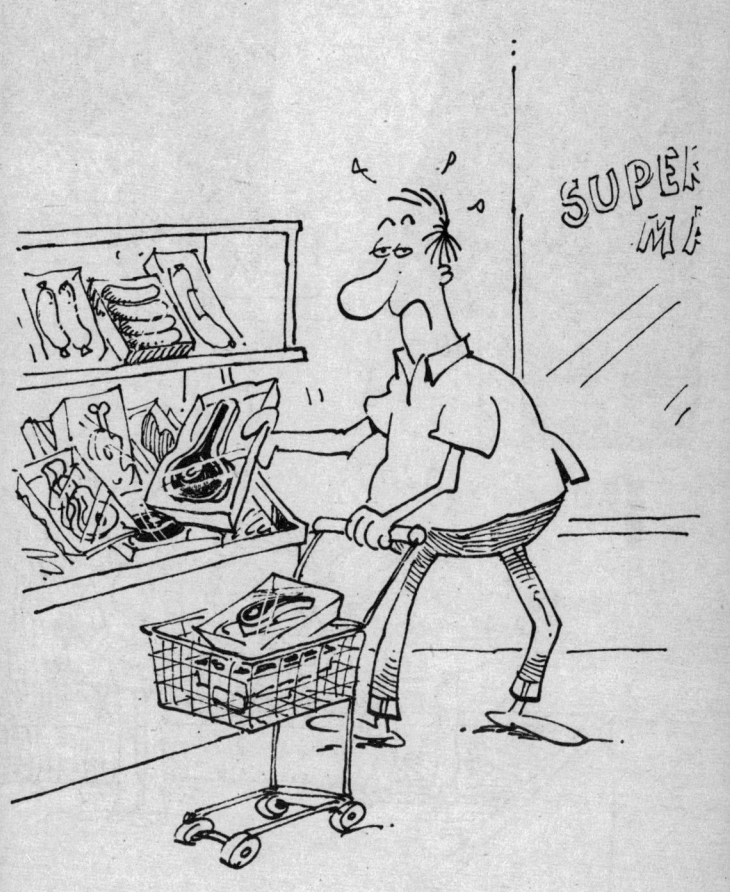

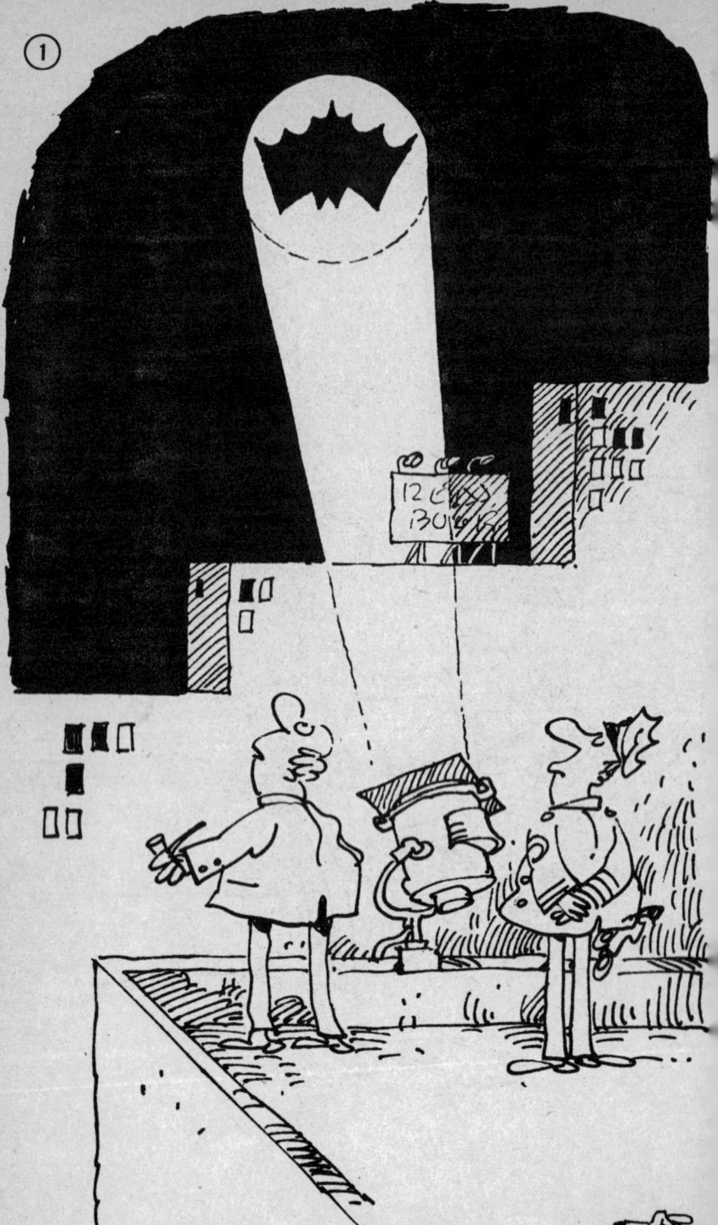
1

2

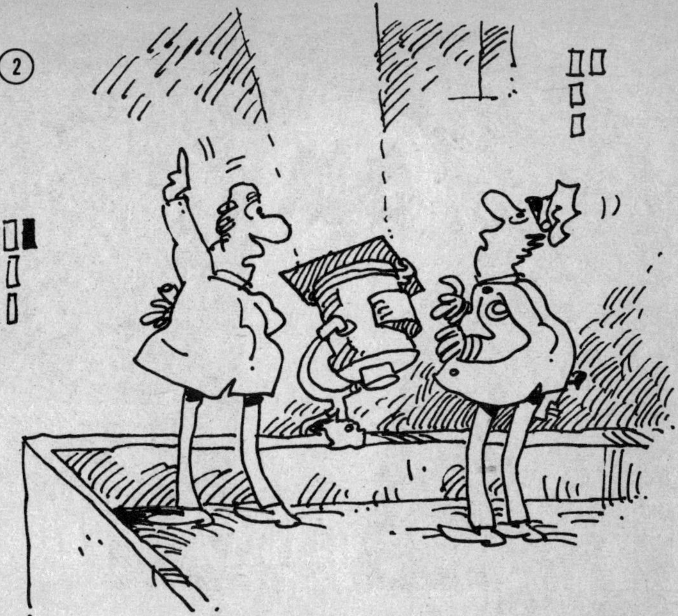

3

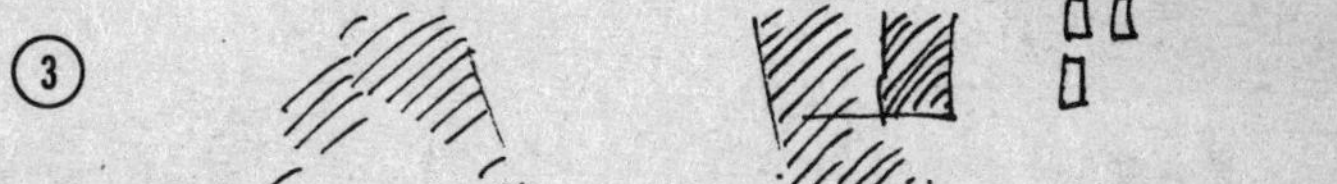

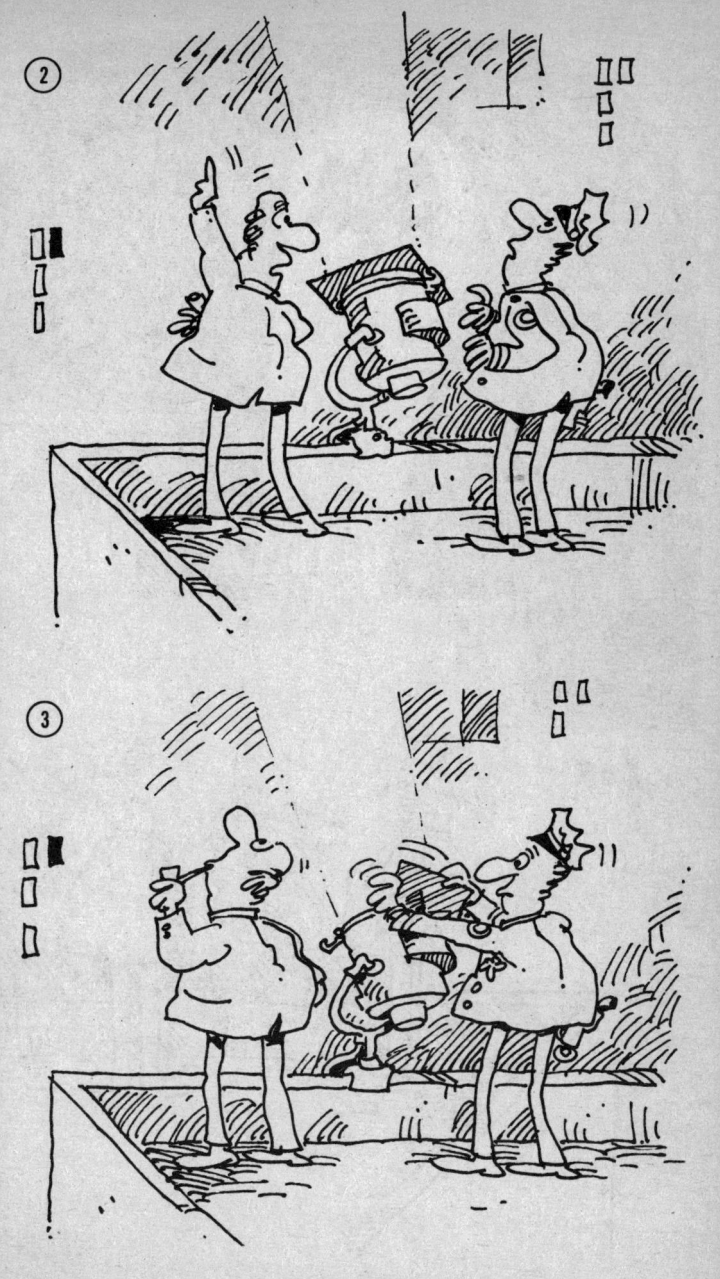

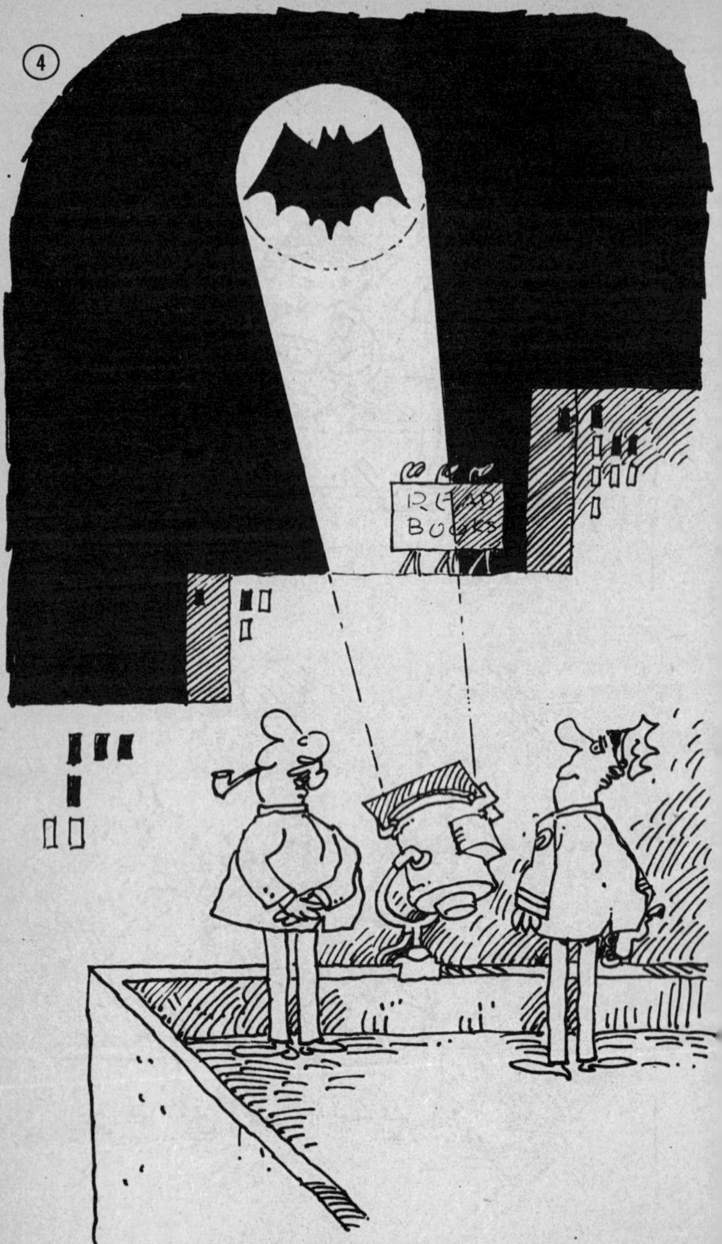
4
READ
BOOKS

1

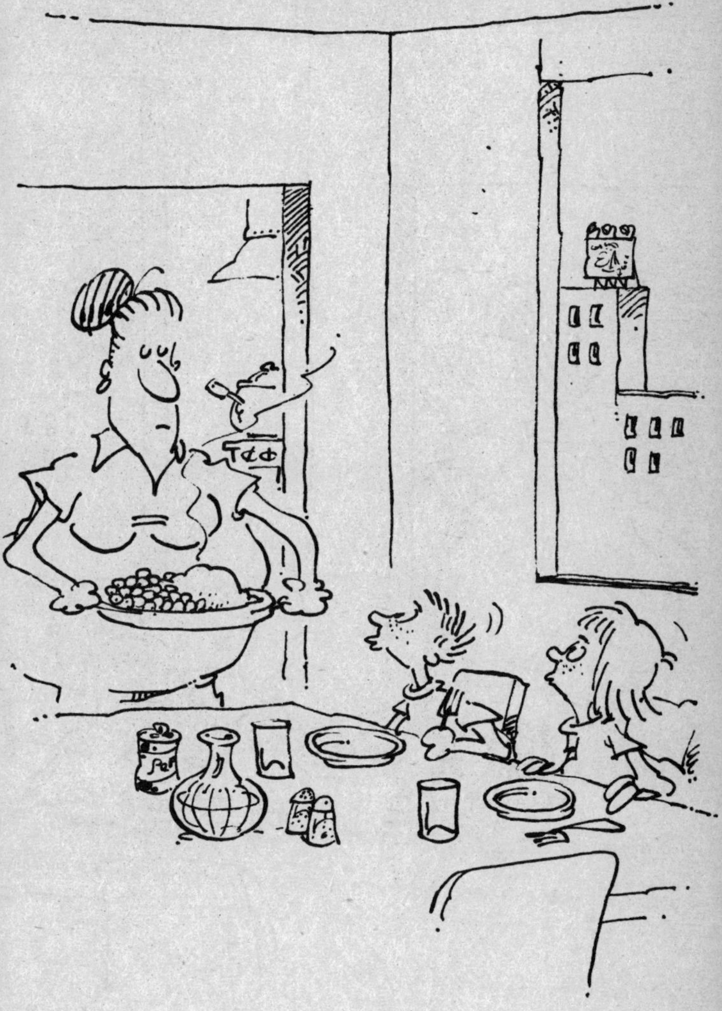

(2)

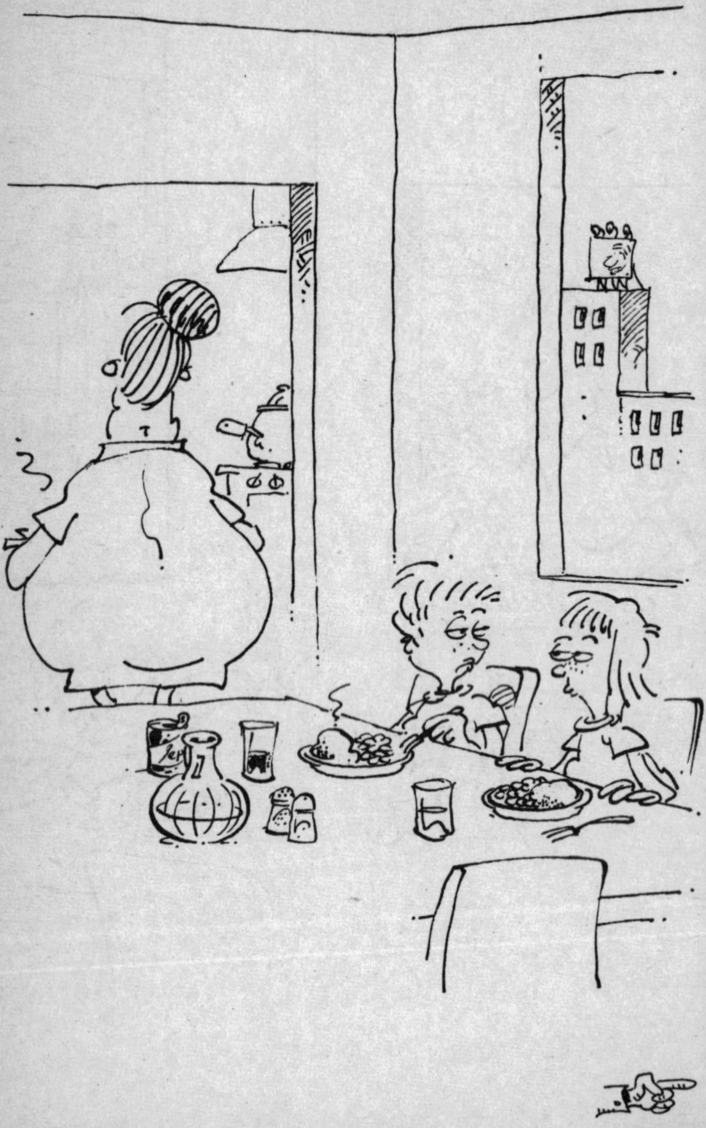

3

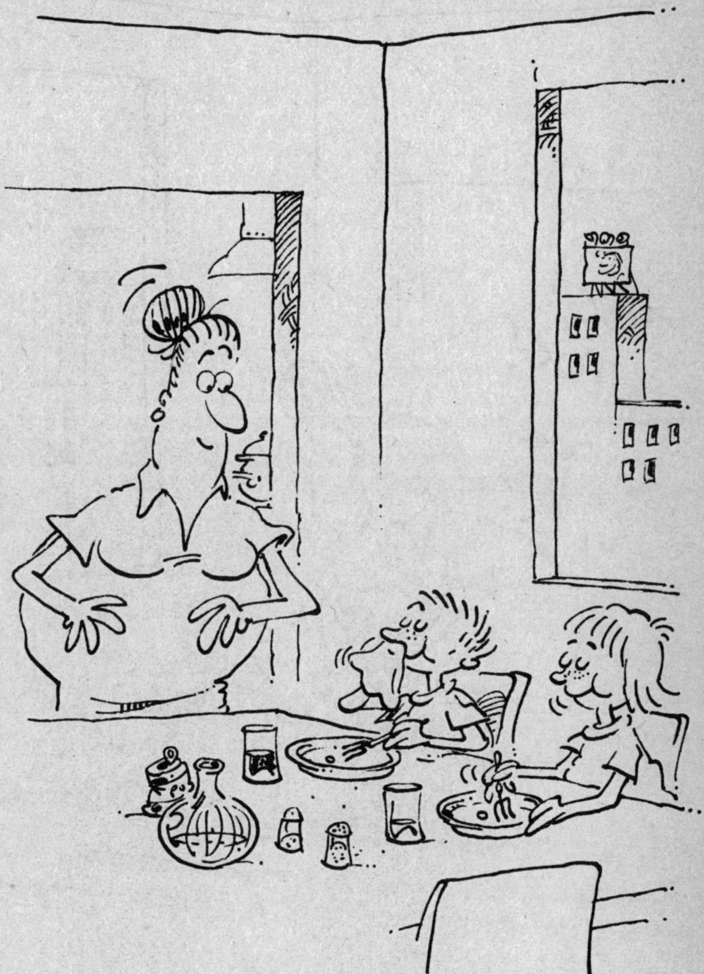

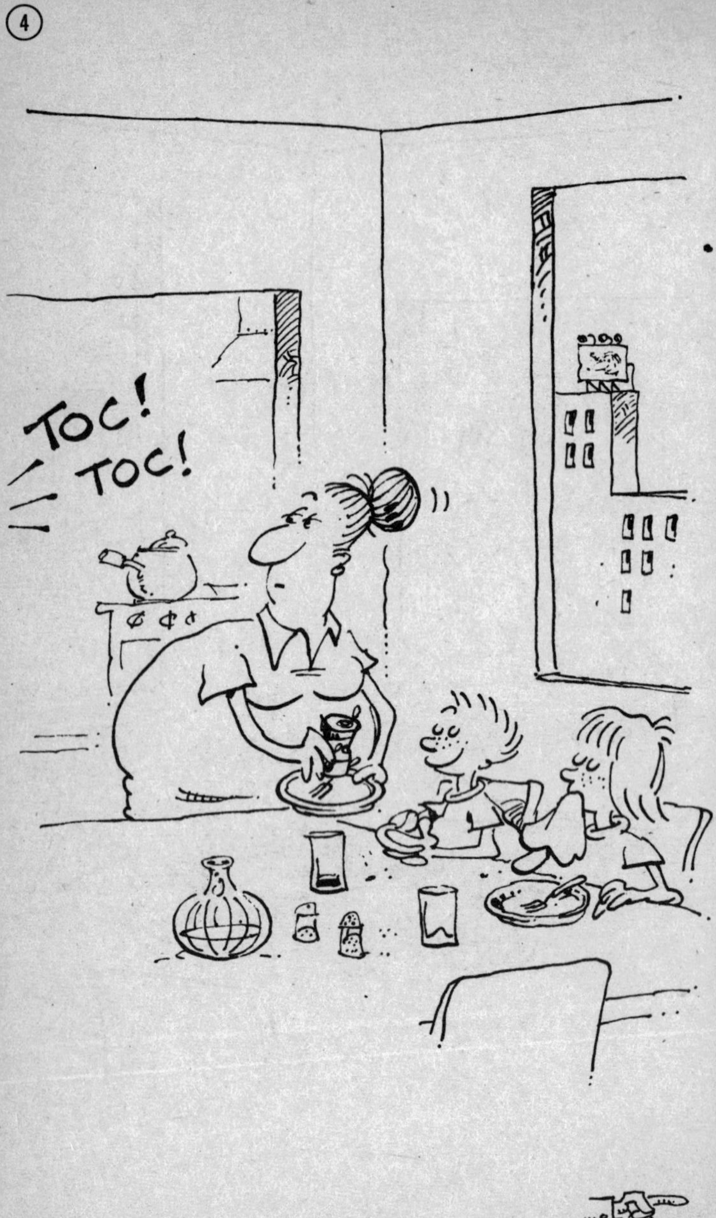
4
TOC!
TOC!

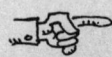

5

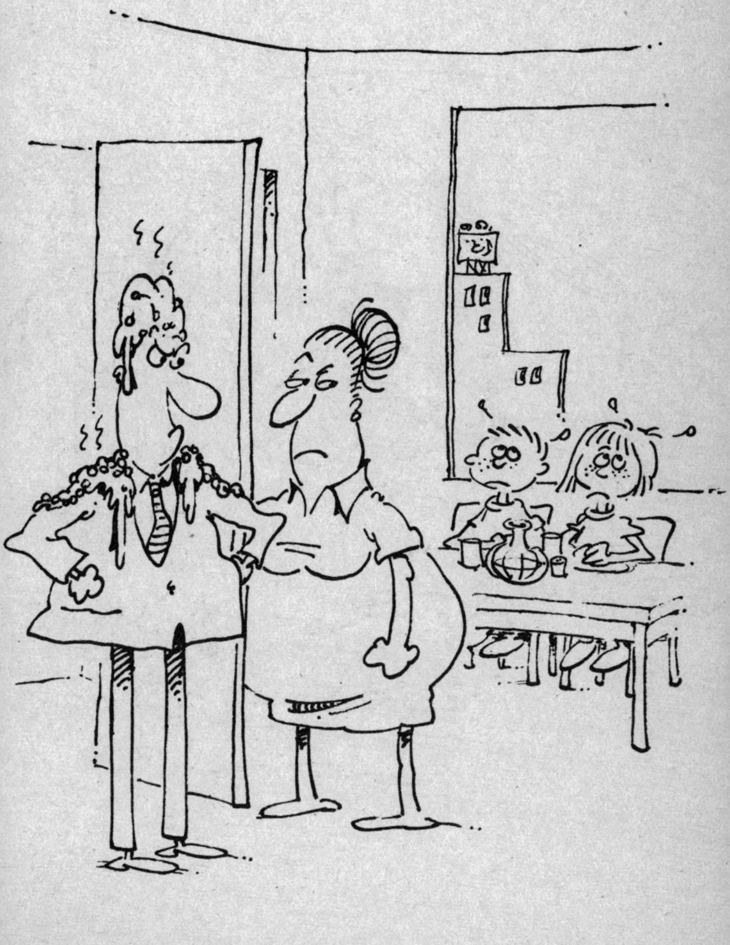

①

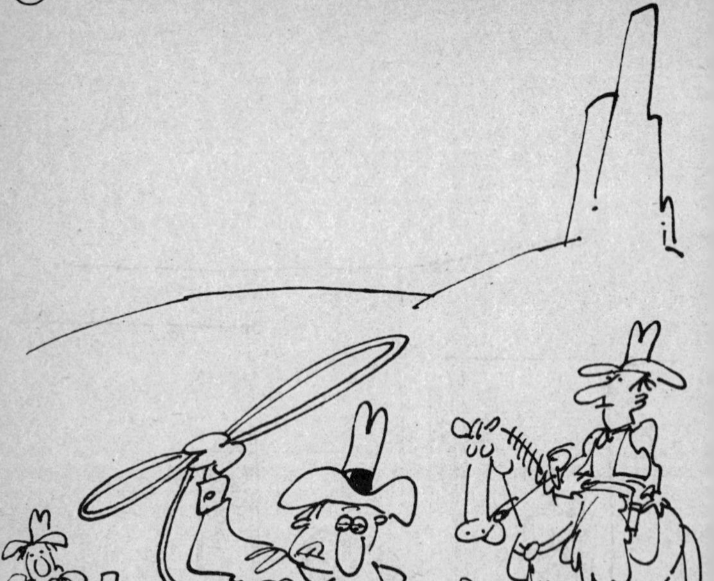

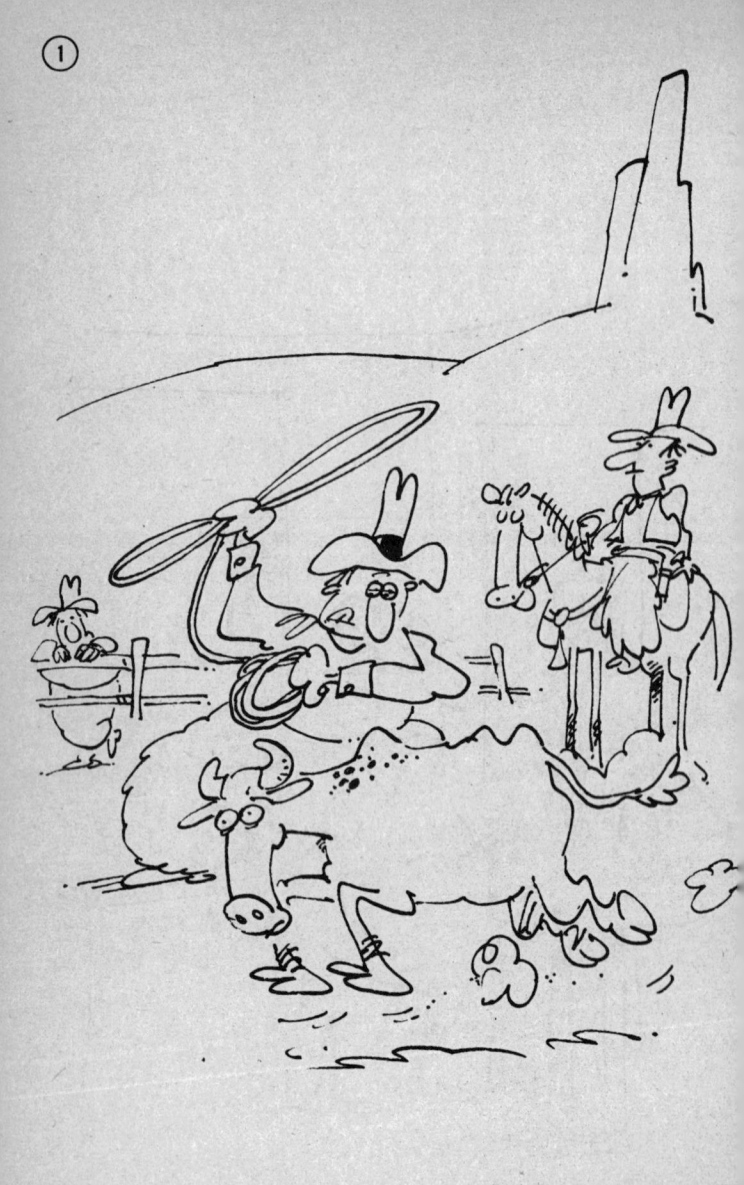

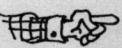

3

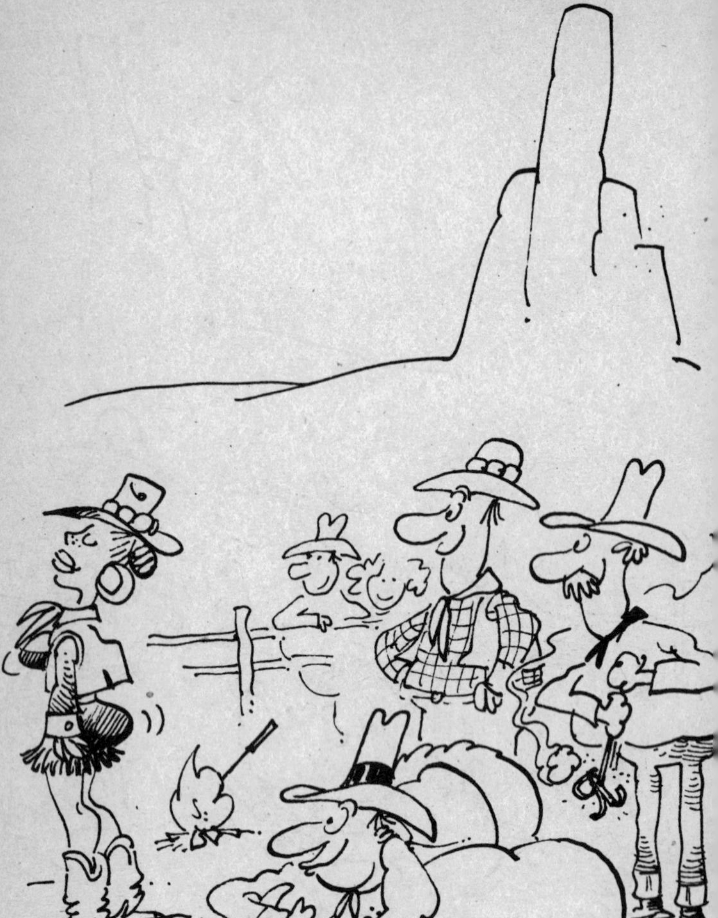

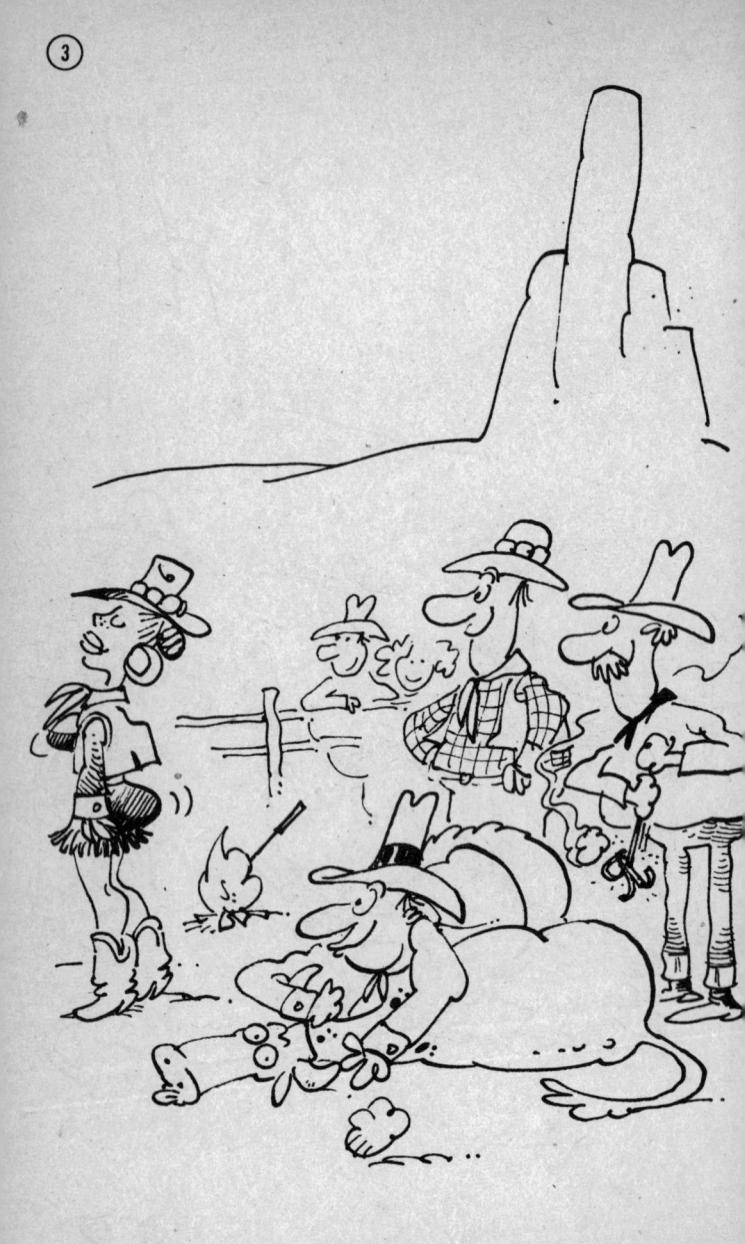

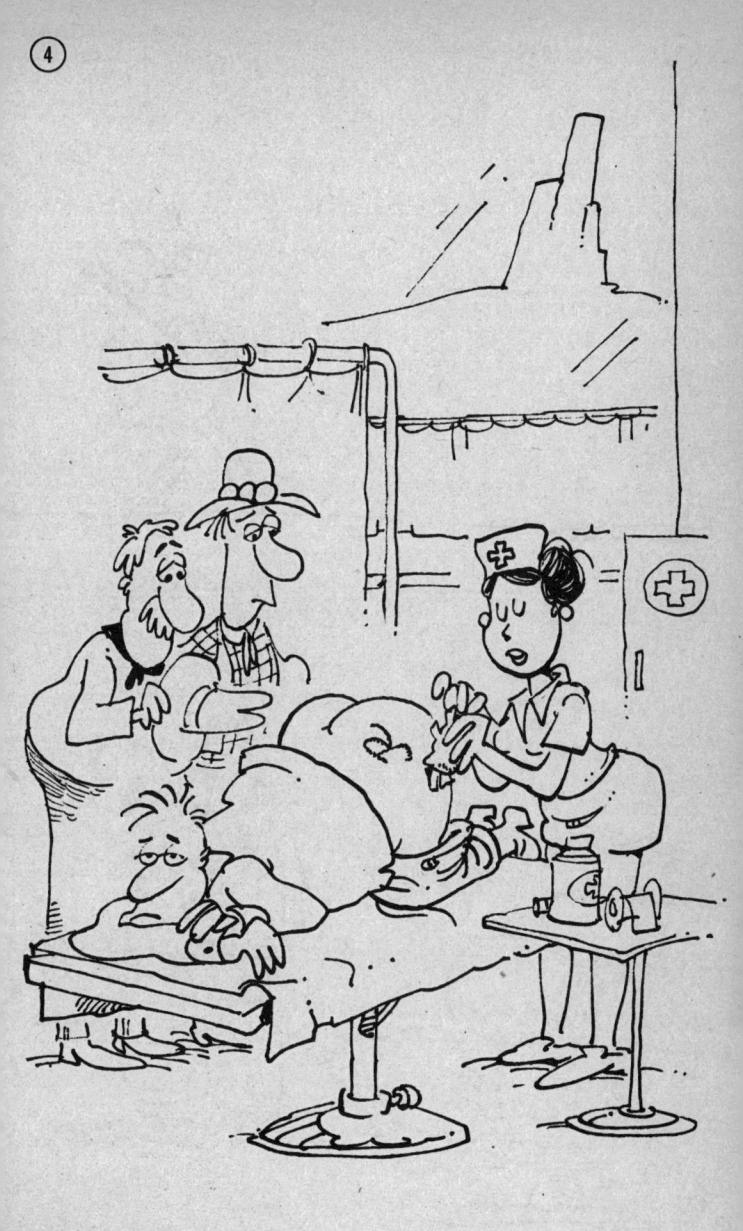

1

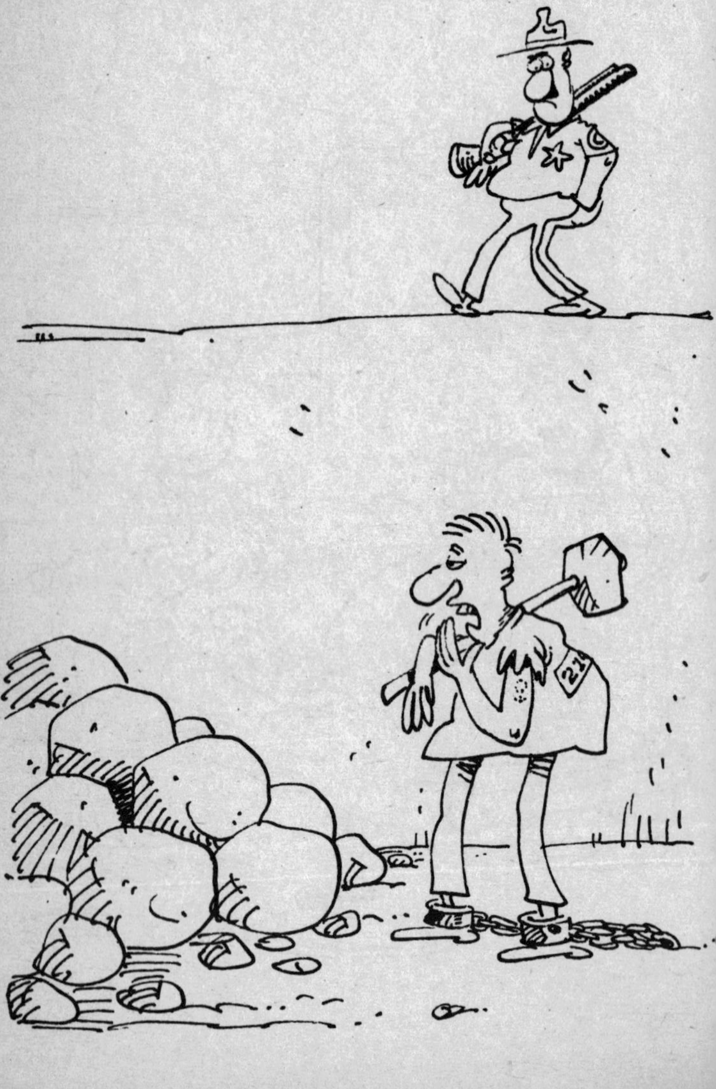

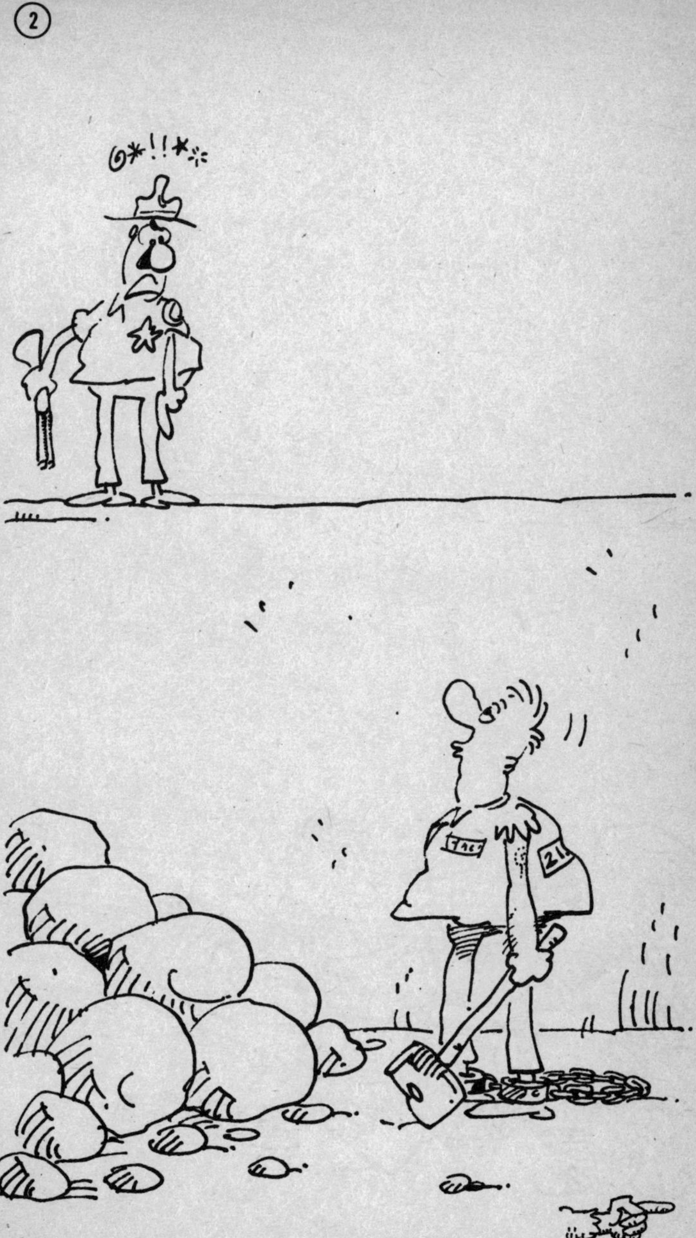
2

3

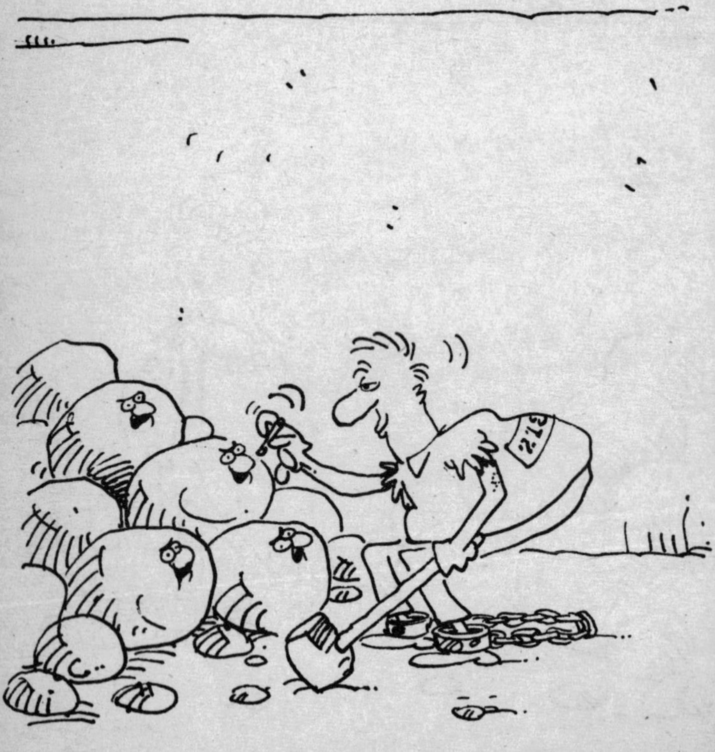

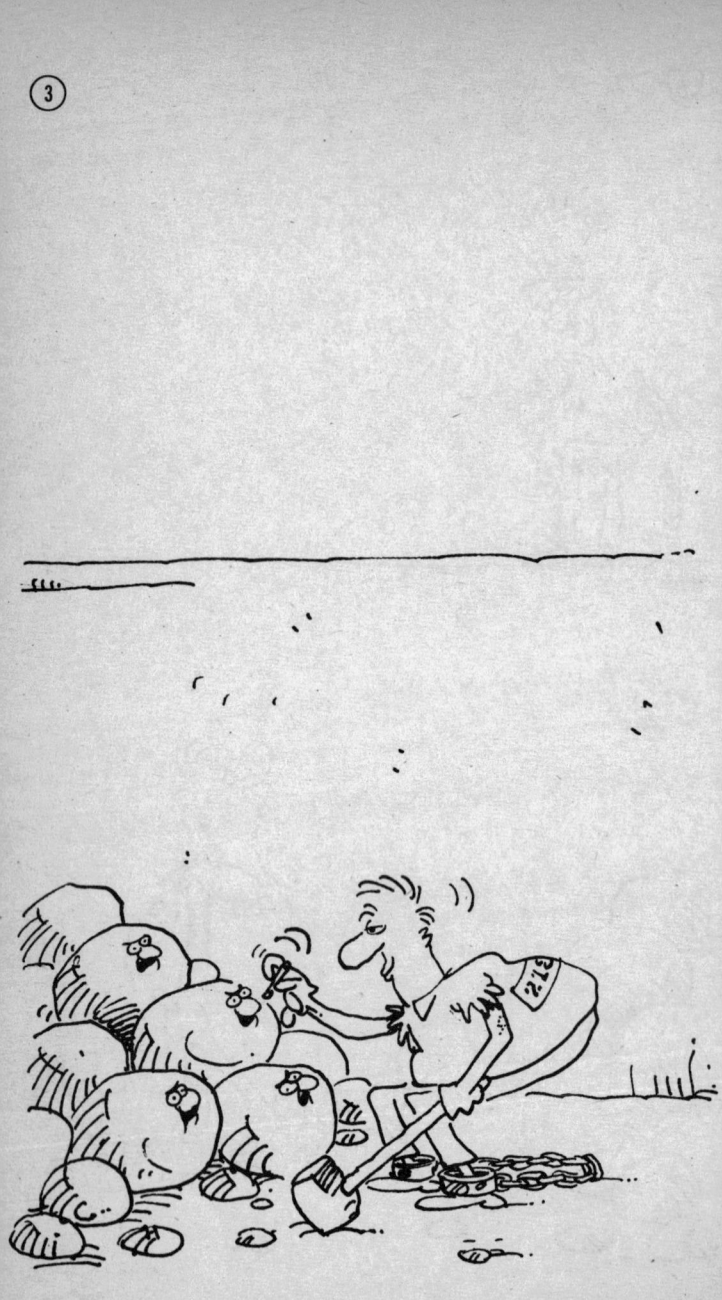

4

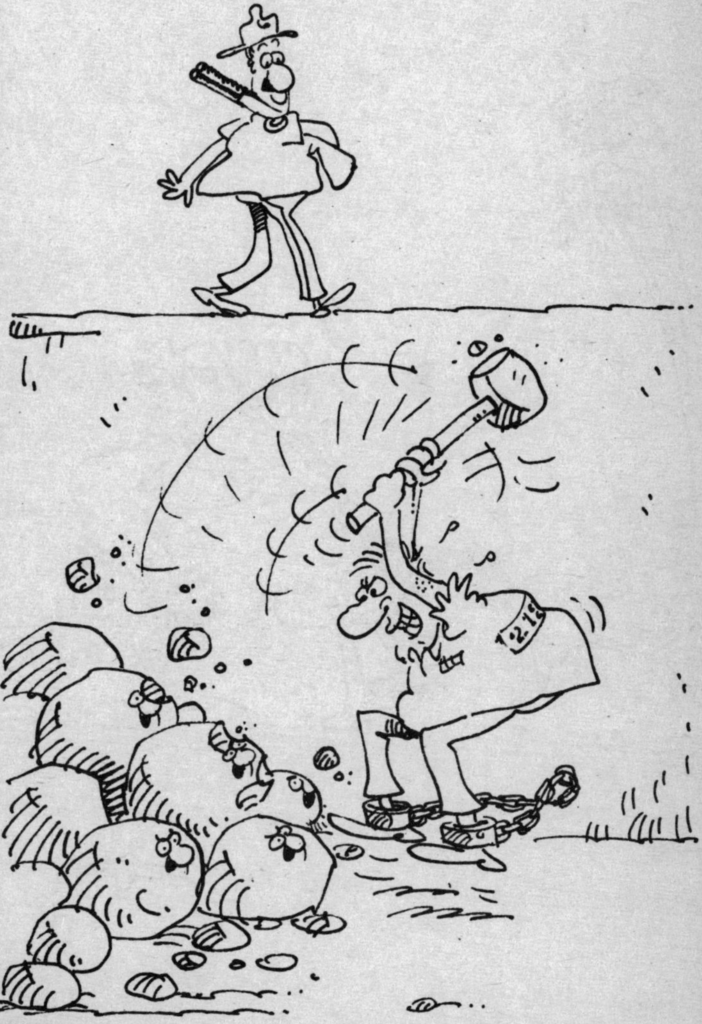

①

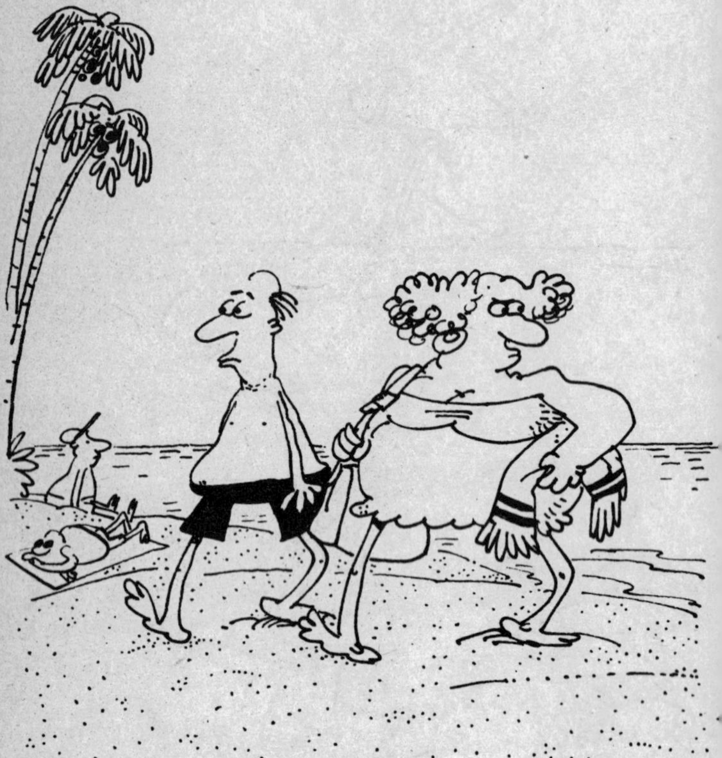

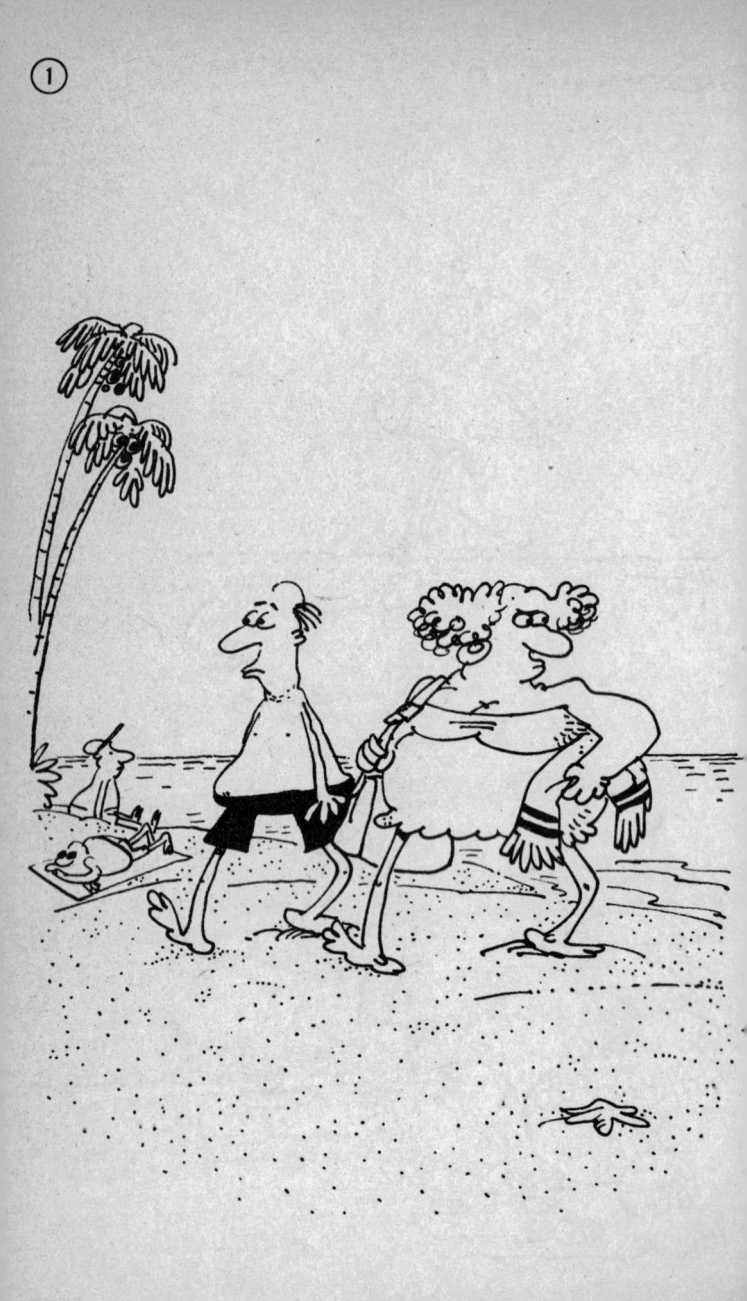

2

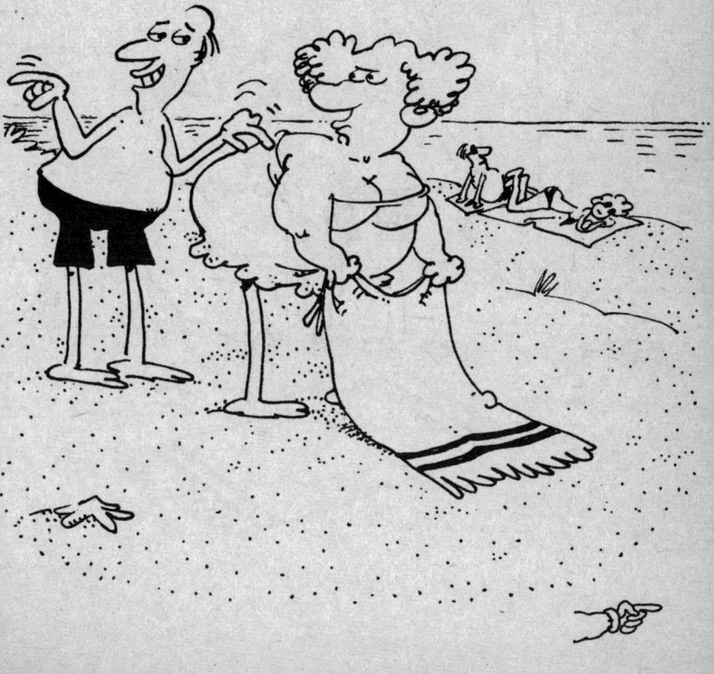

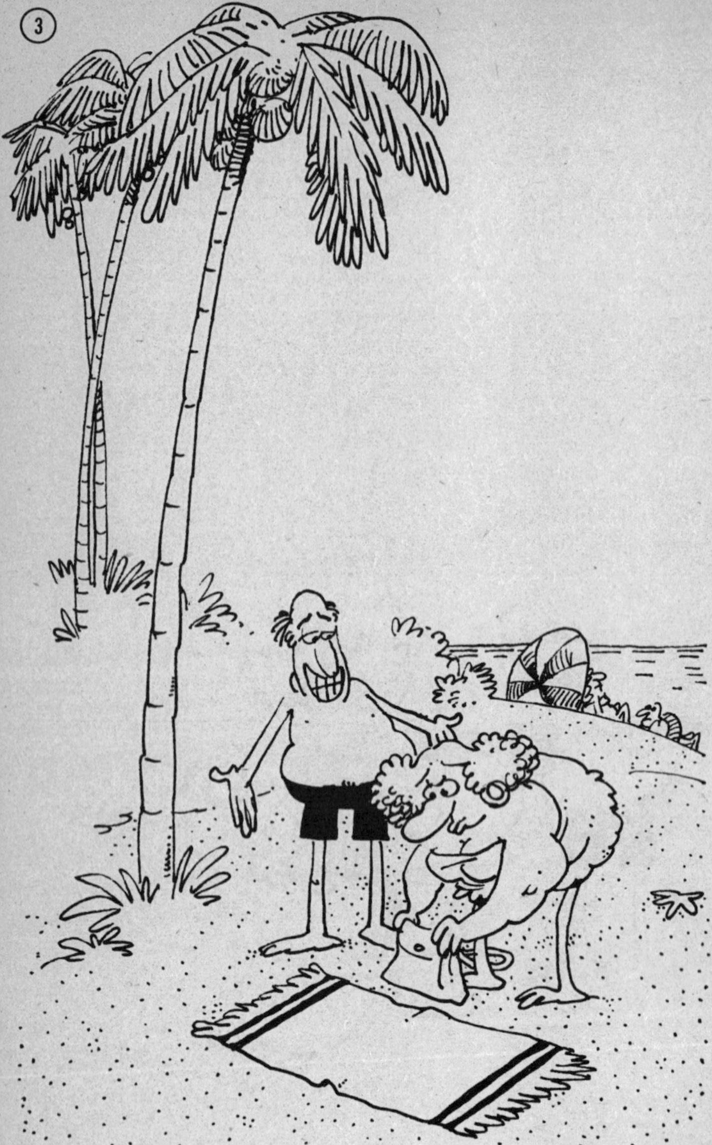

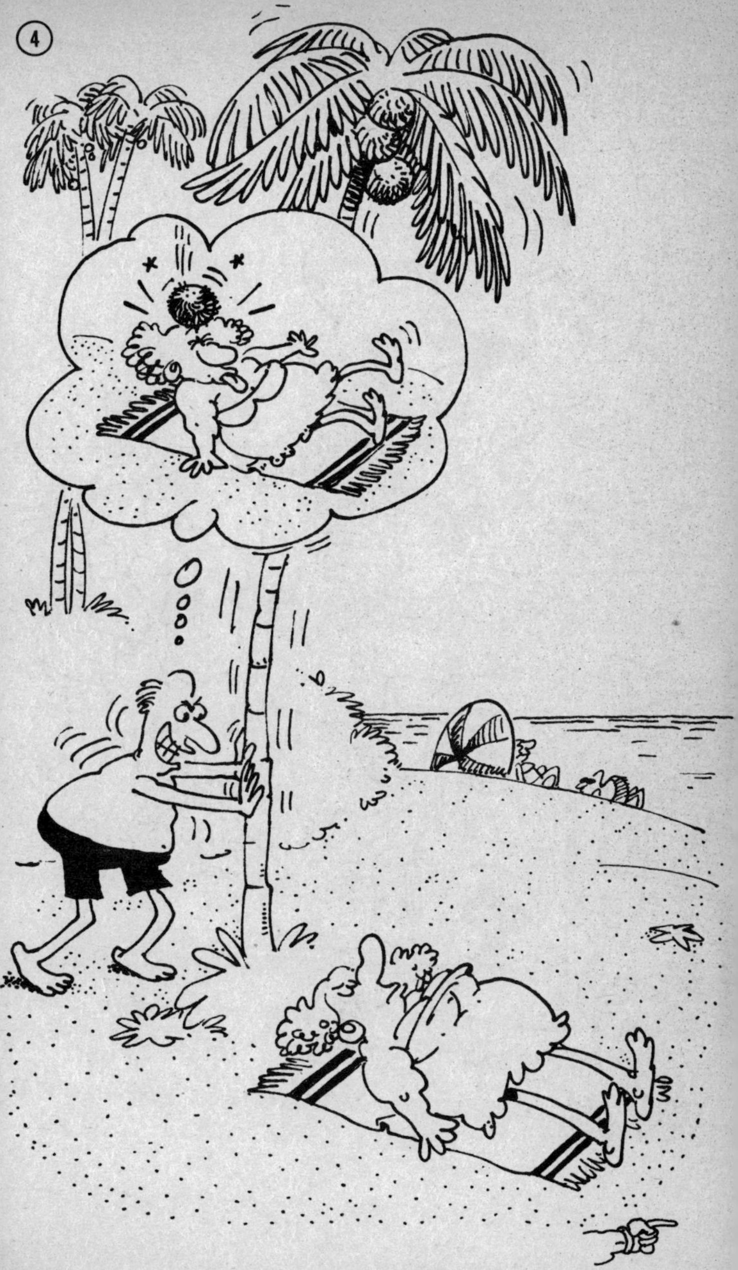
4

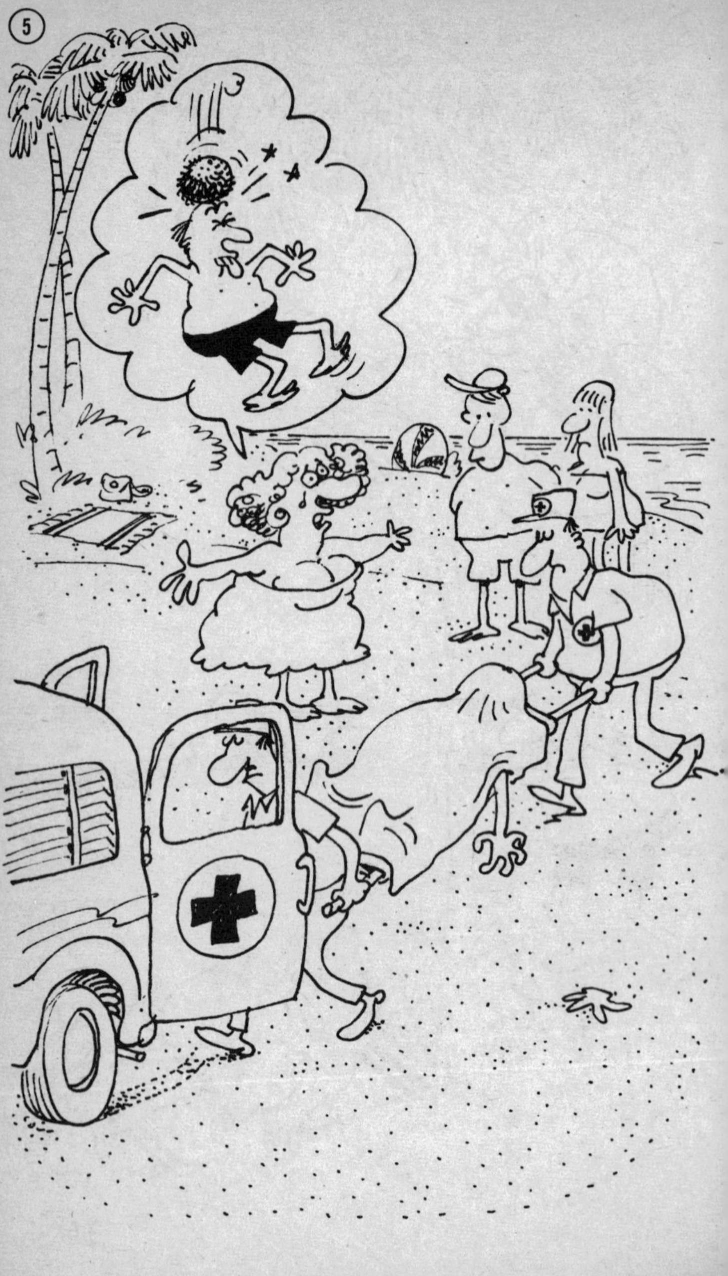
5

①

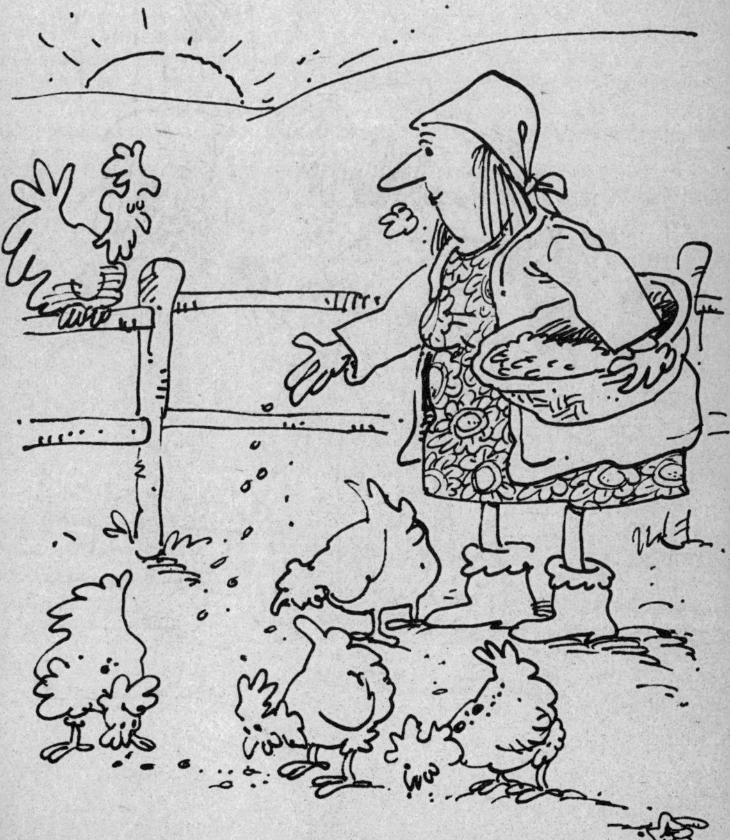

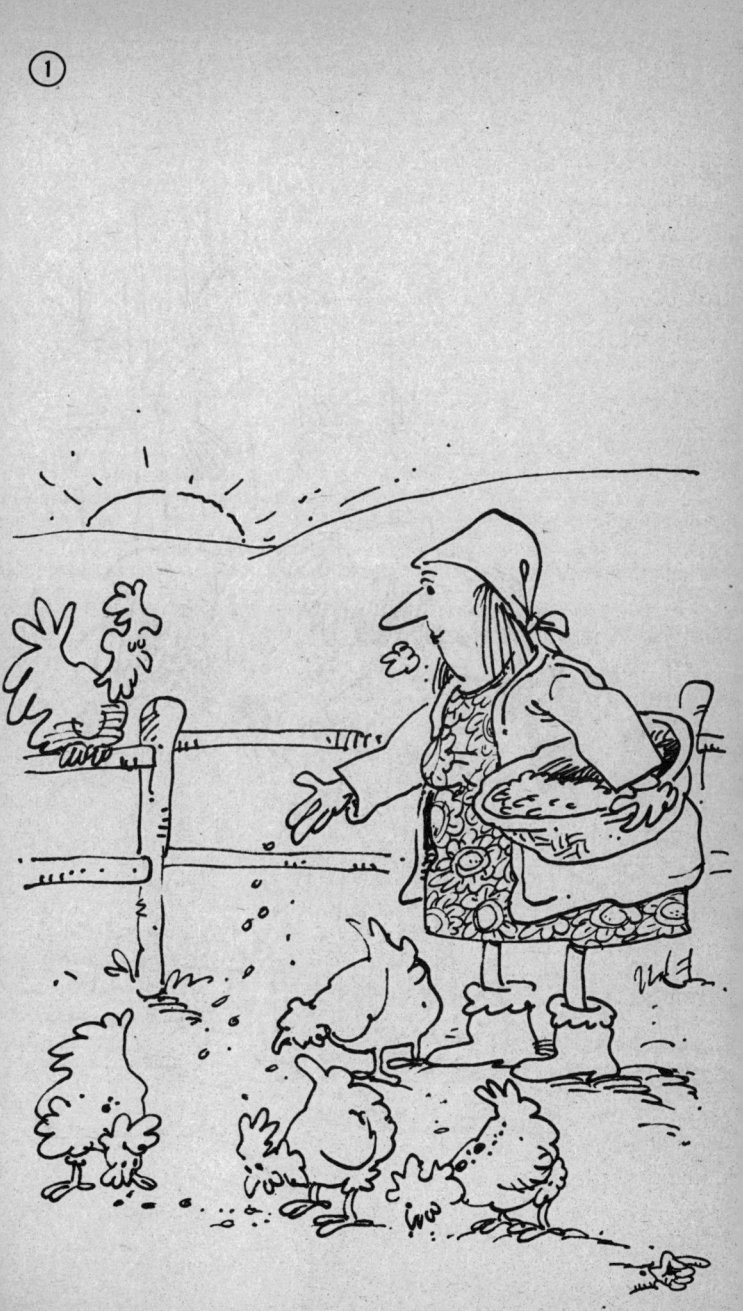

(2)

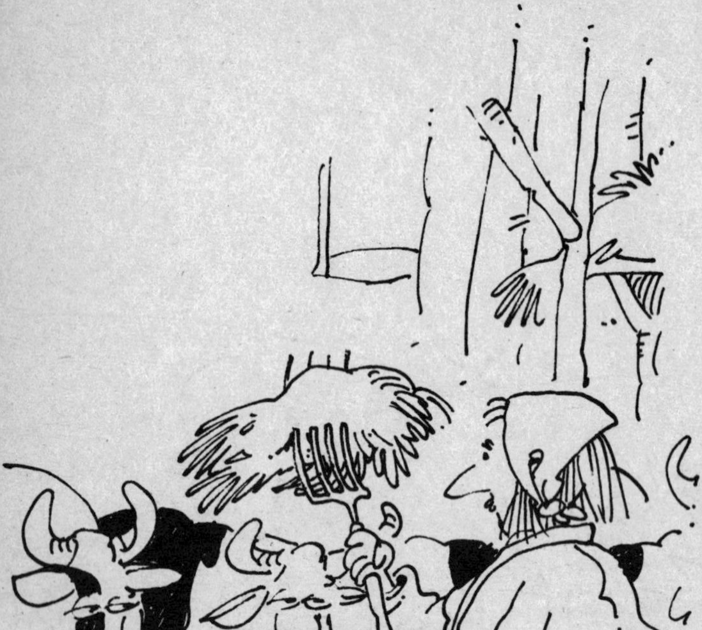

3

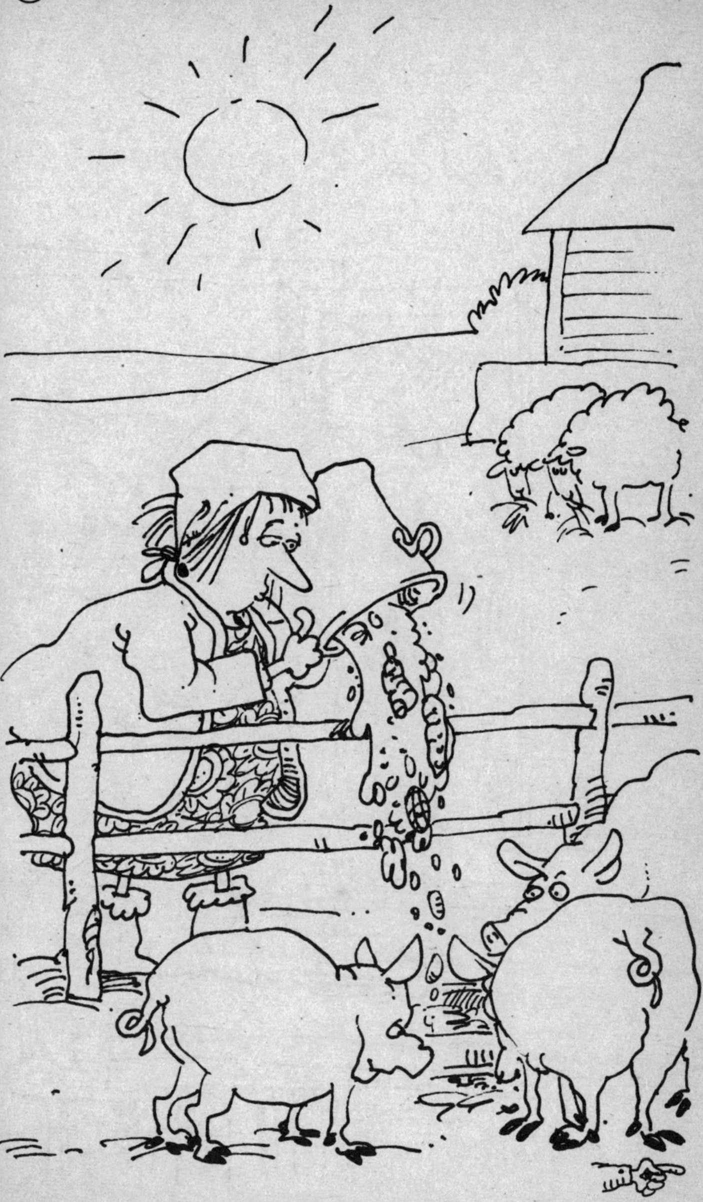

4

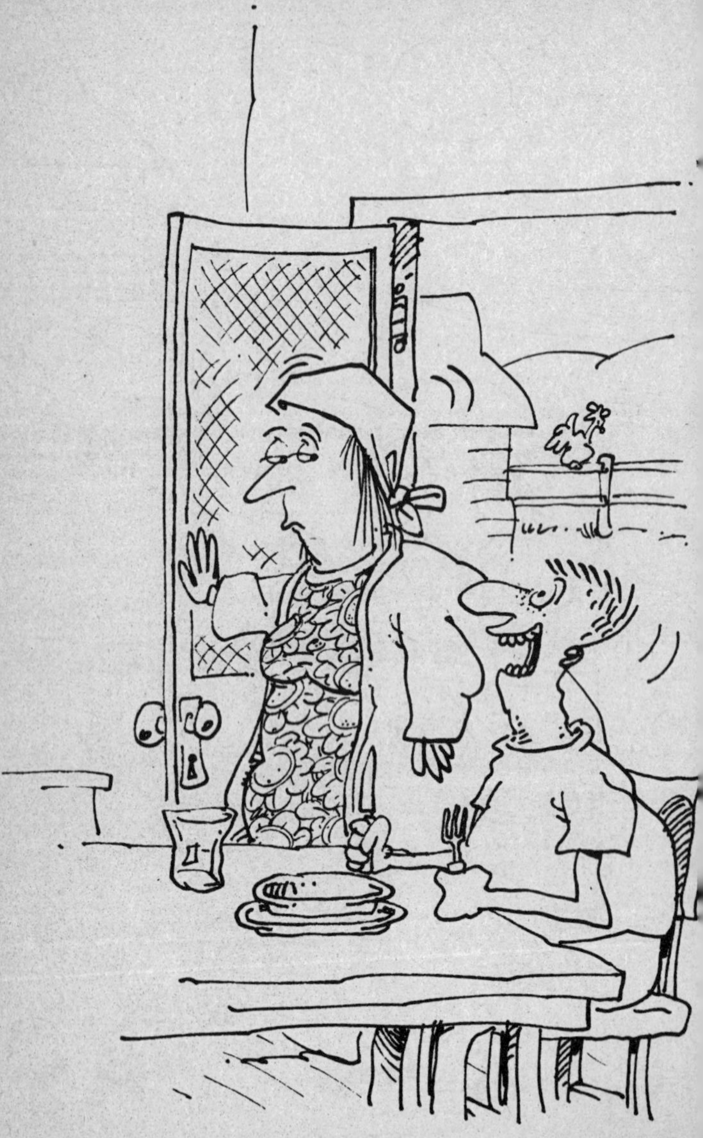

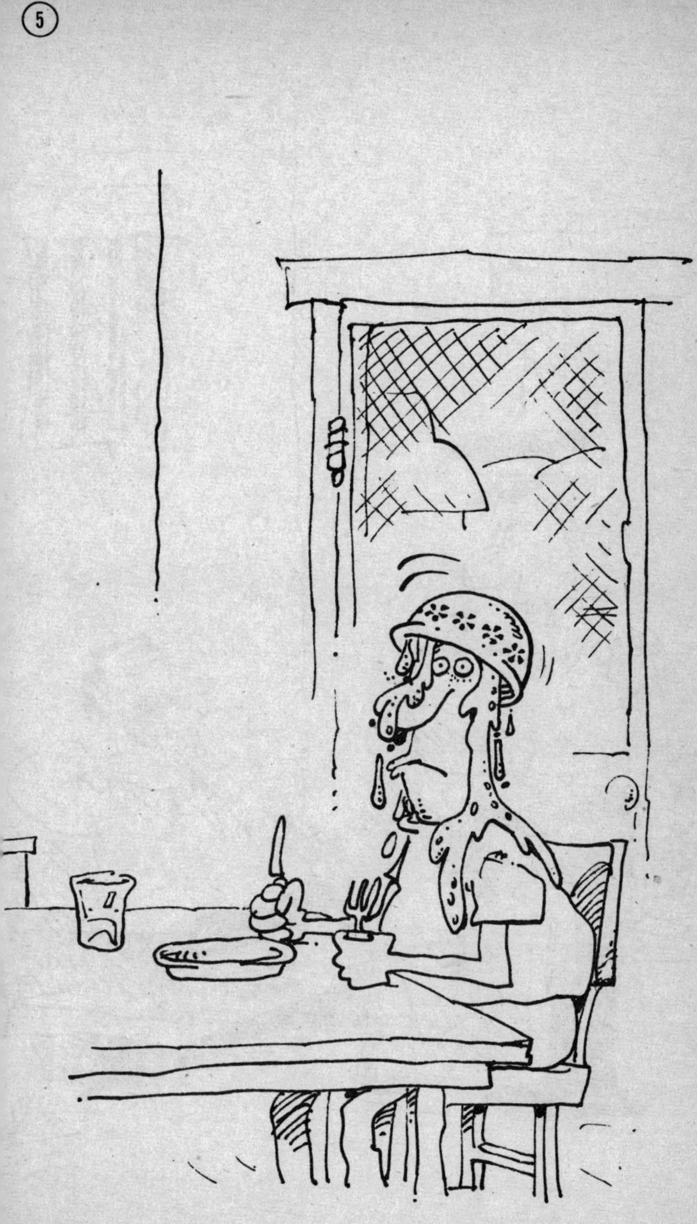

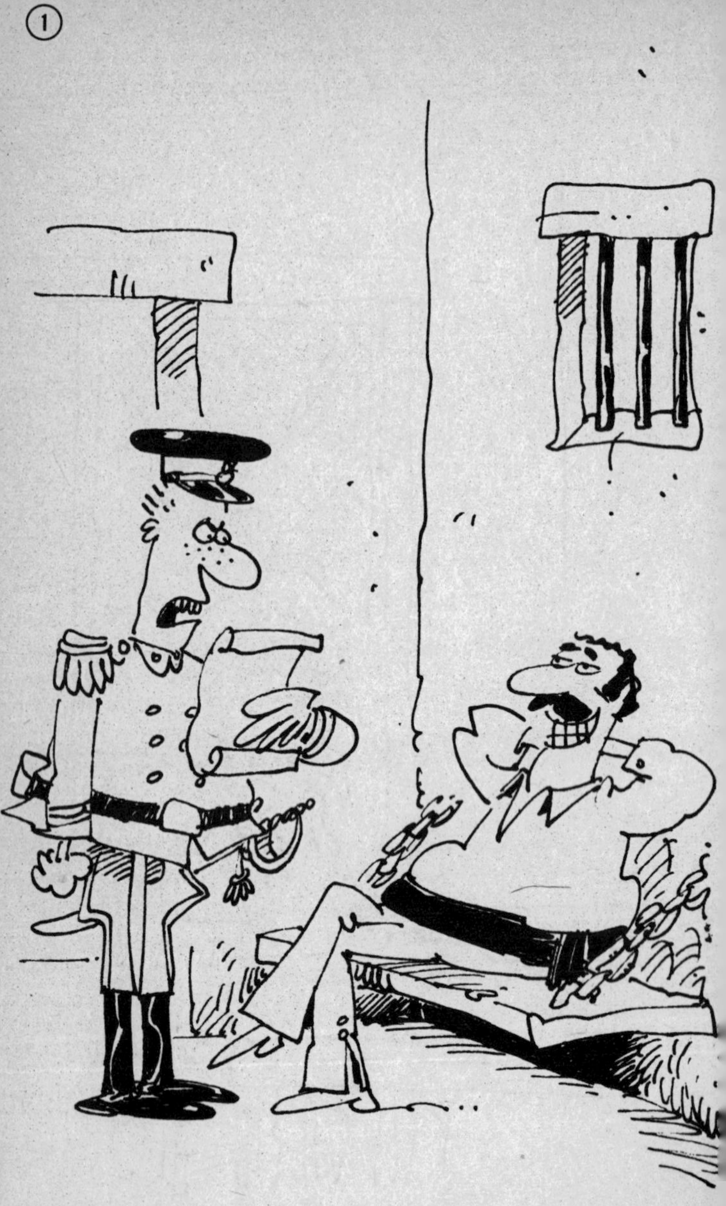
1

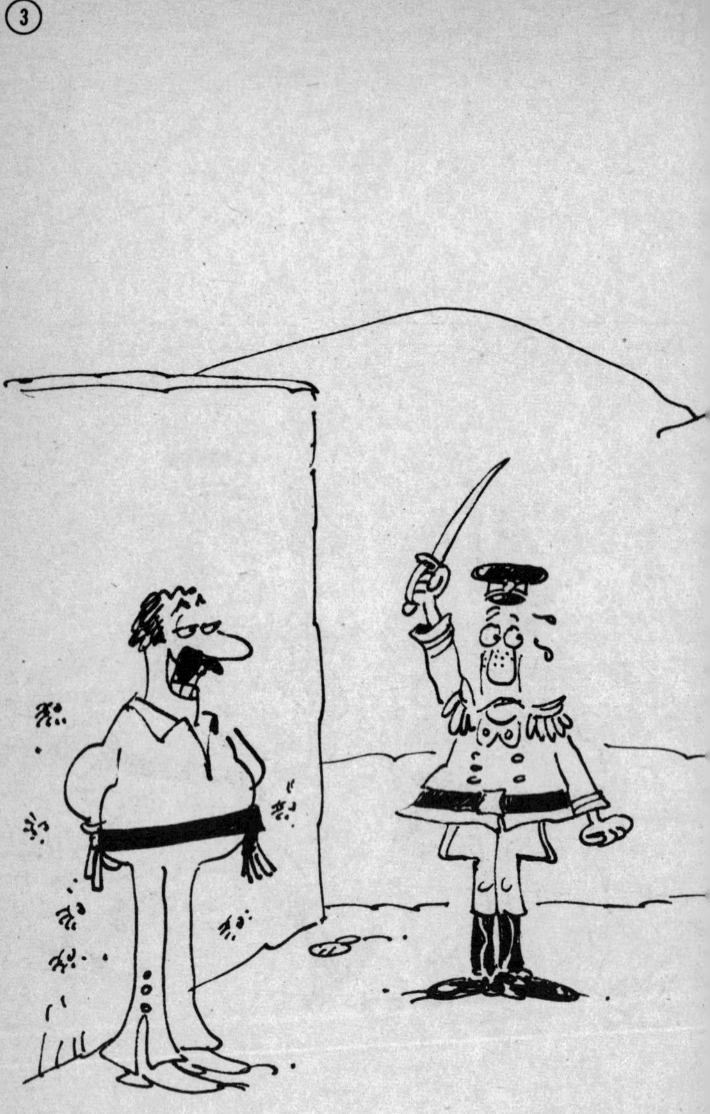
3

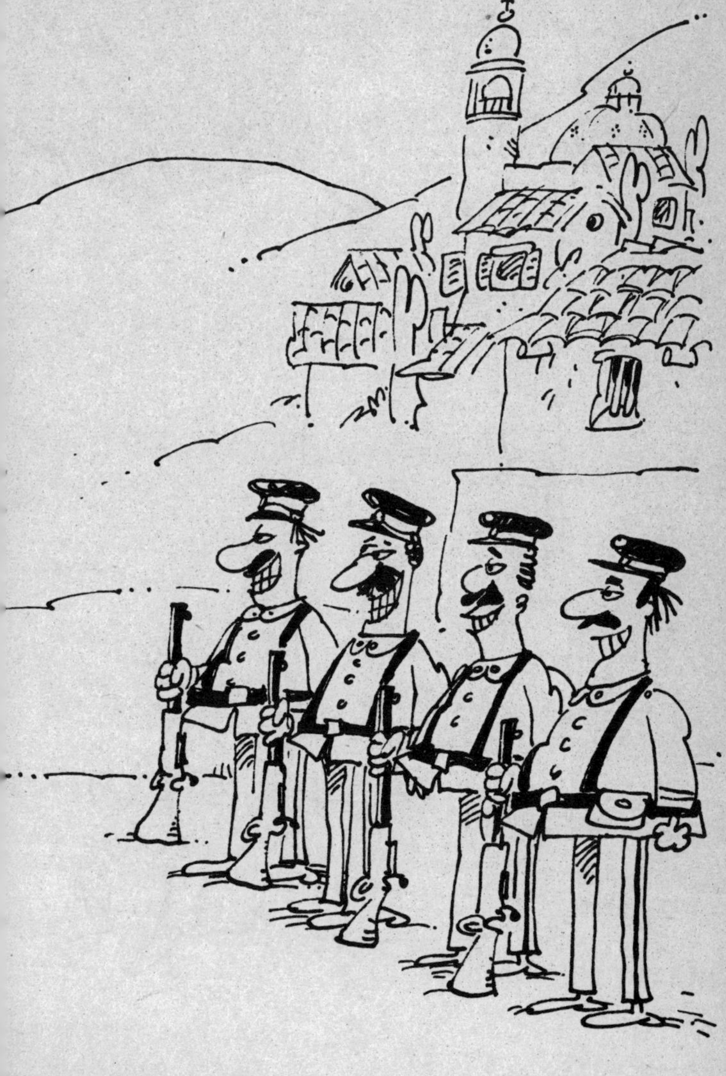

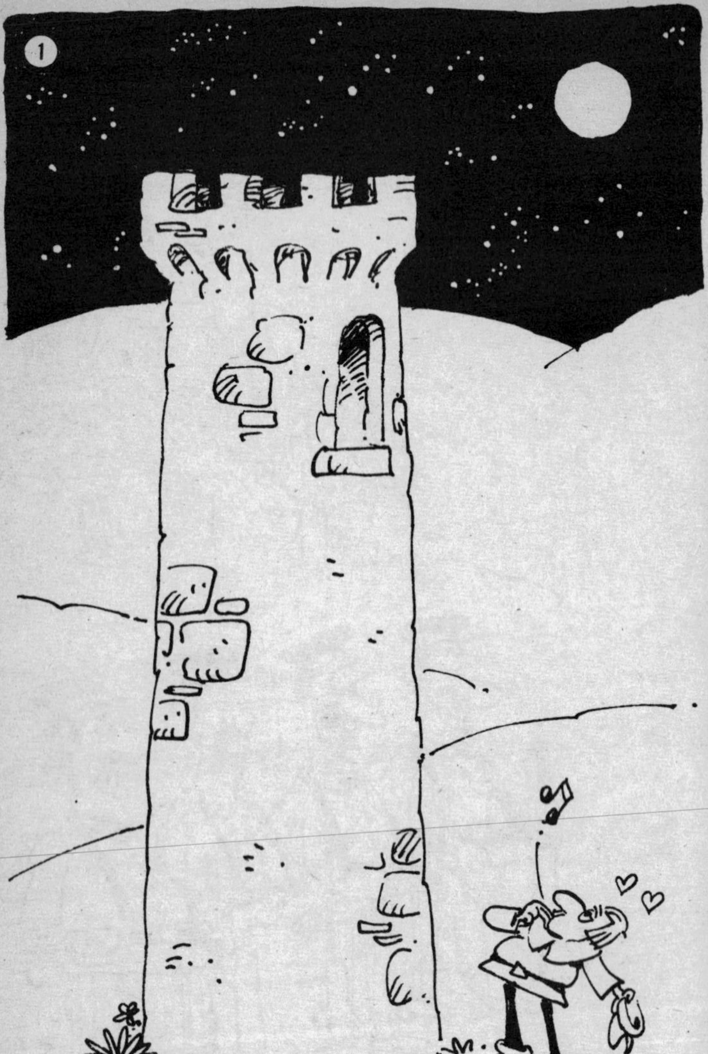
1

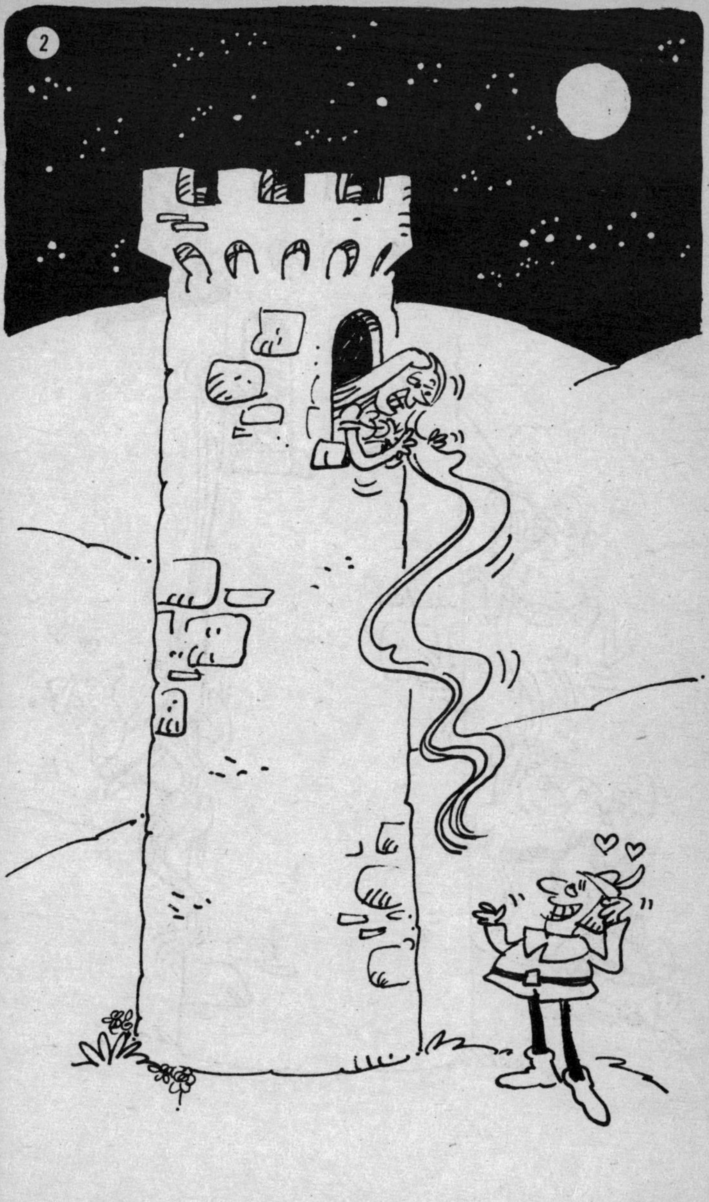
2

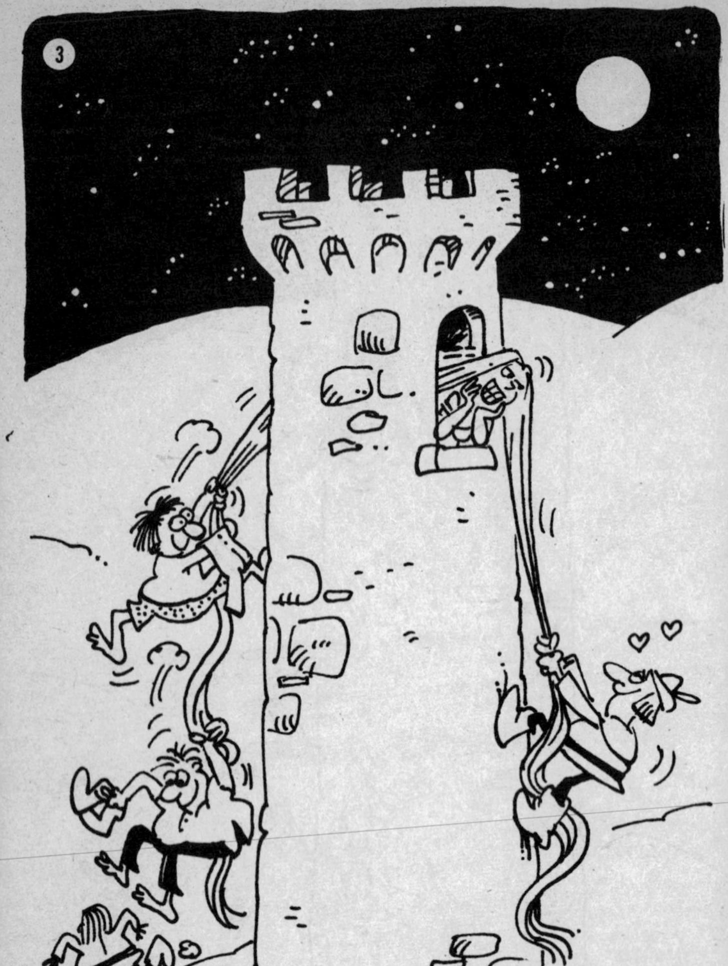
3

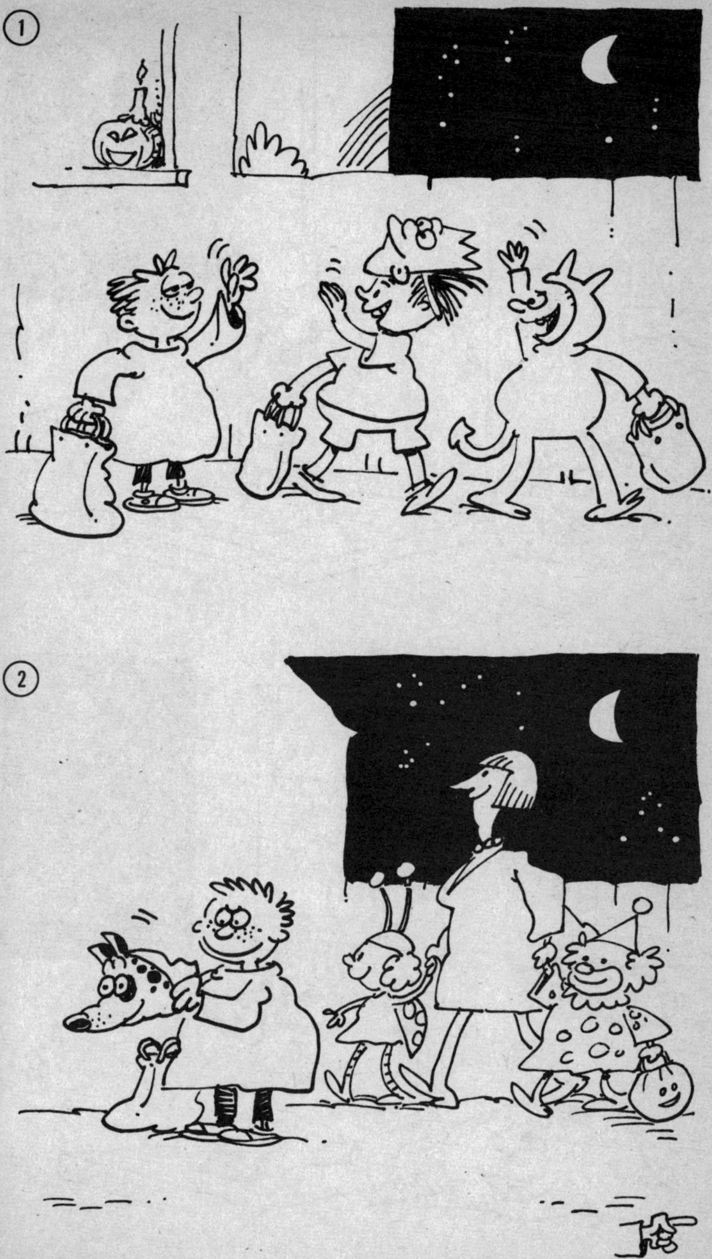
1
2

3

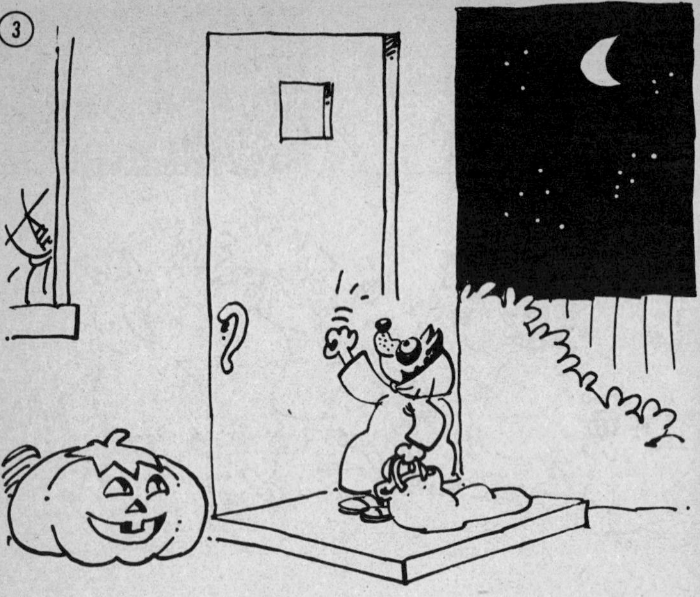

4

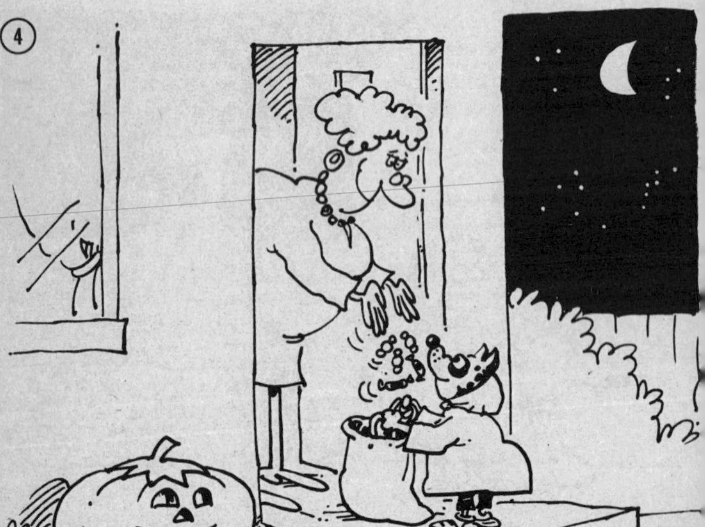

5

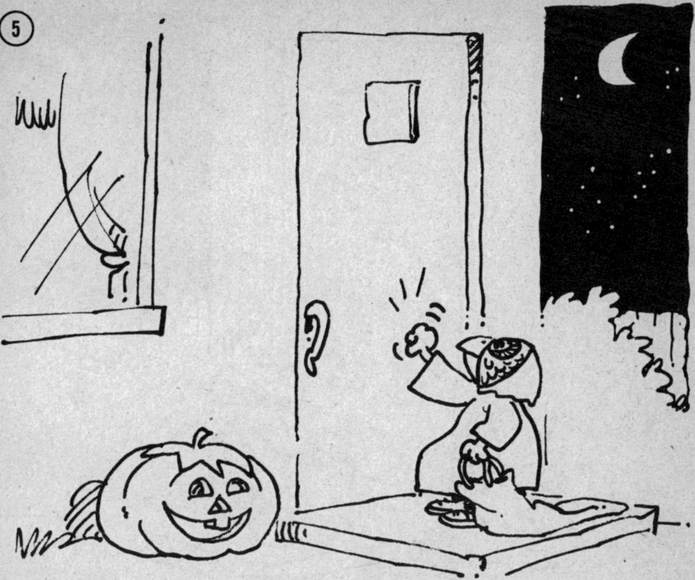

6

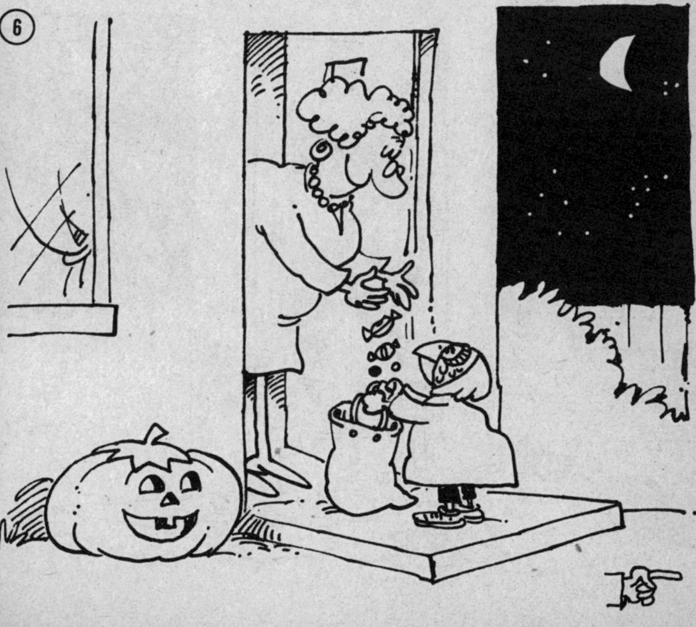

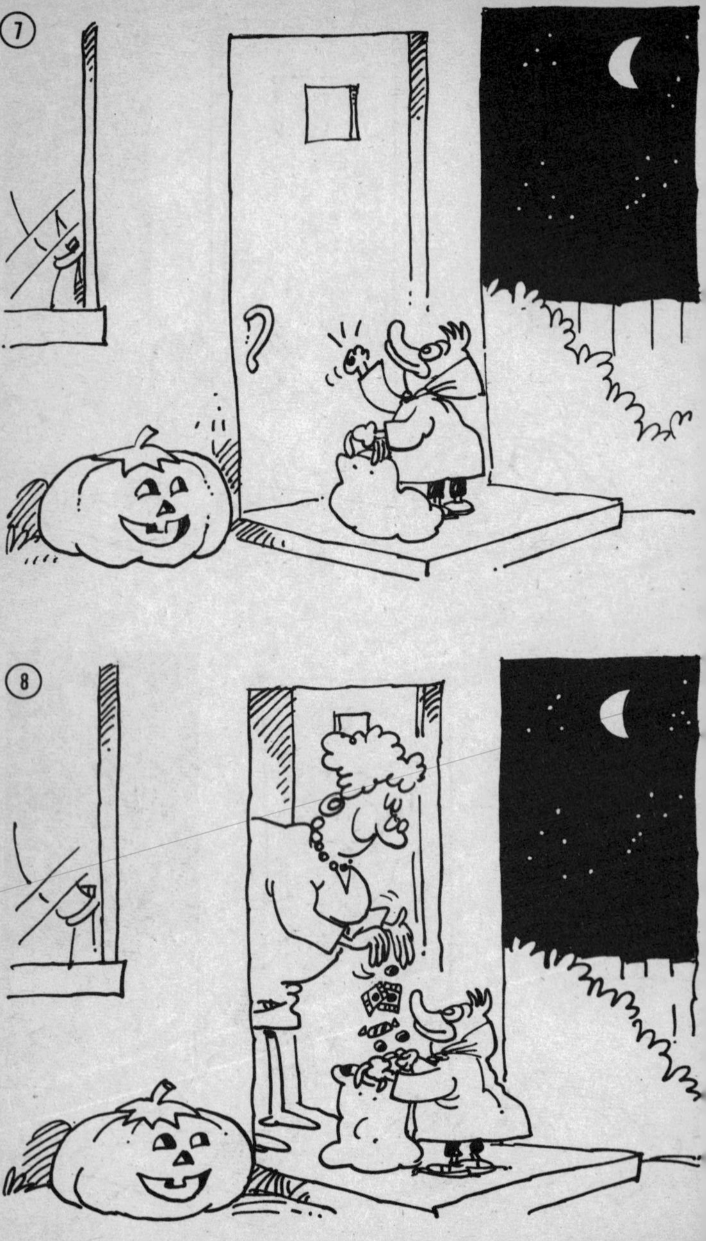
7
8

9

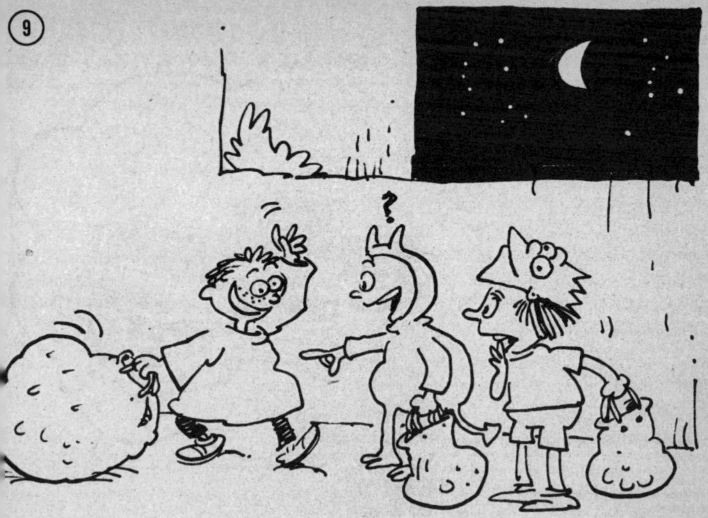

10

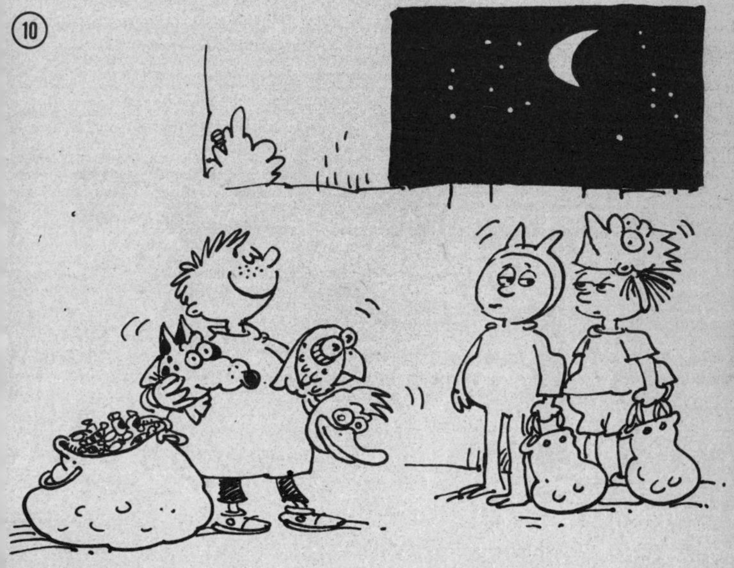

1

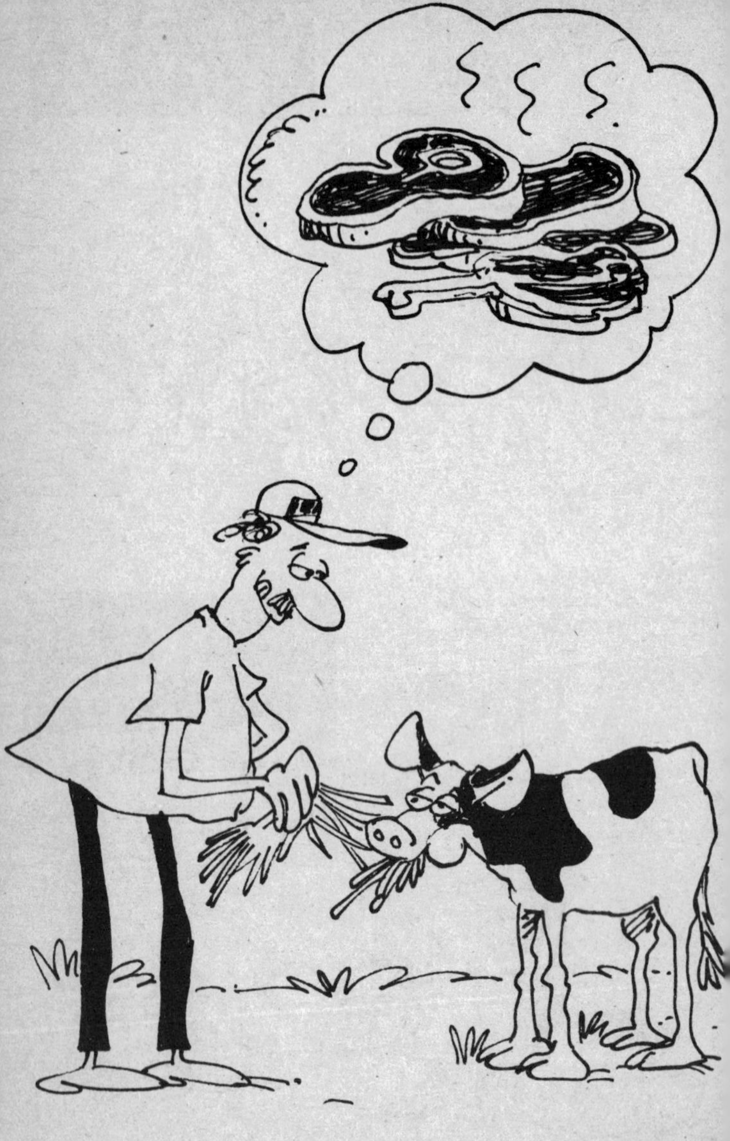

2

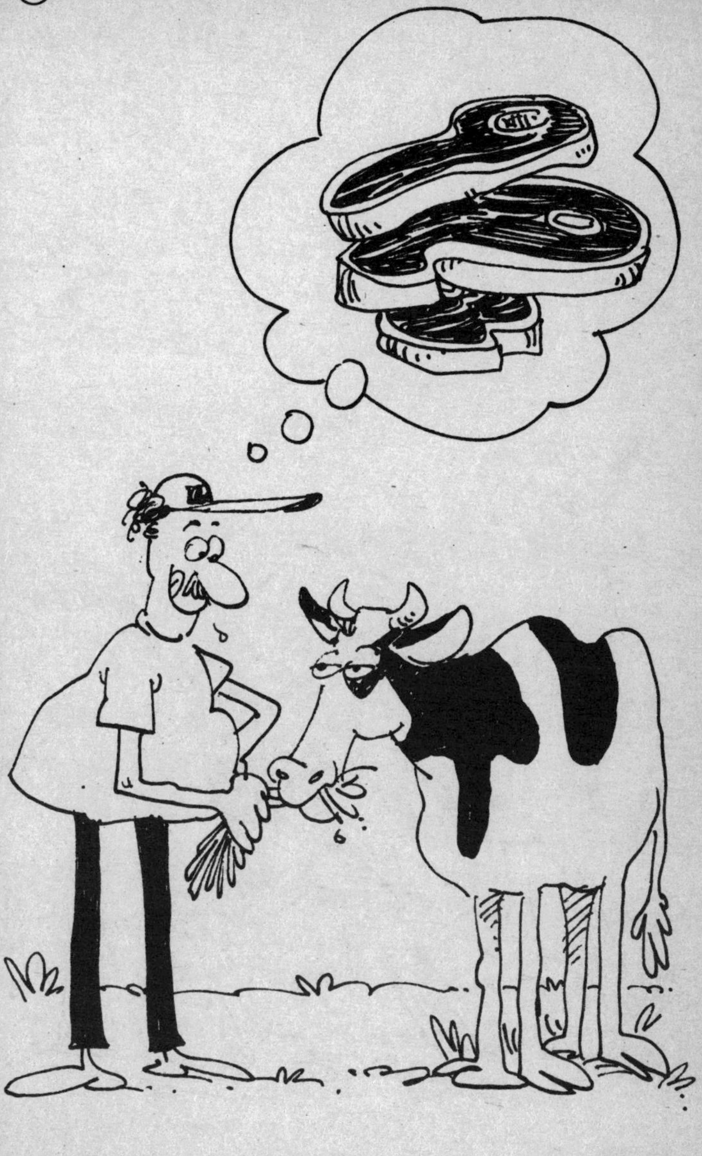

③

(4)

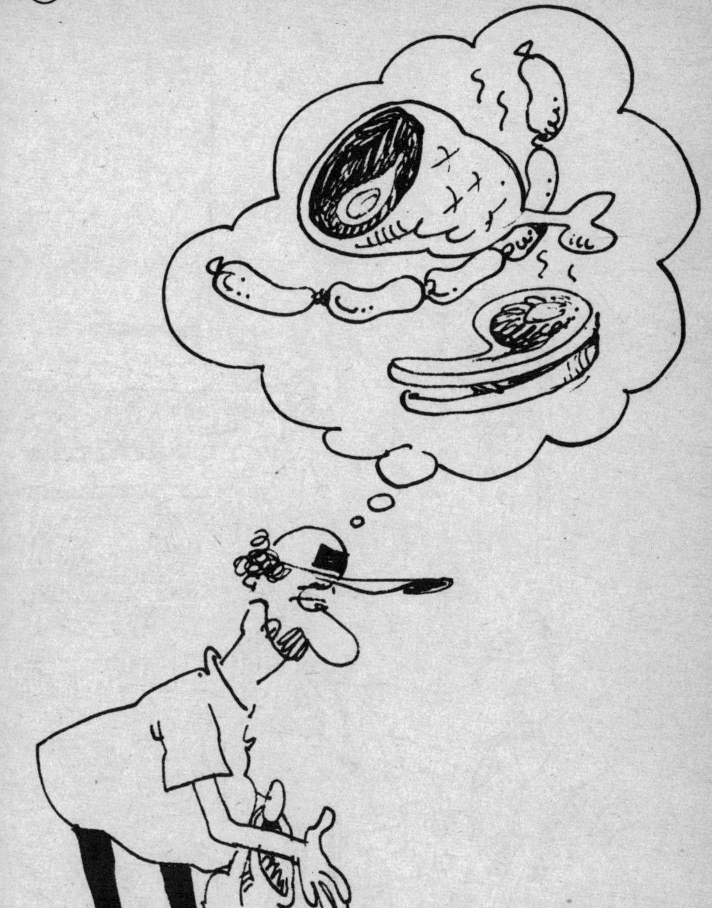

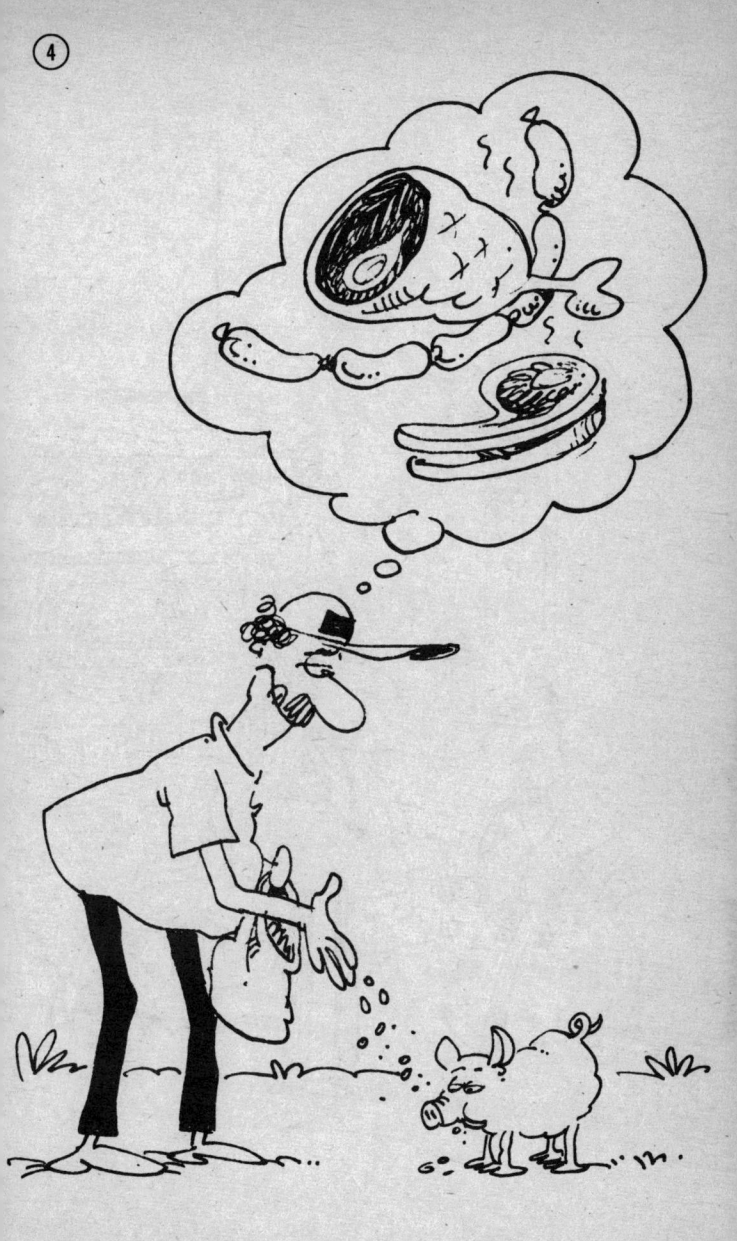

①

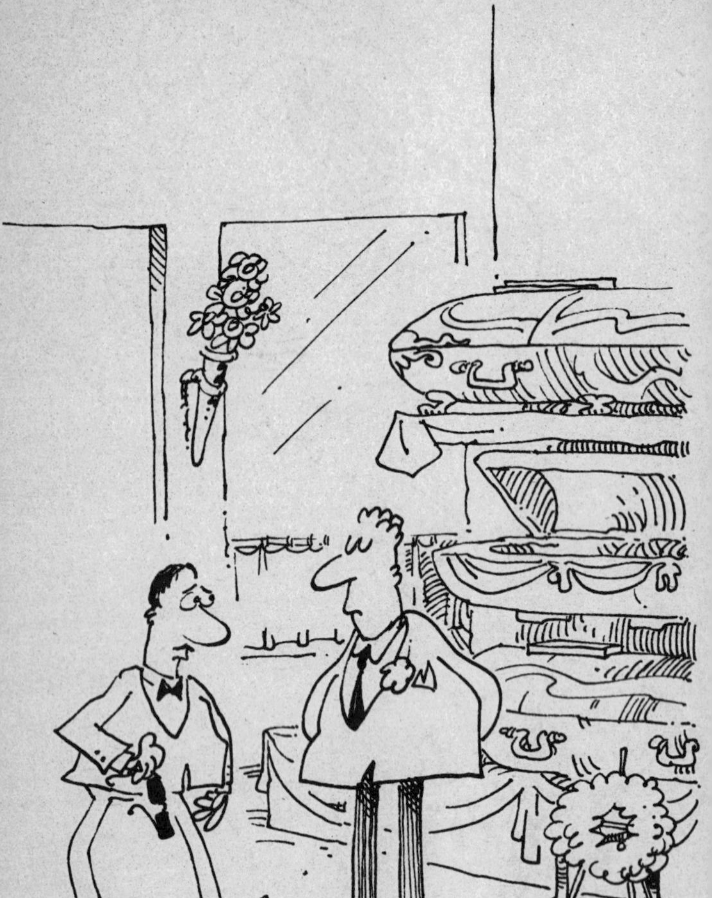

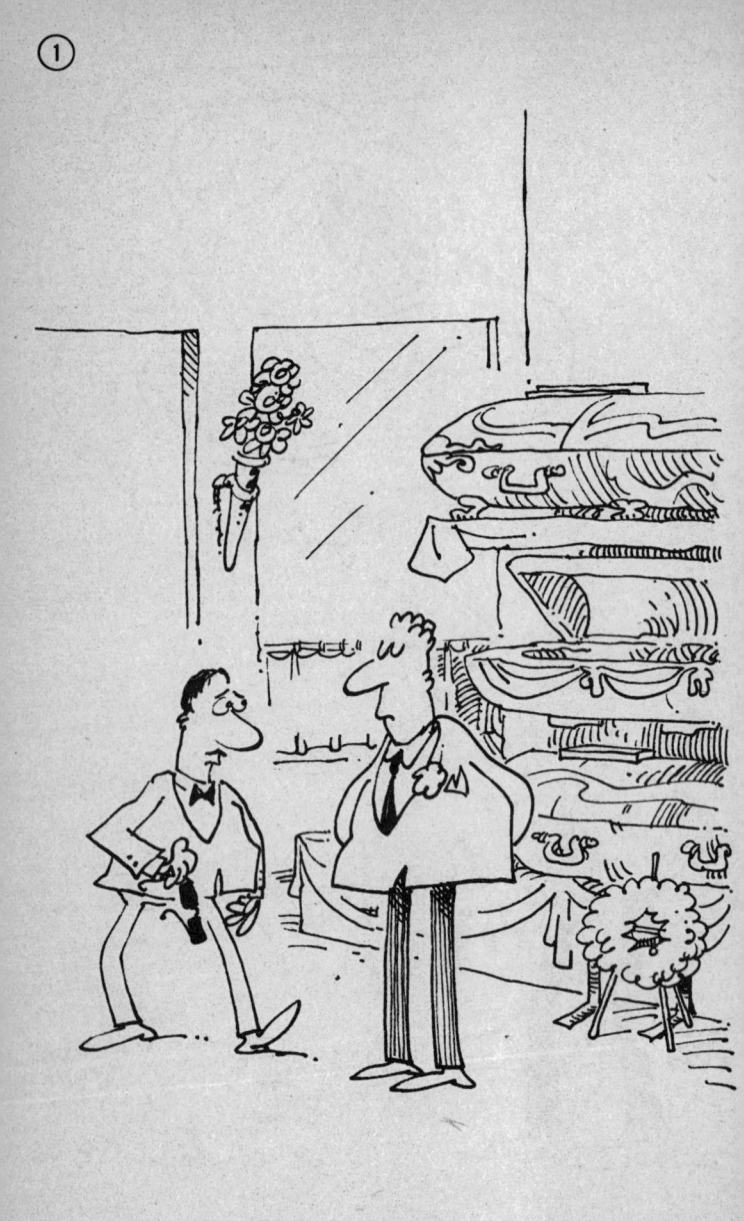

②

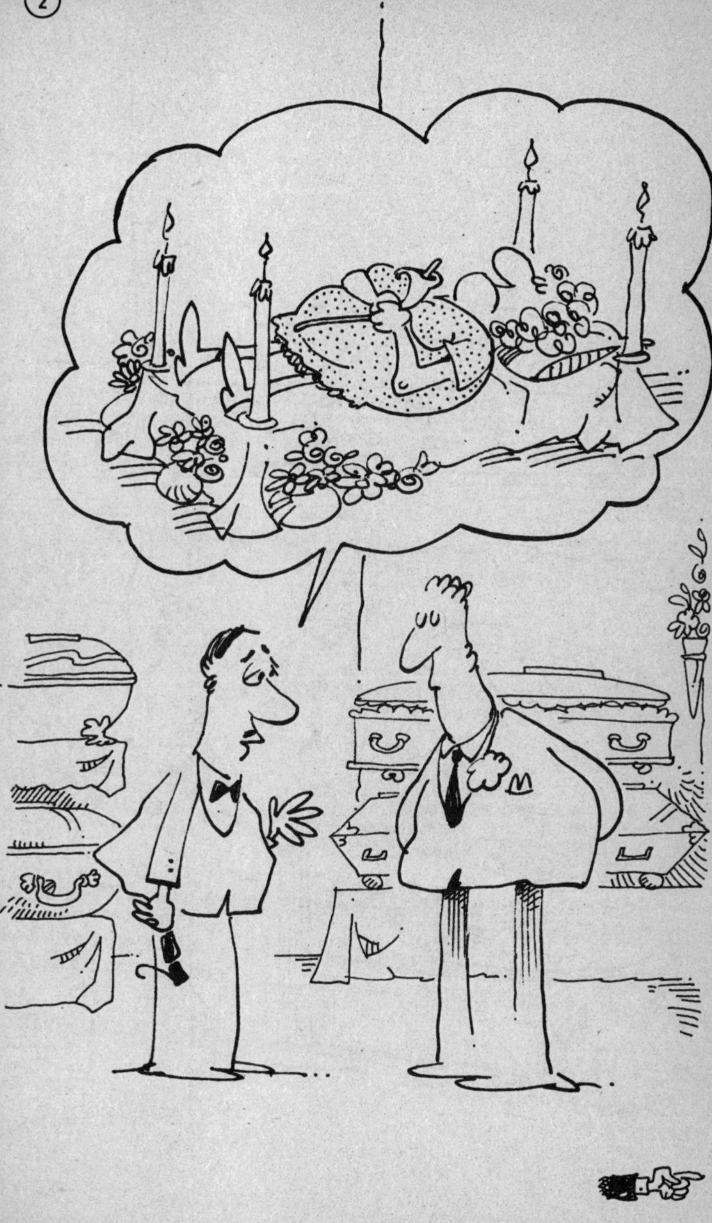

(3)

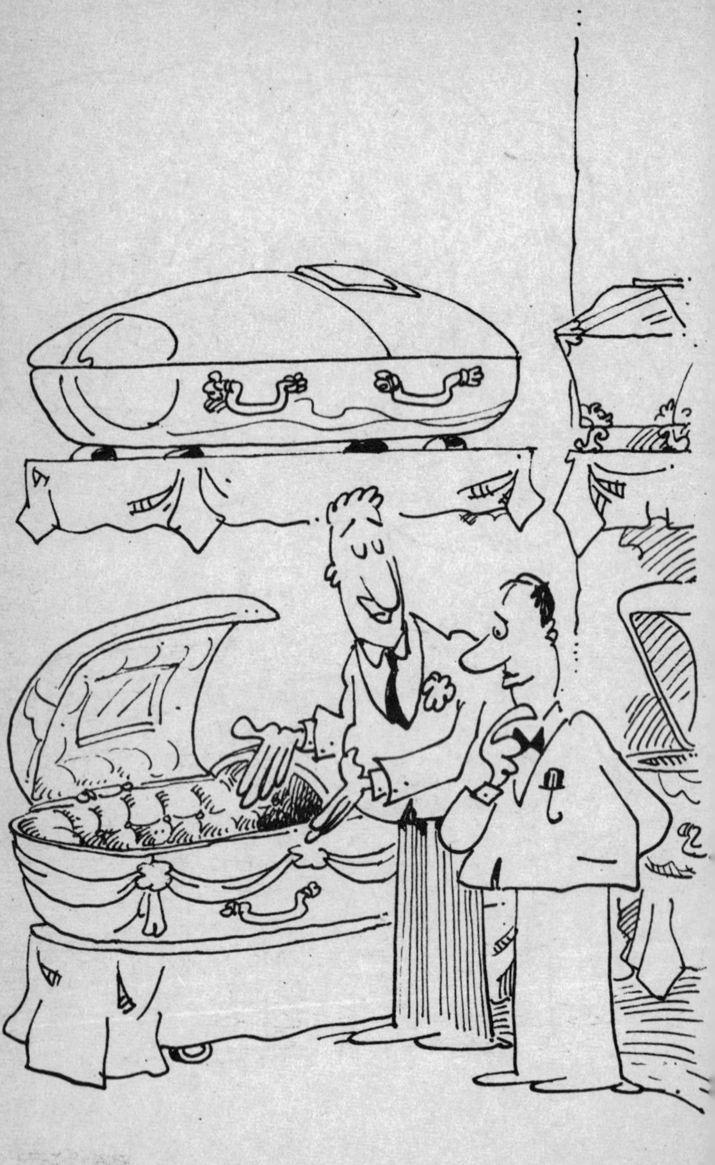

4

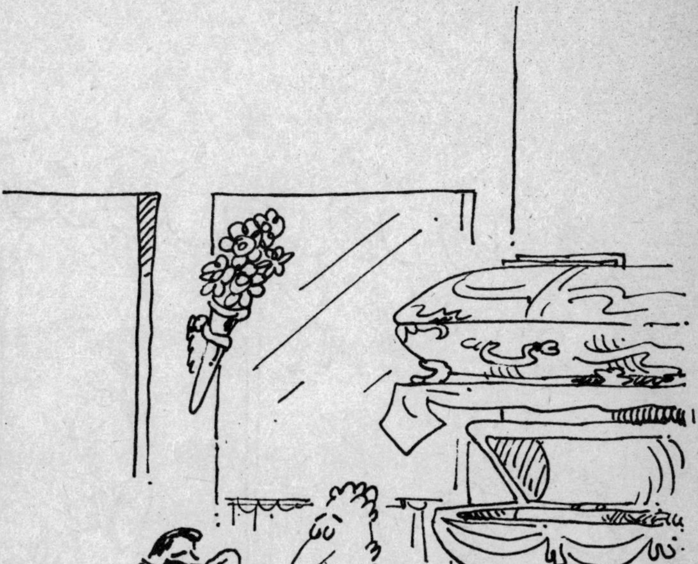

5

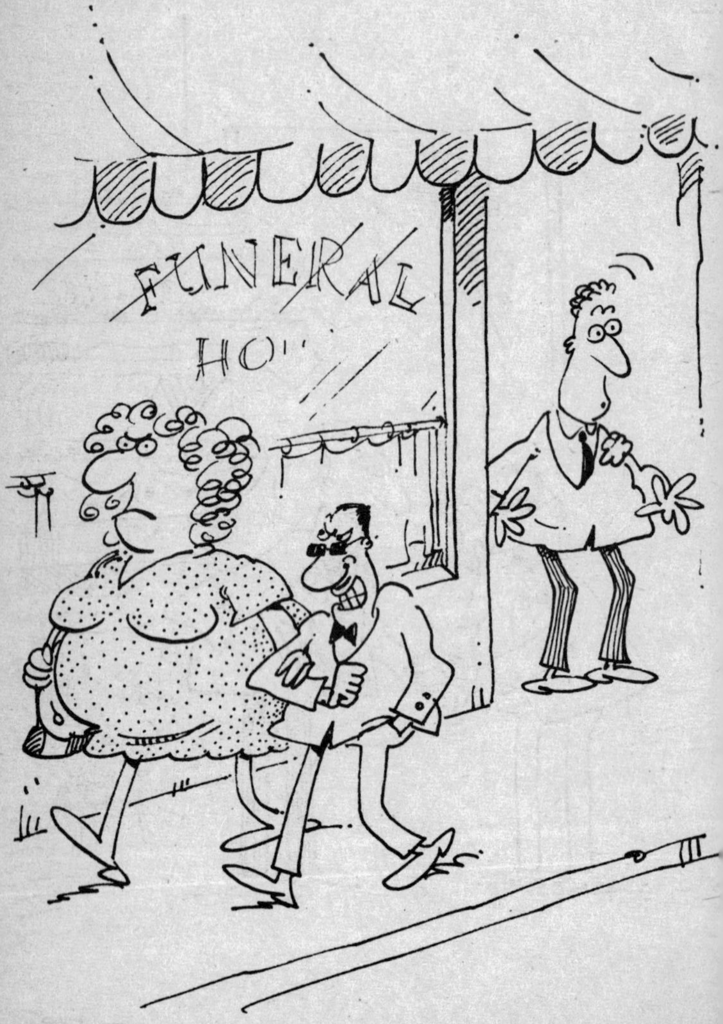
FUNERAL
HO

(1)

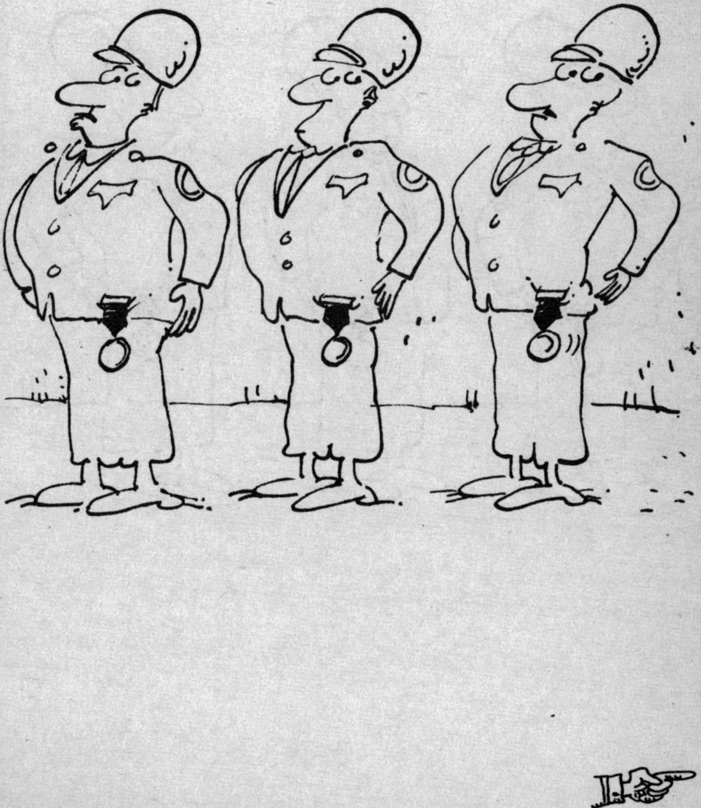

①

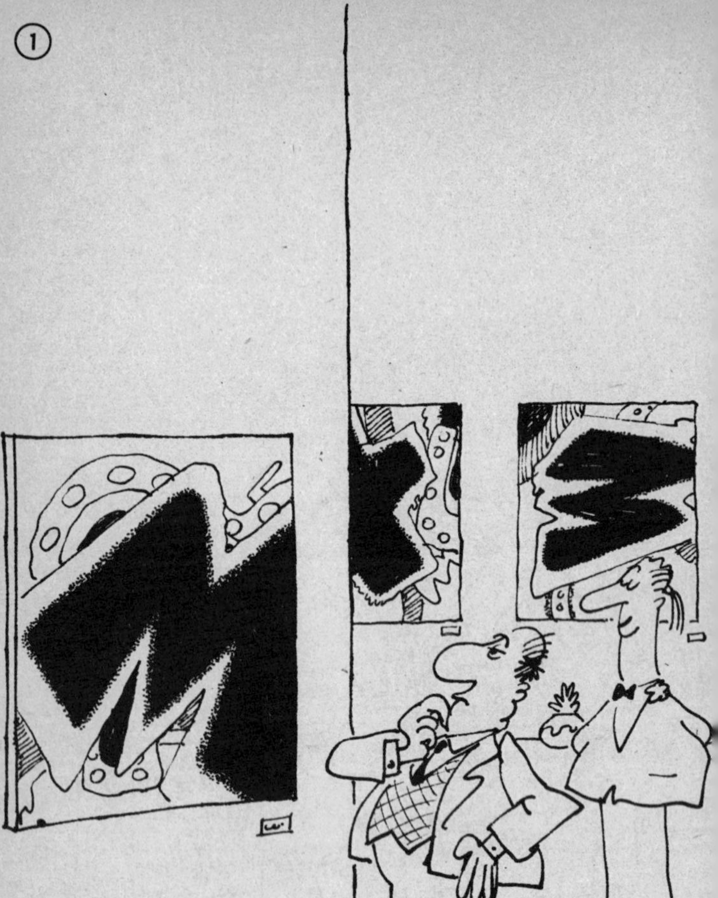

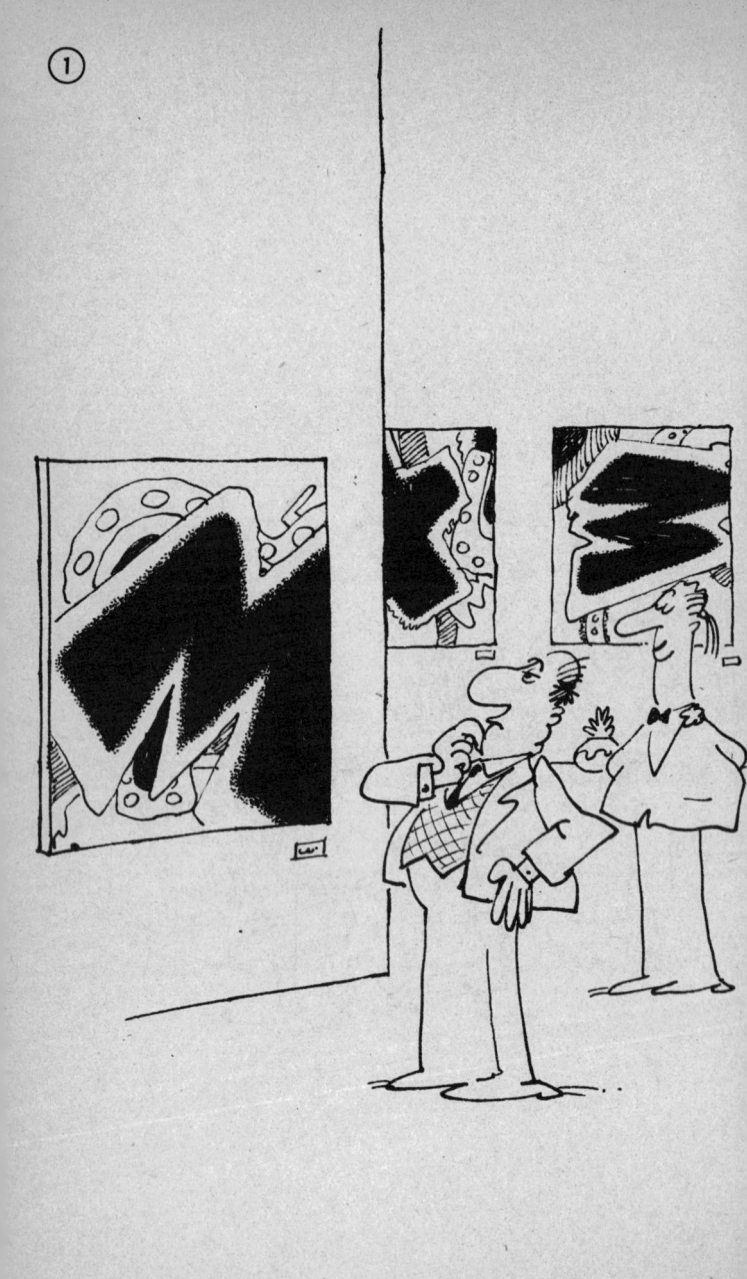

2

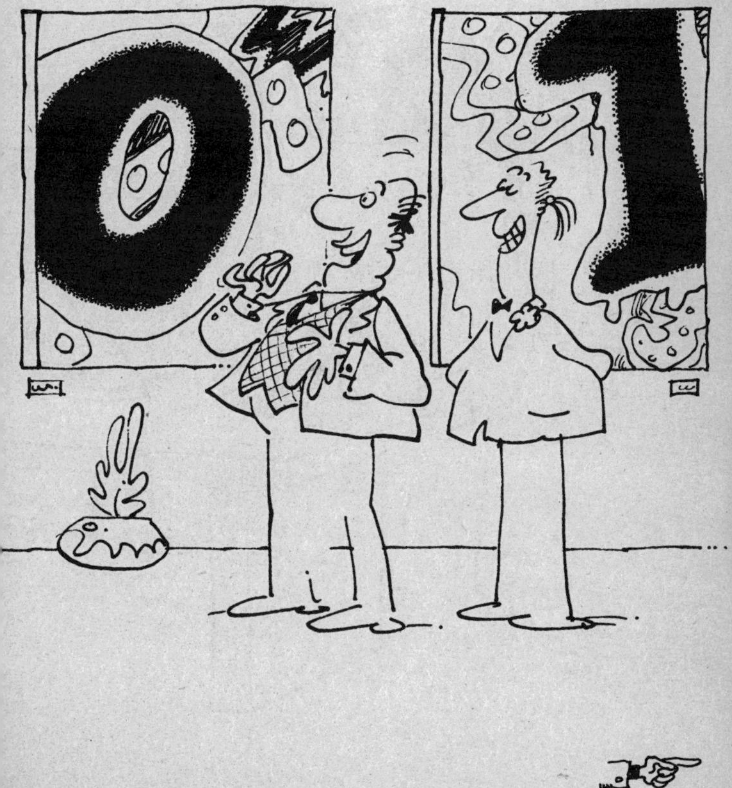

3

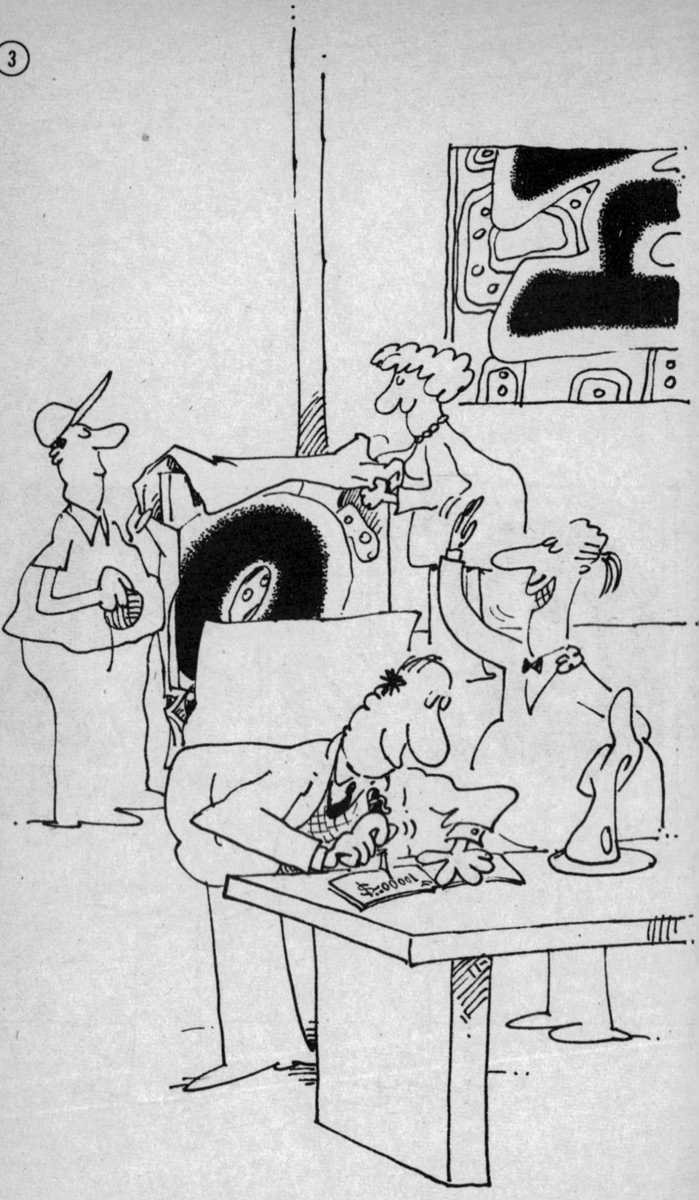

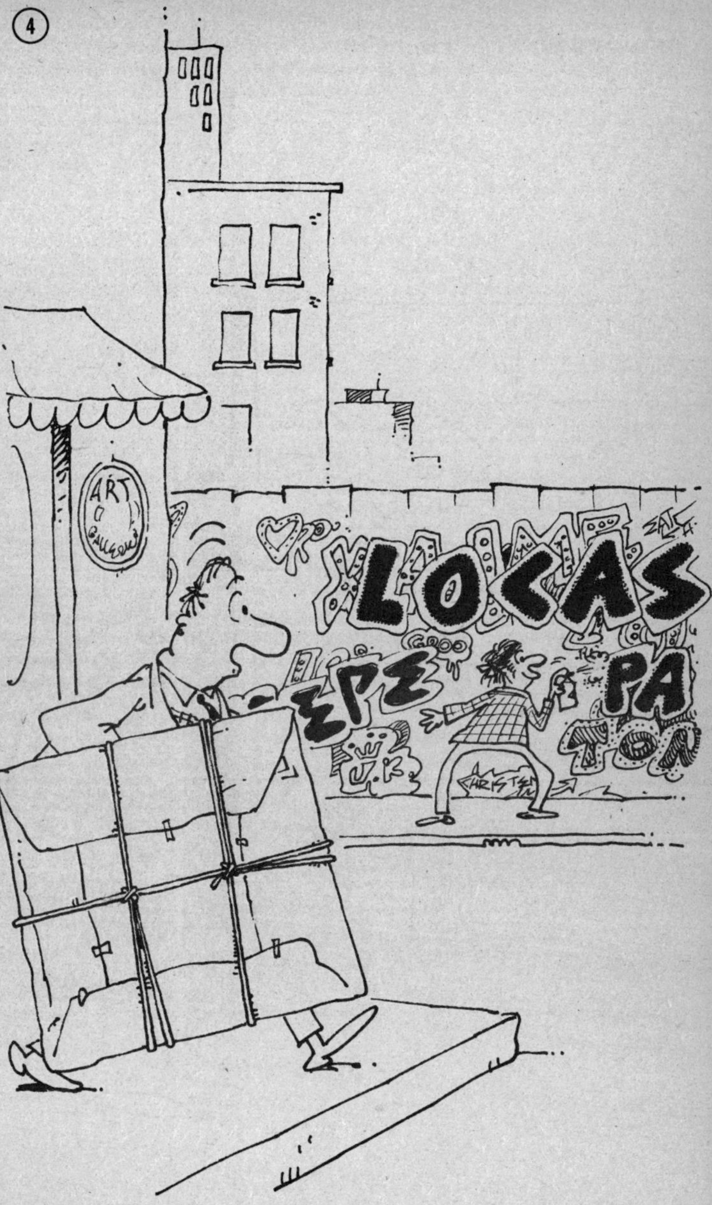
4
ART
LOCAS
PA

1

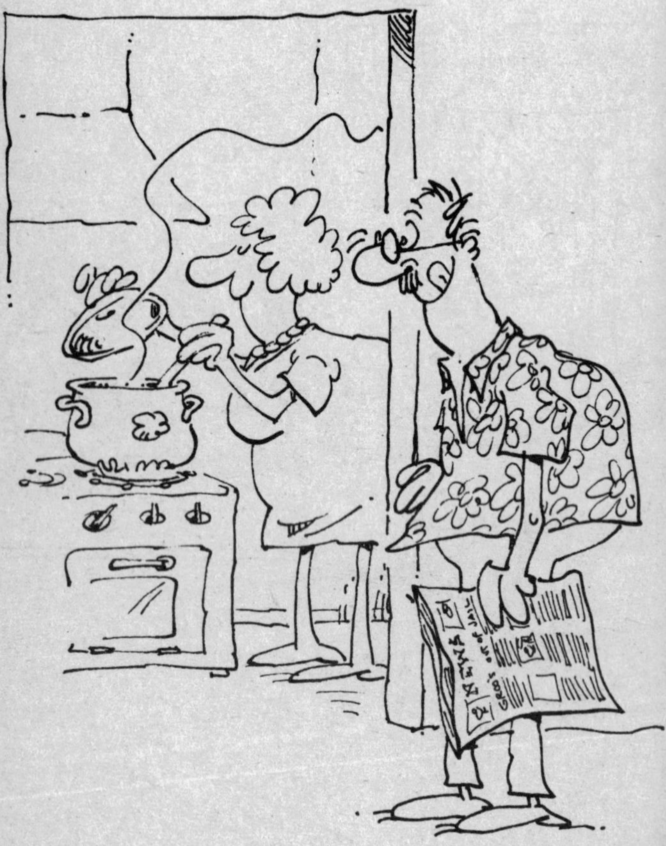
GROO'S OUT OF JAIL

2

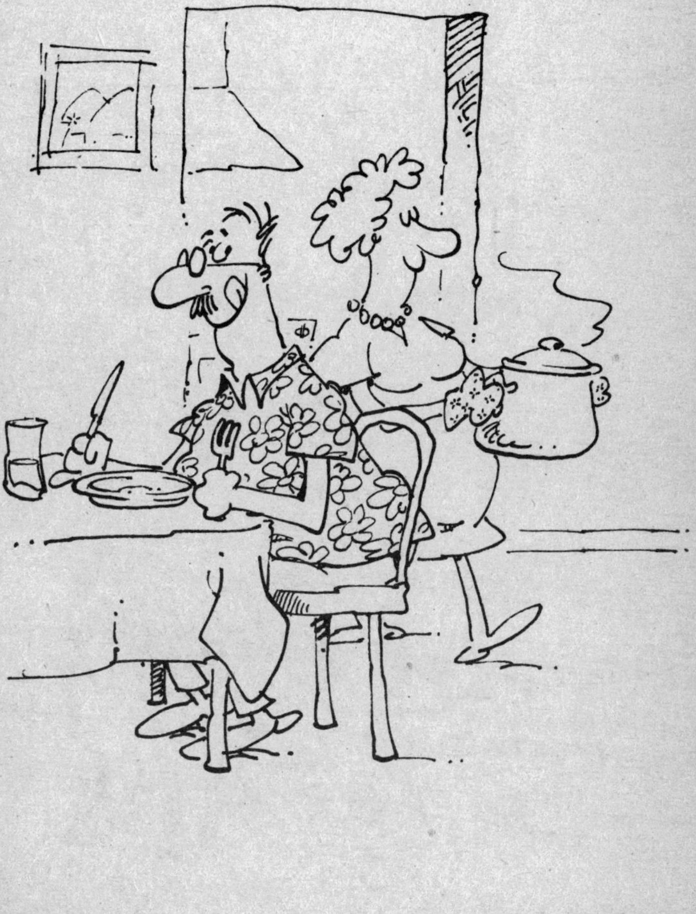

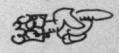

3

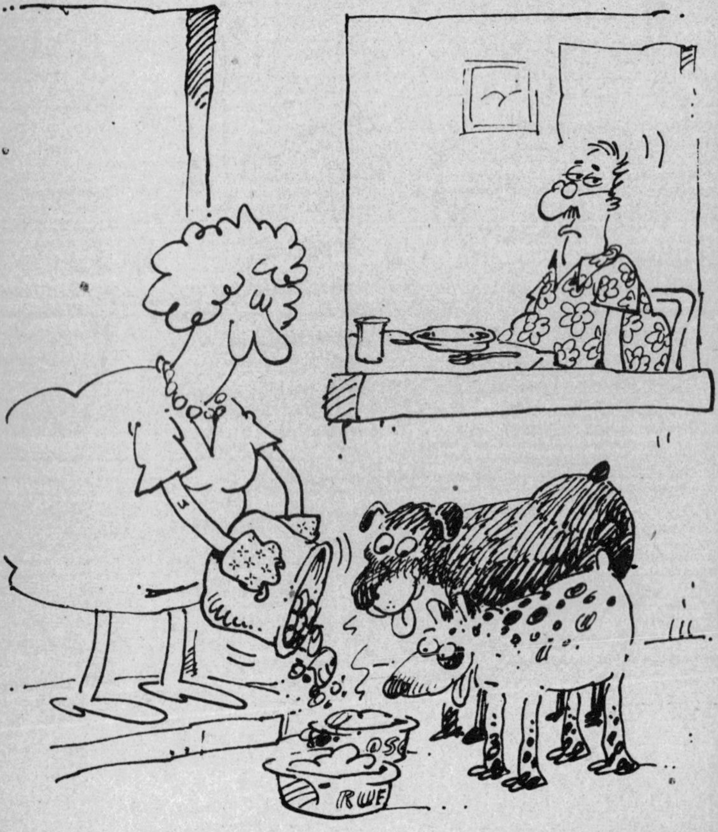
RWE

1

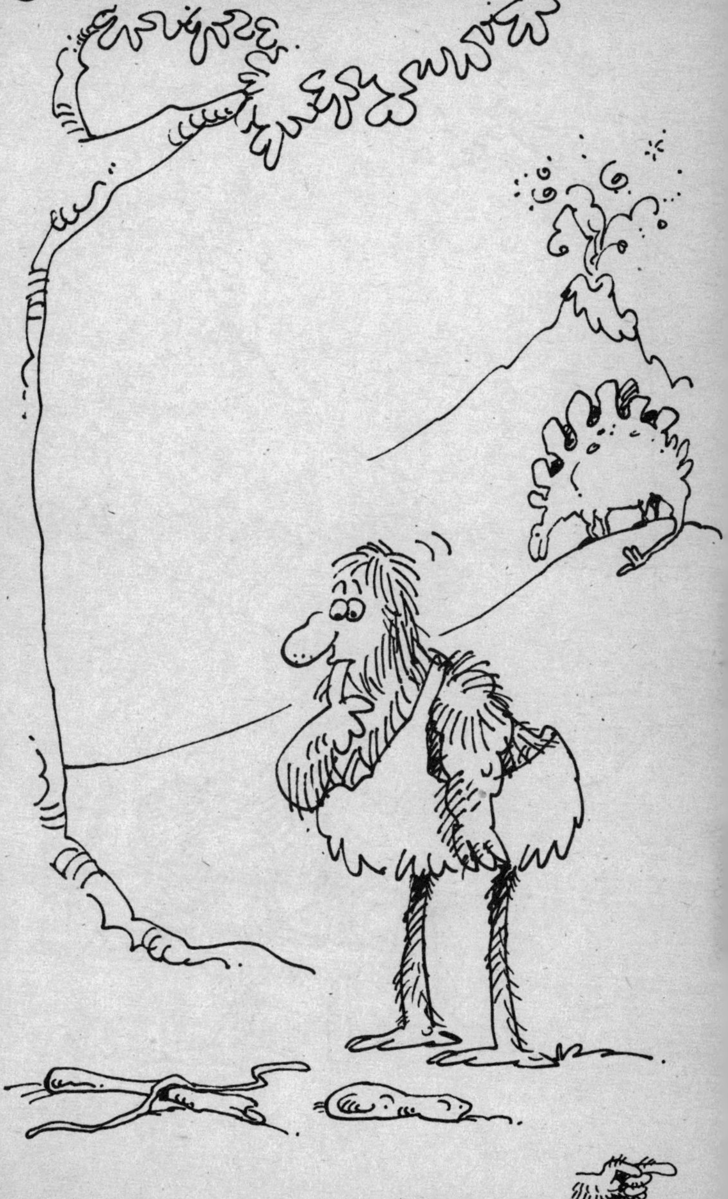

2

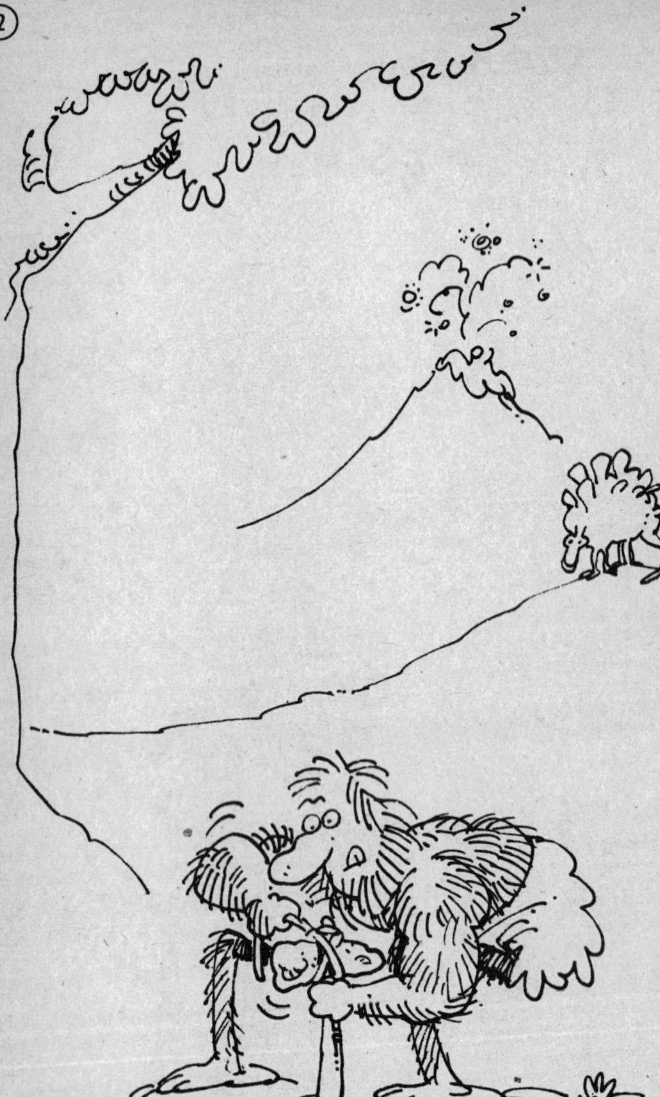

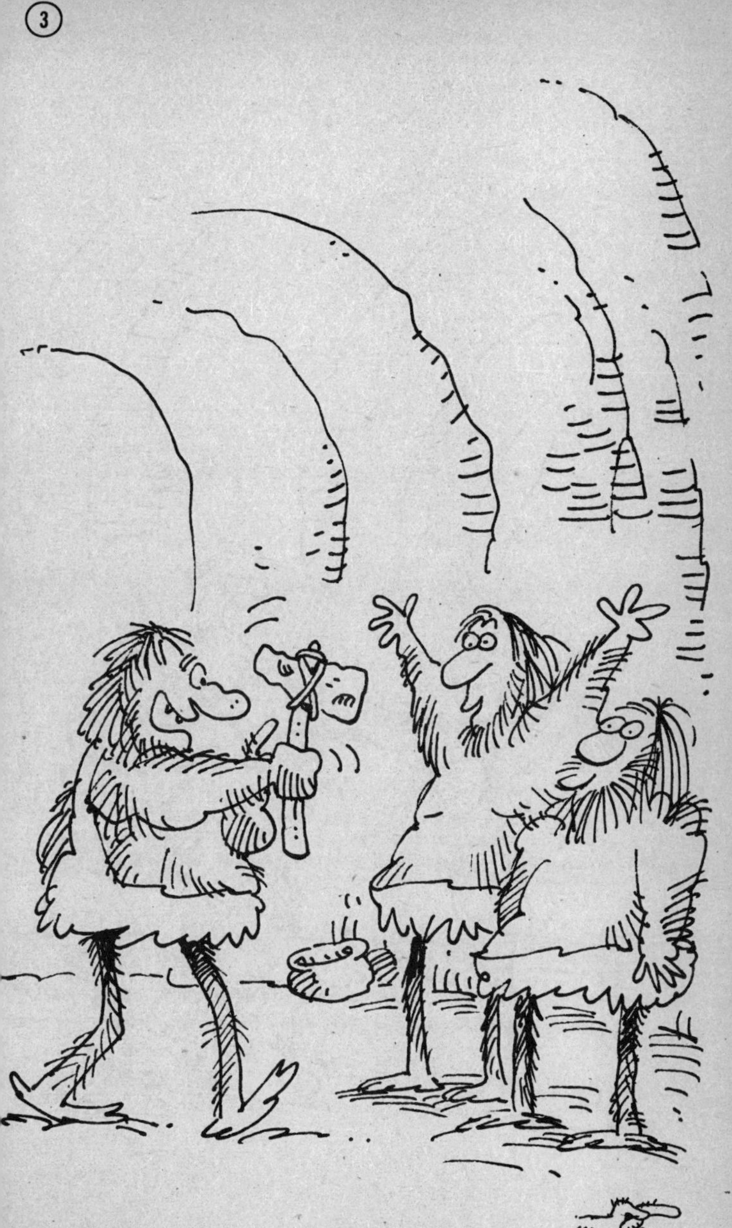
3

4

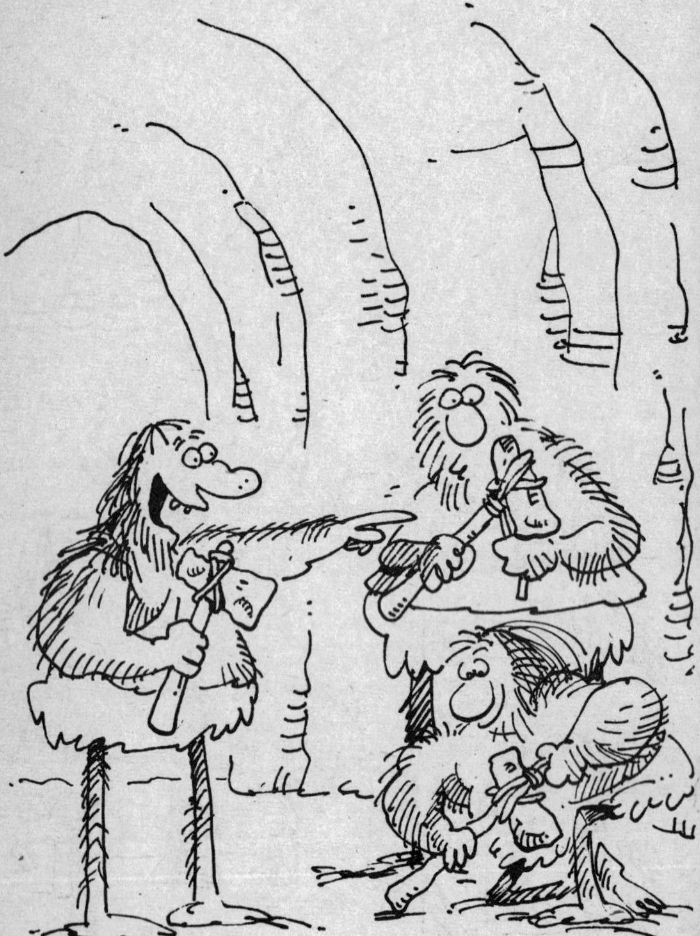

5

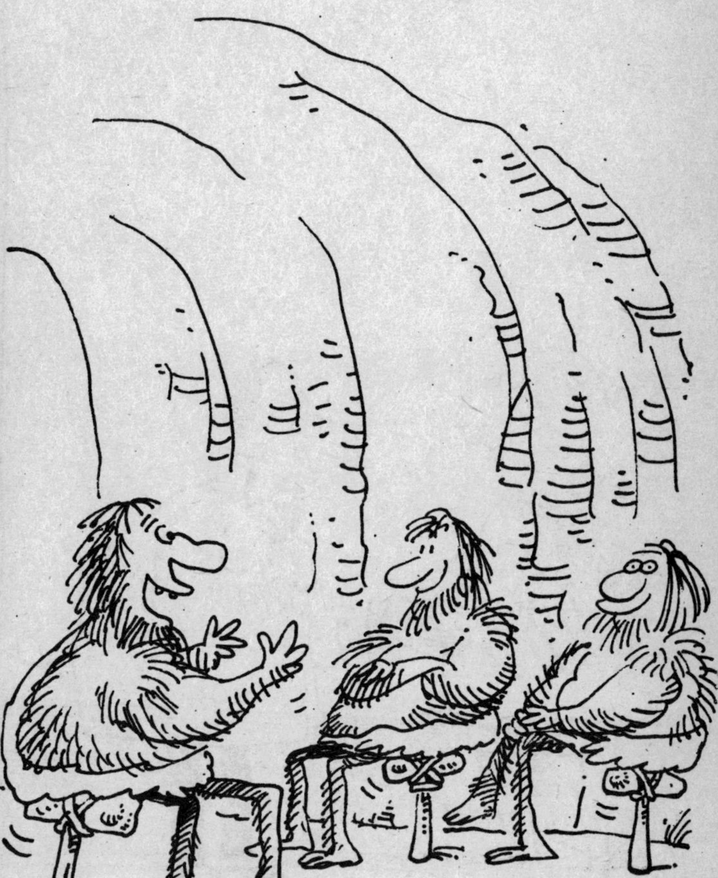

①

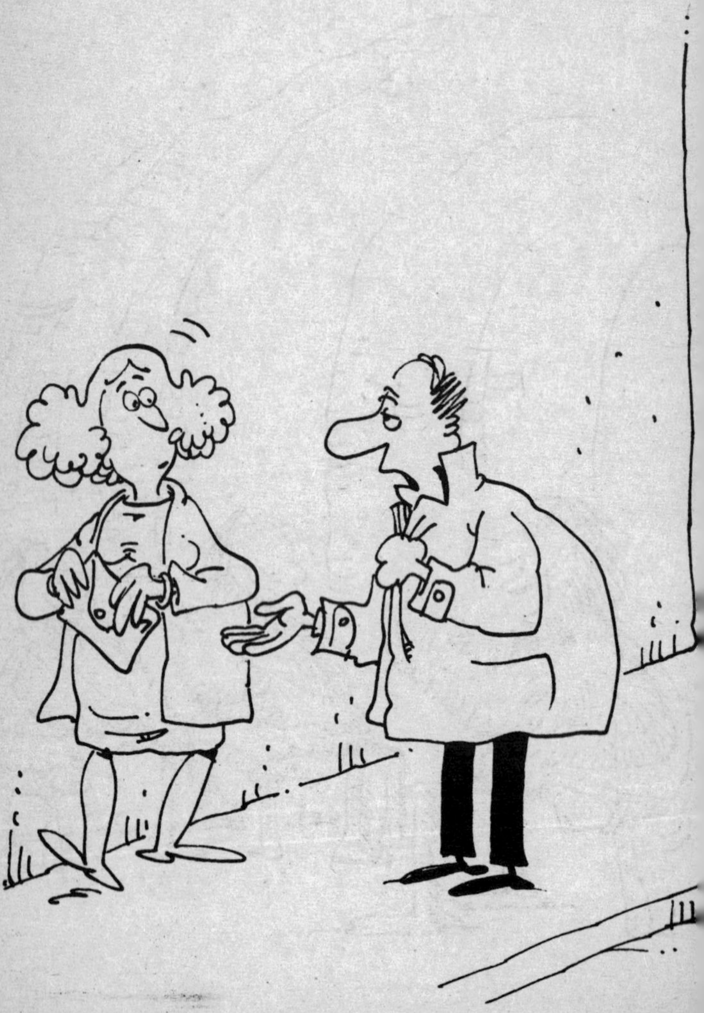

②

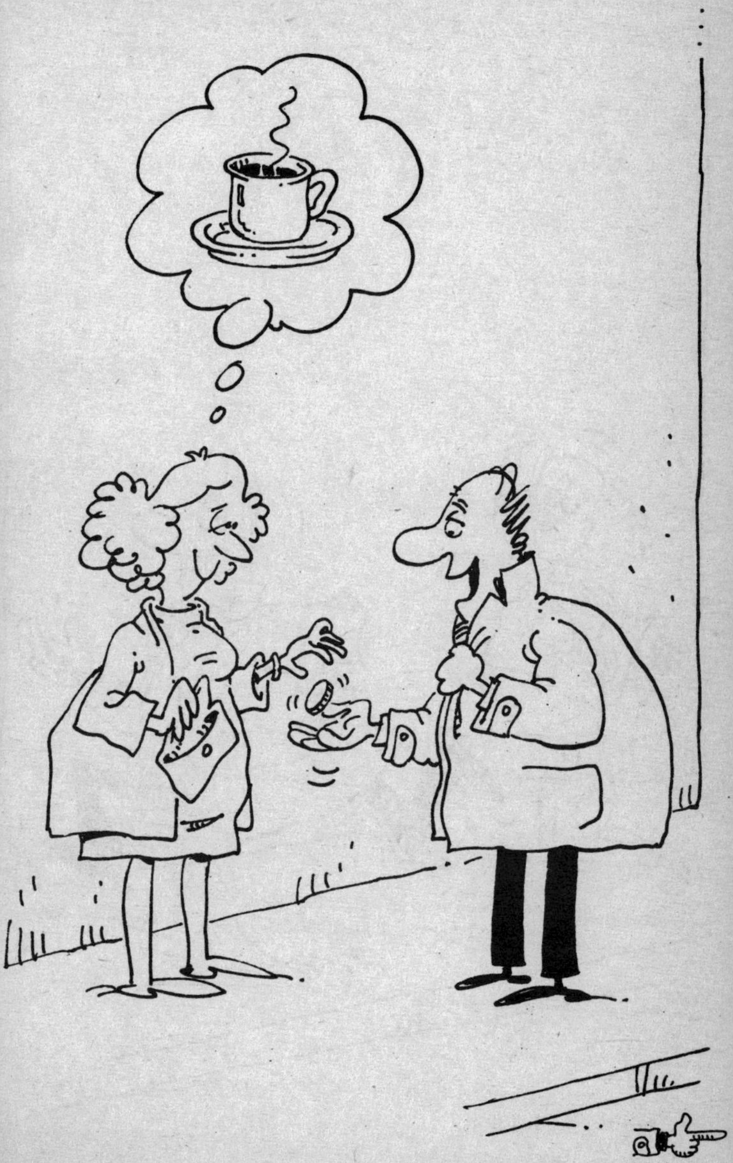

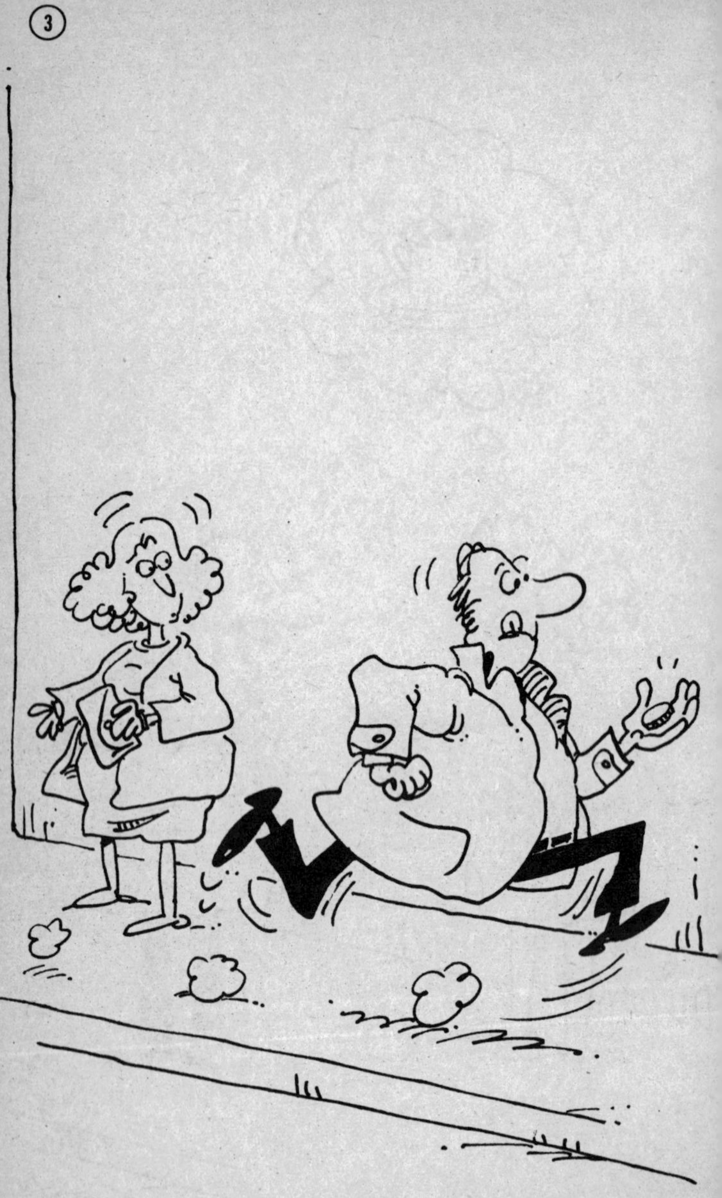
3

4

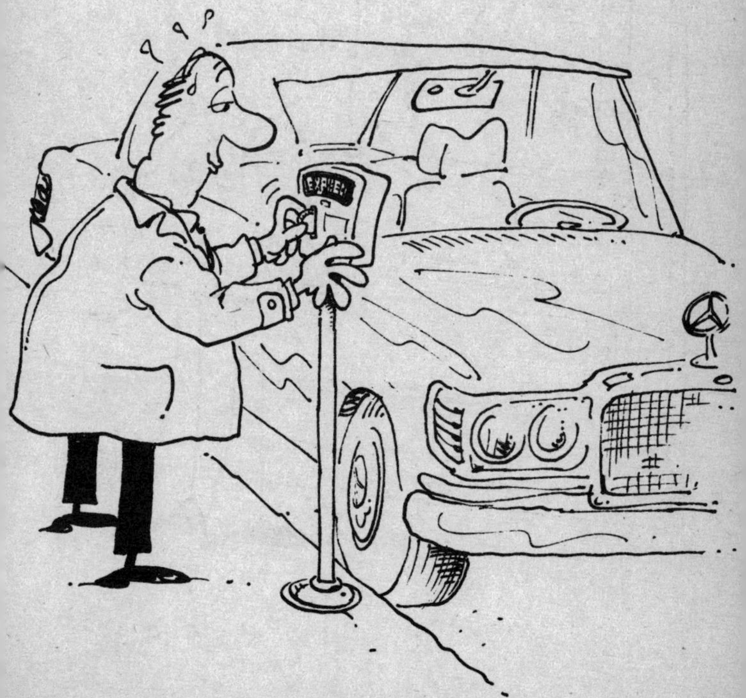
EXPIRED

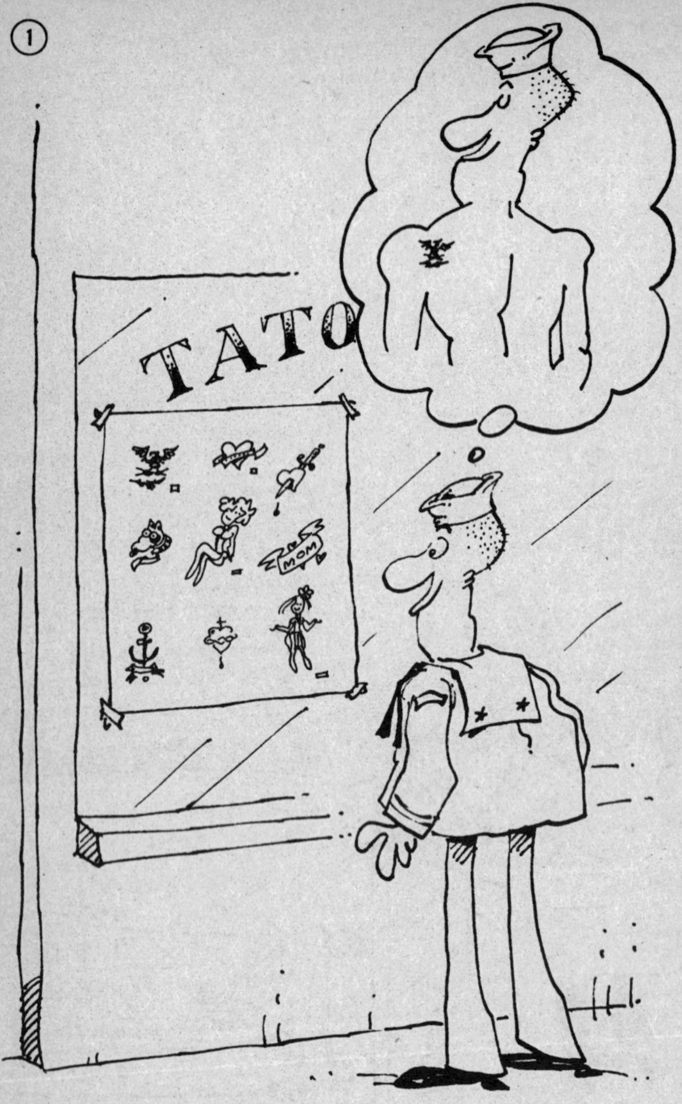
TATO
MOM

(2)

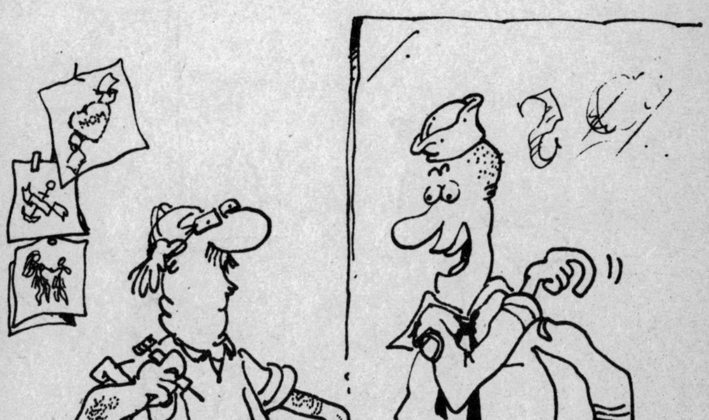
MOM

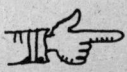

3

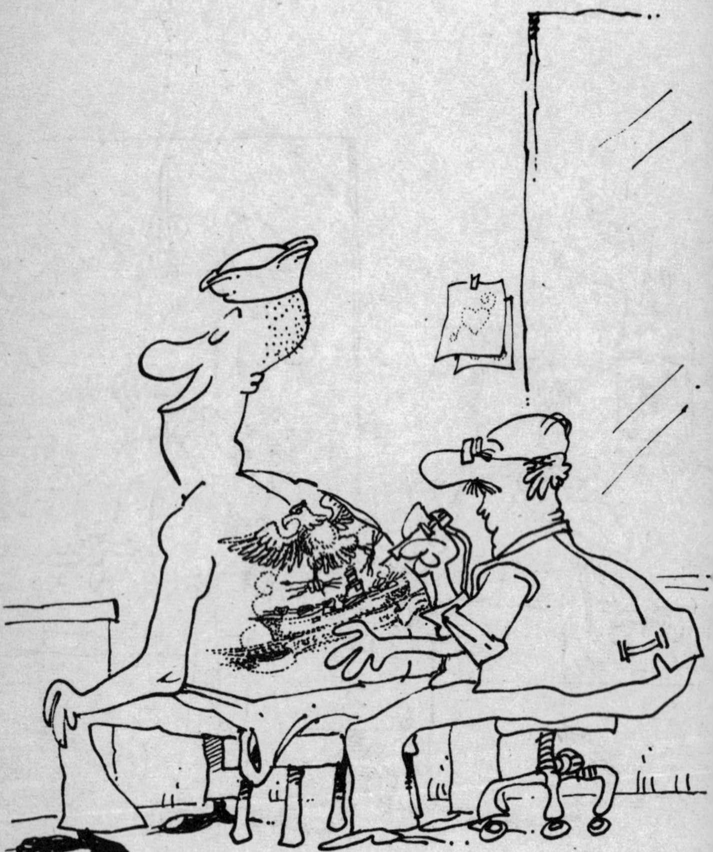

①

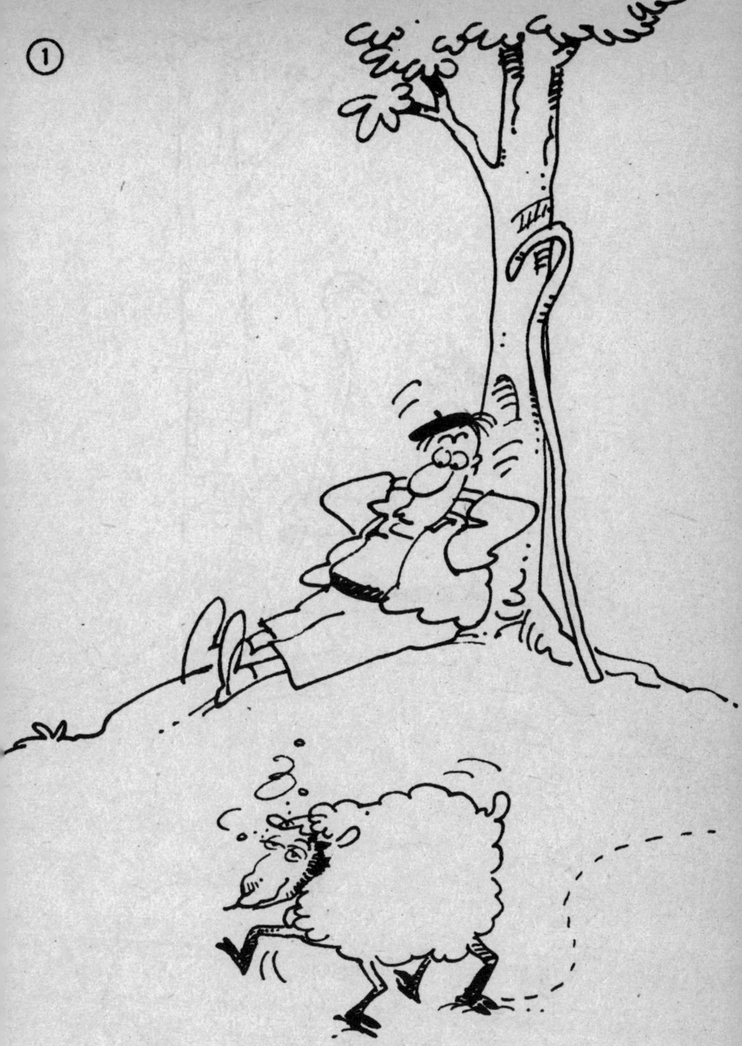

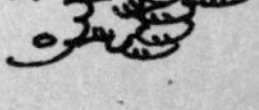

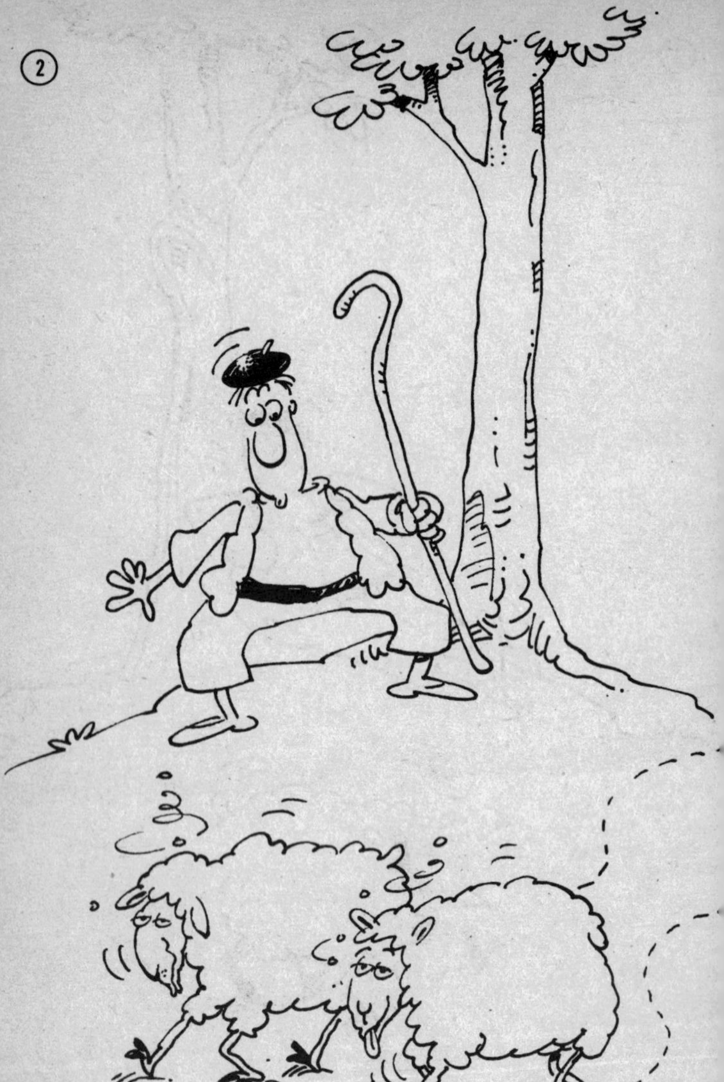

3

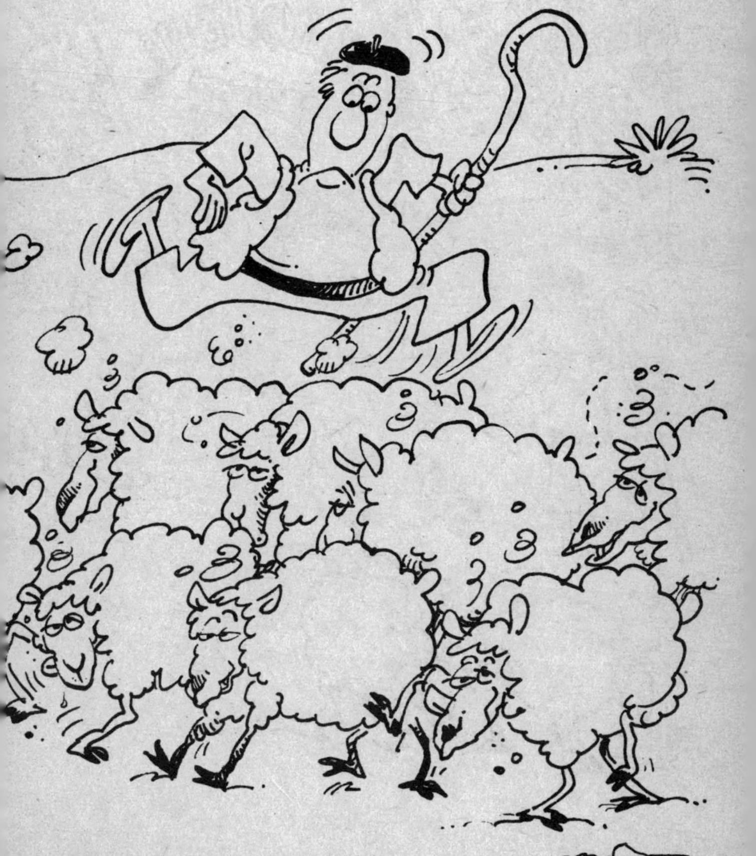

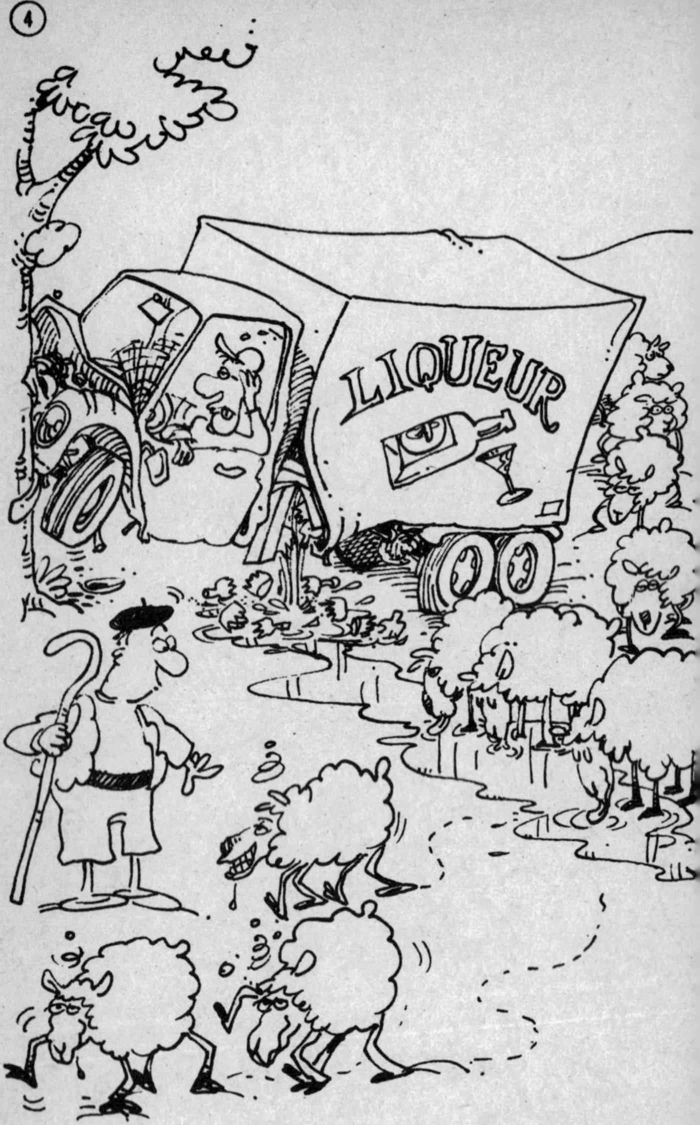
4
LIQUEUR

(1)

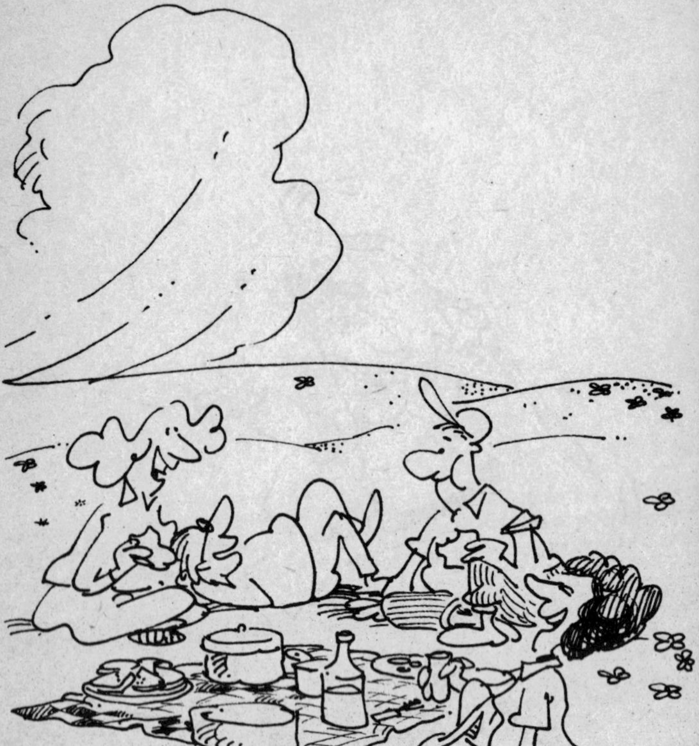

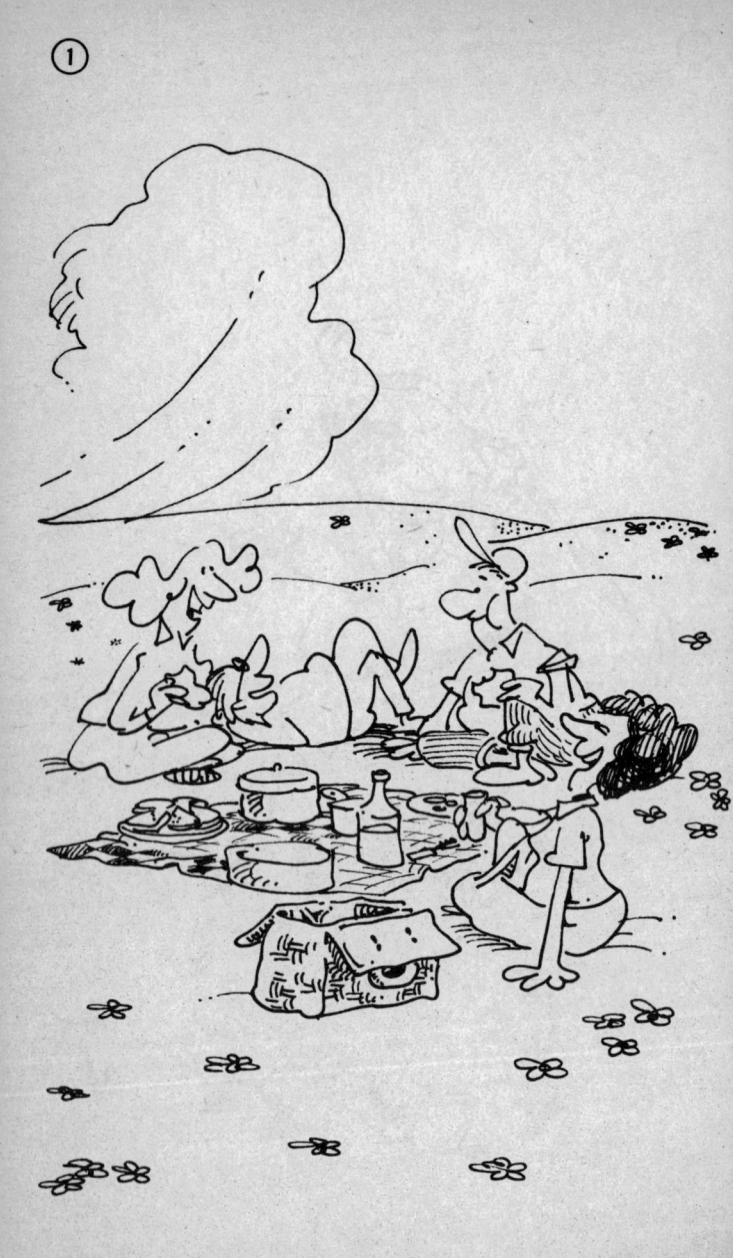

2

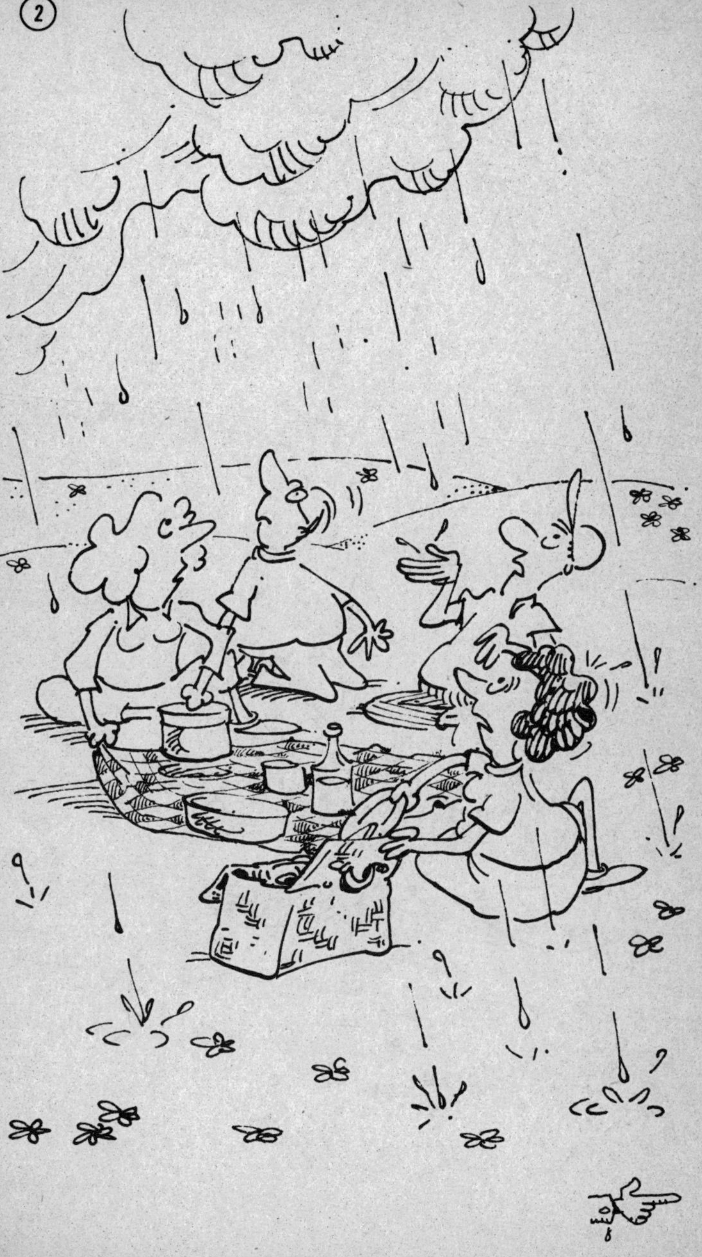

3

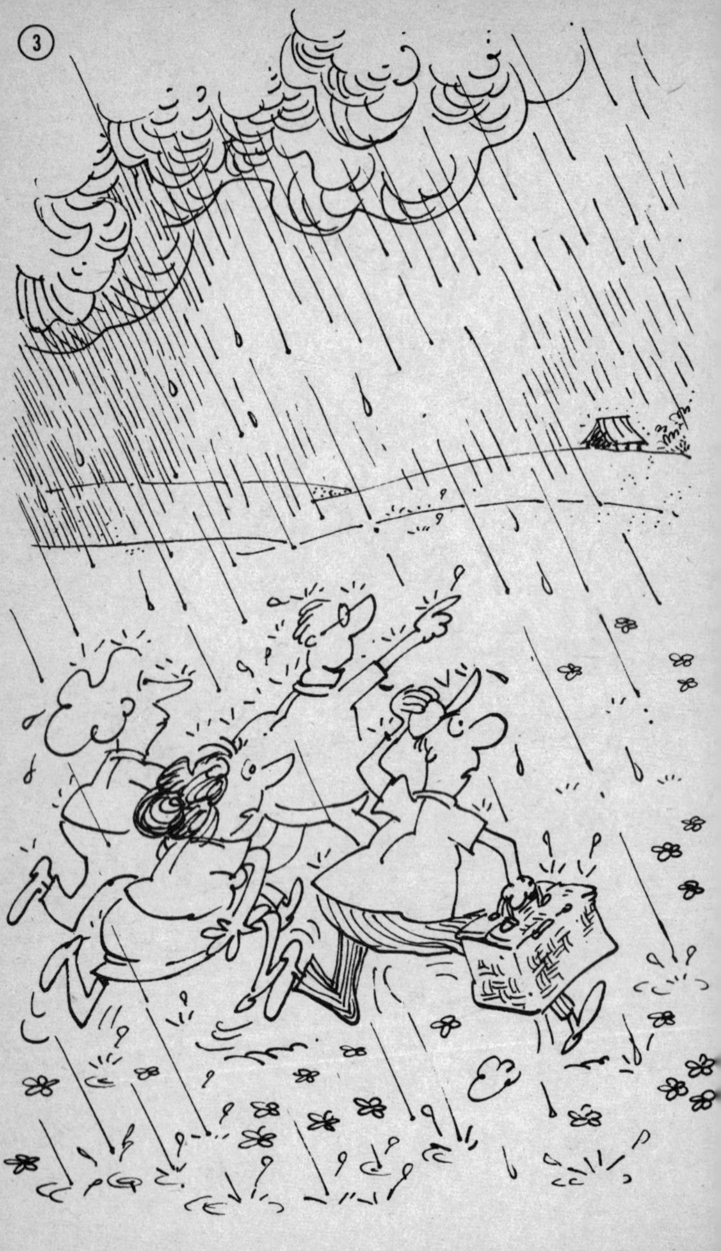

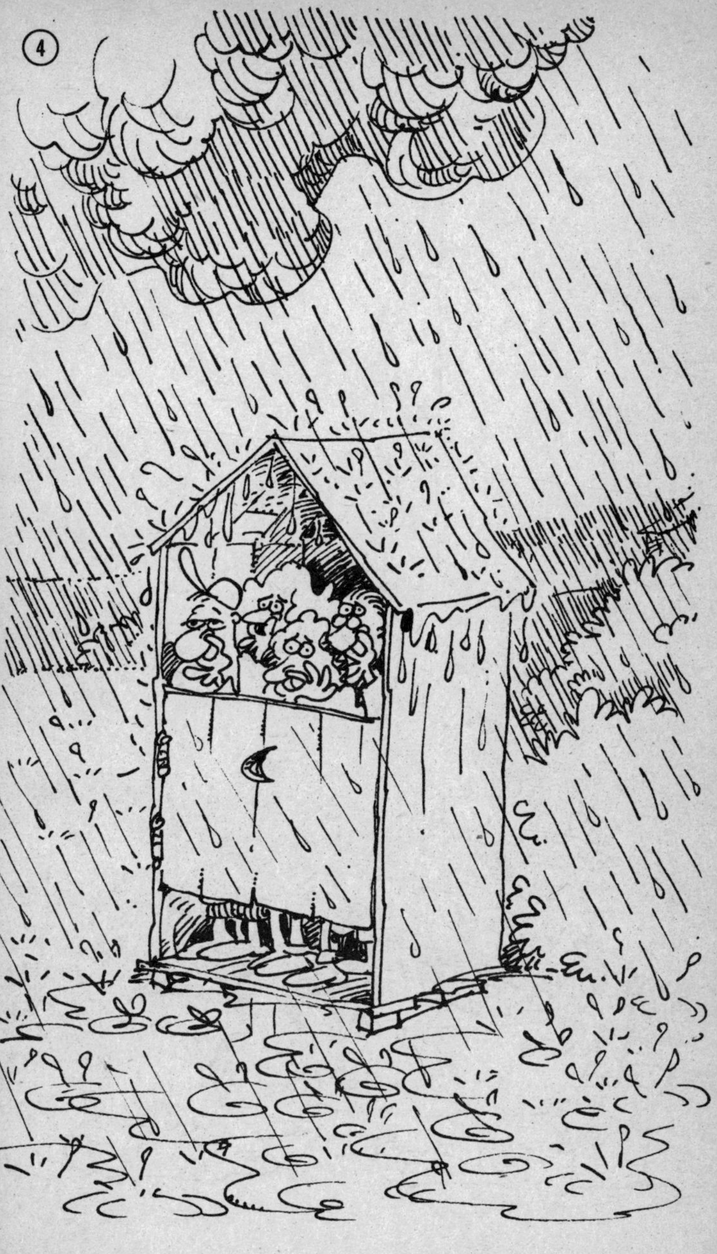
4

1

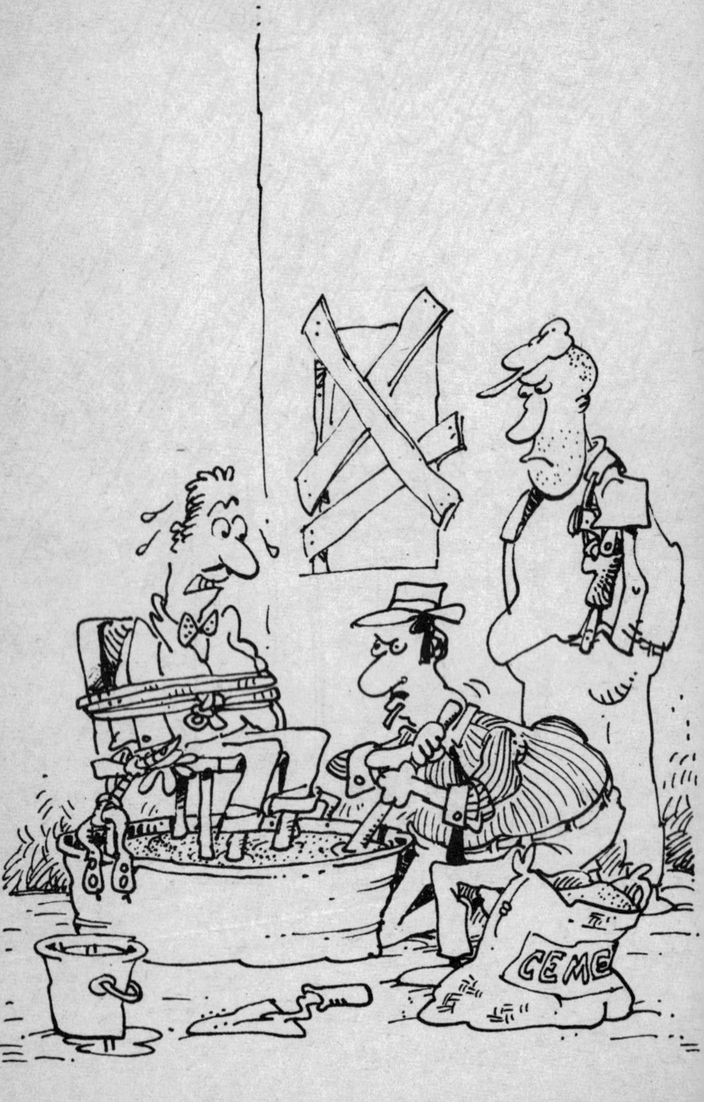
CEME

2

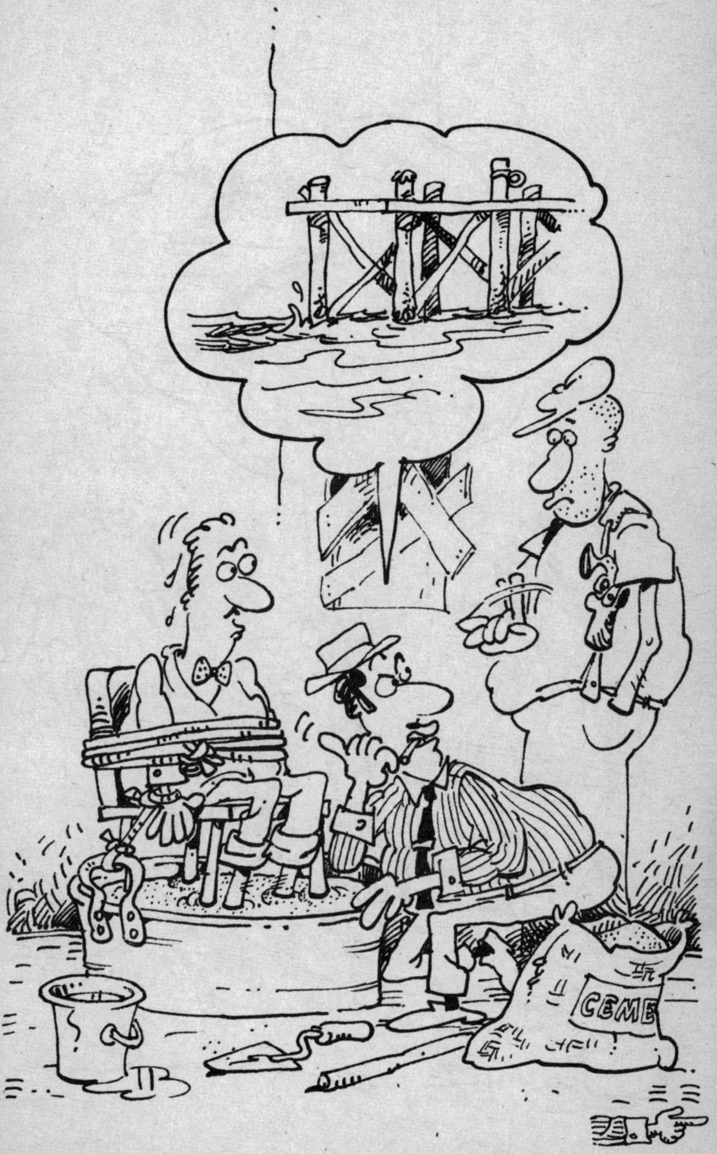
CEME

3

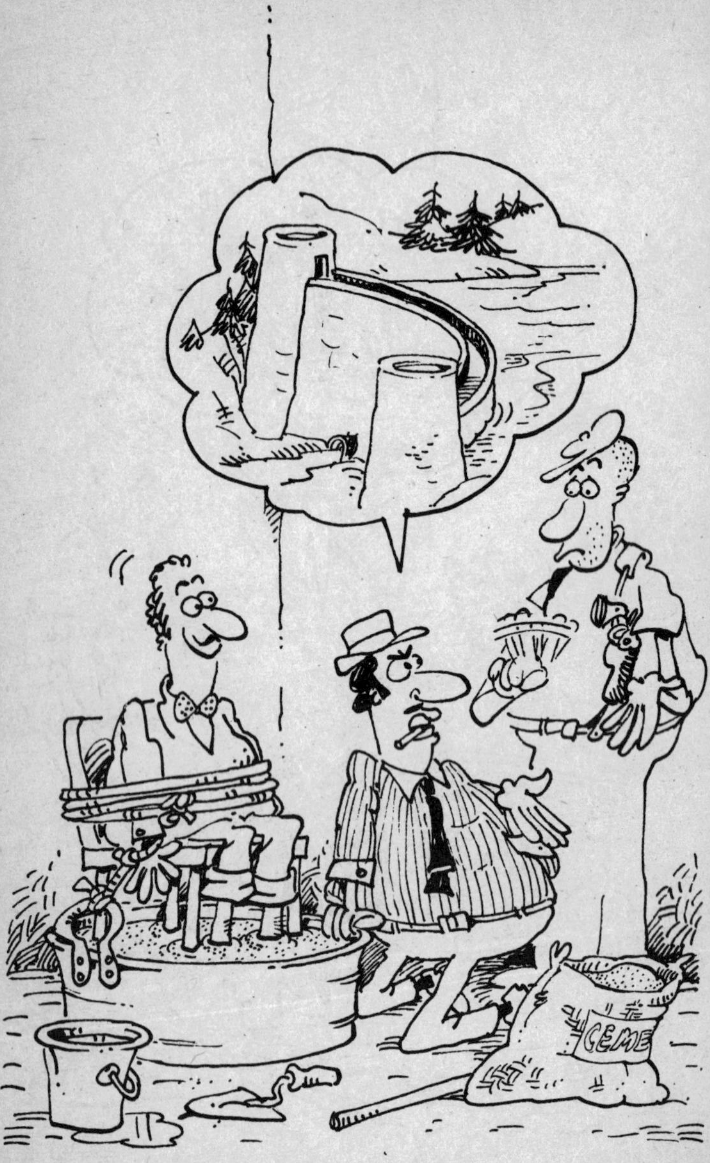
CEME

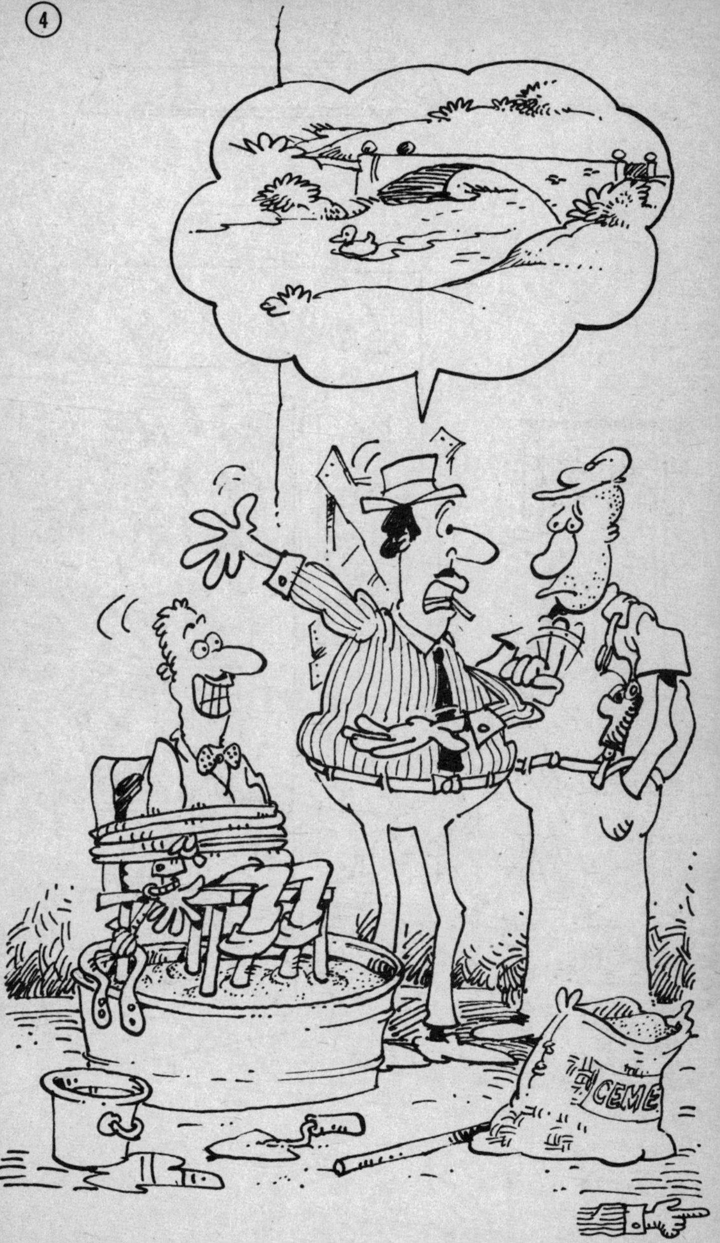
4
CEME

5

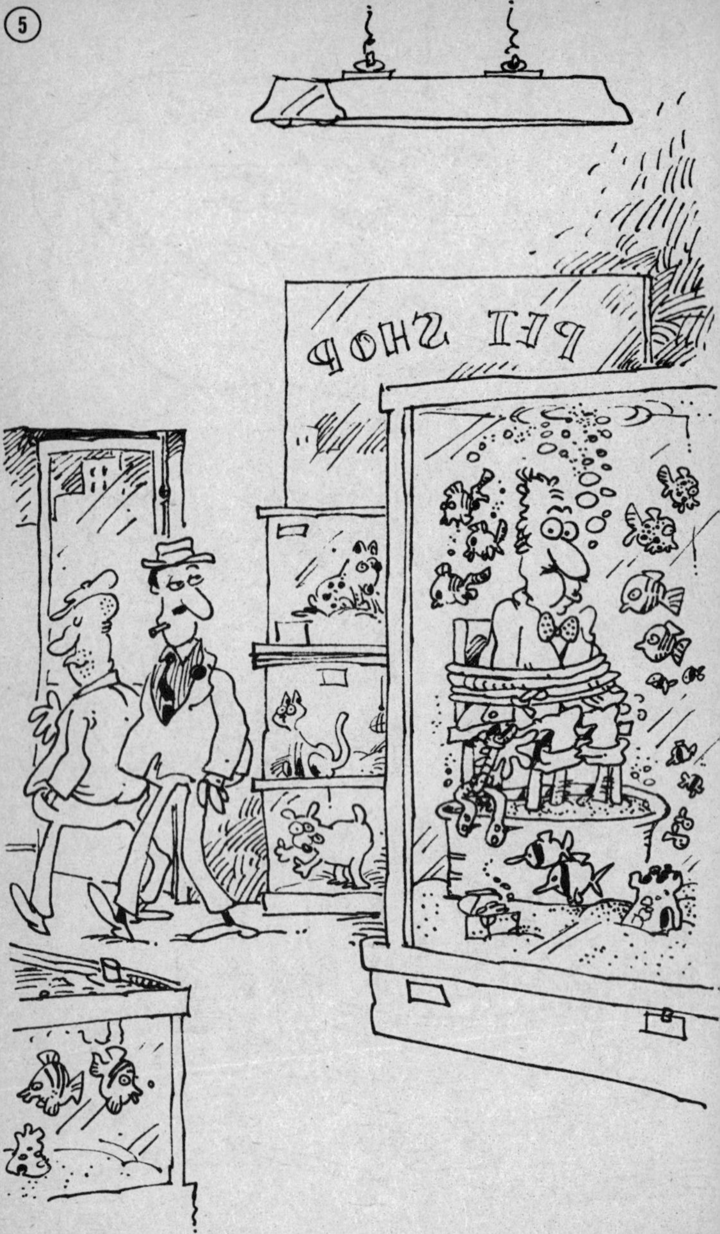
PET SHOP

①

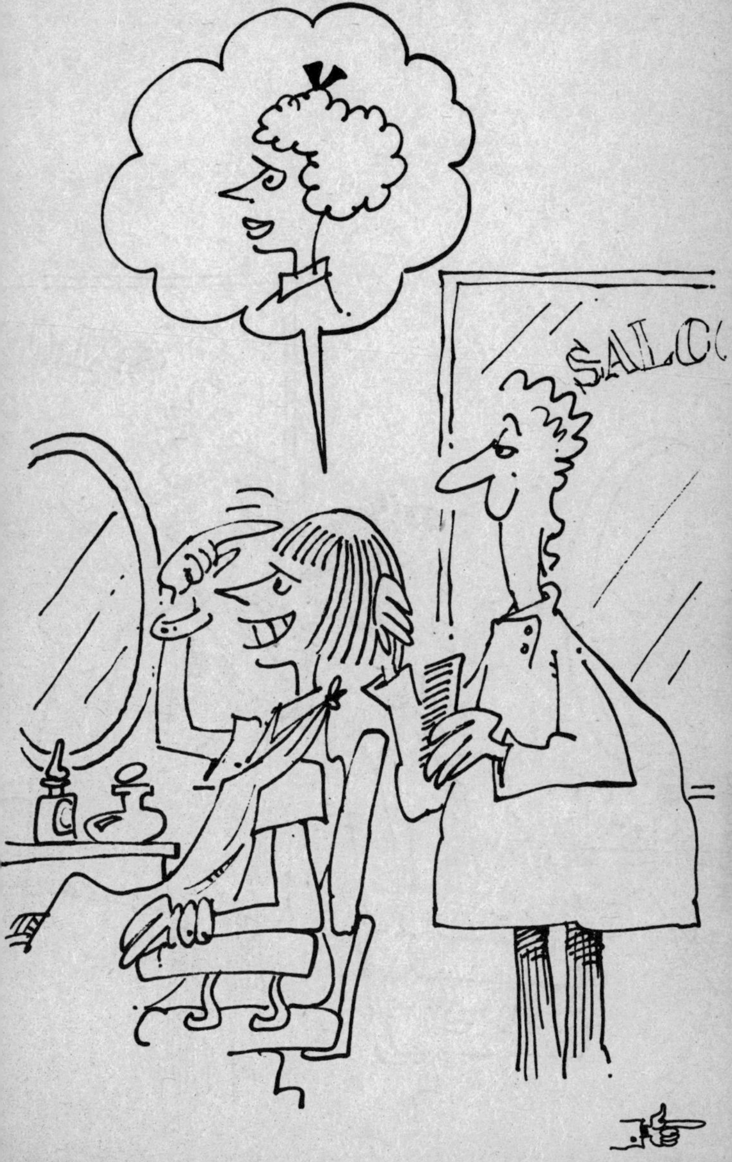

(2)

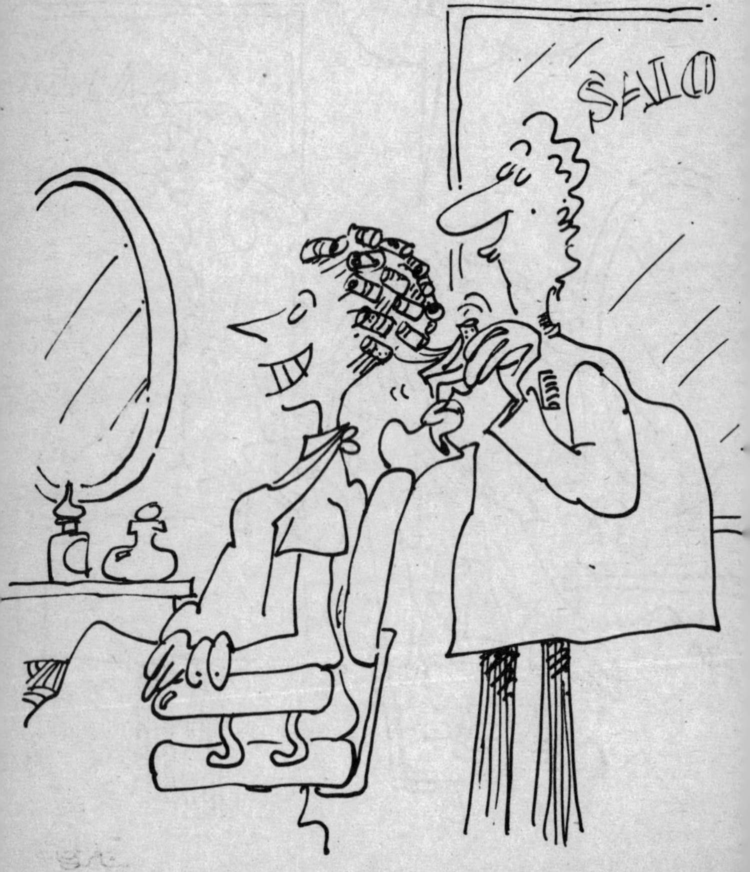

3

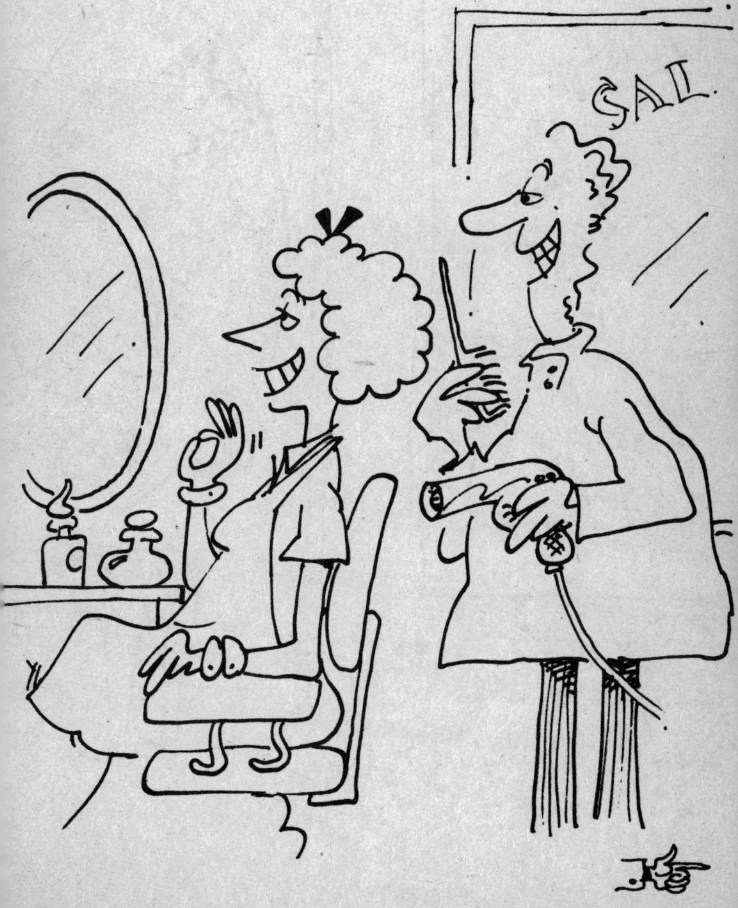
SAL

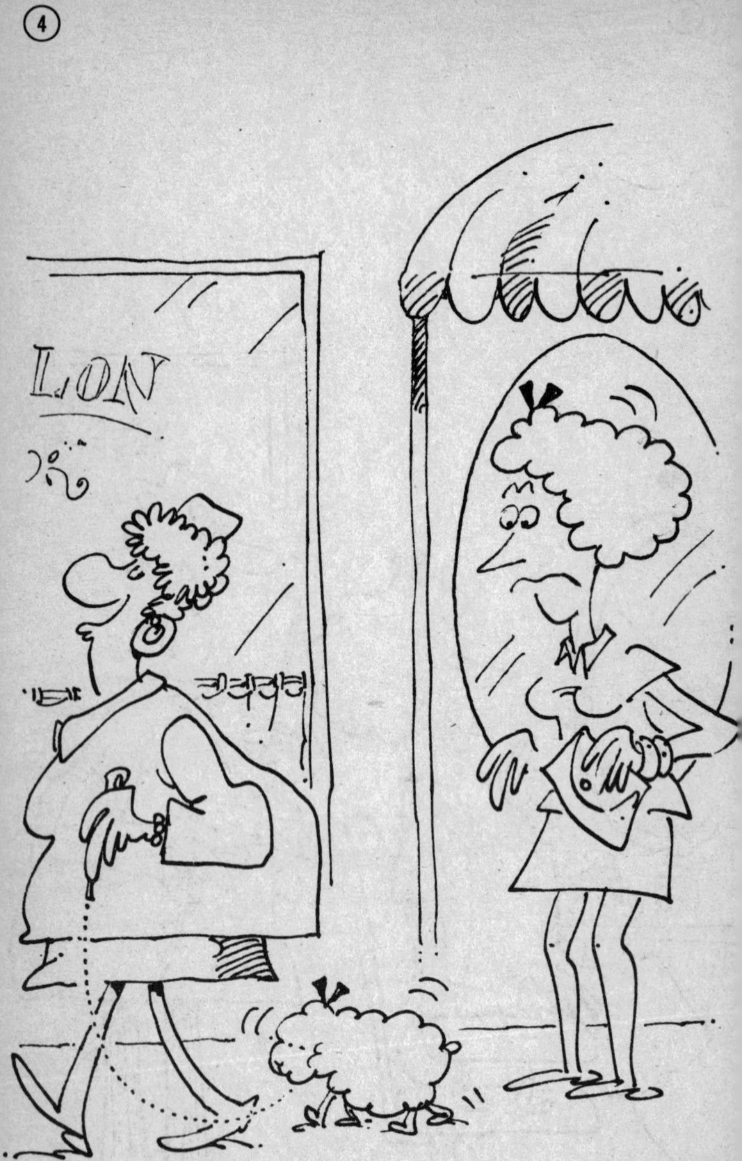
4
LON

5

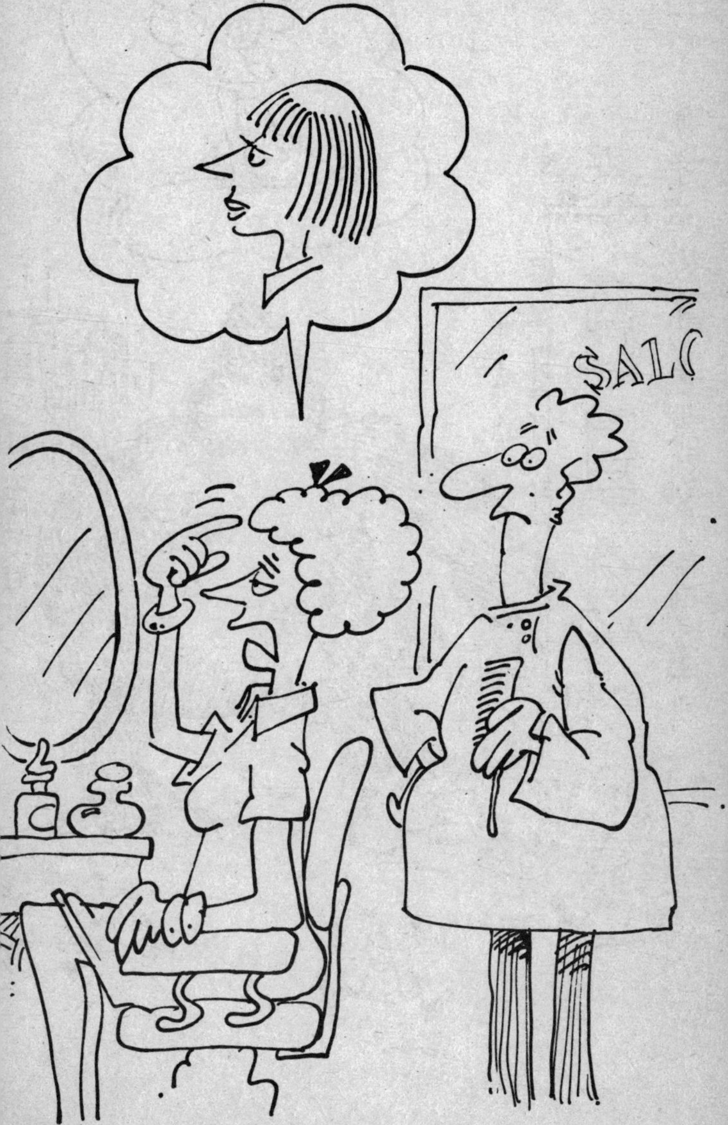
SALC

1

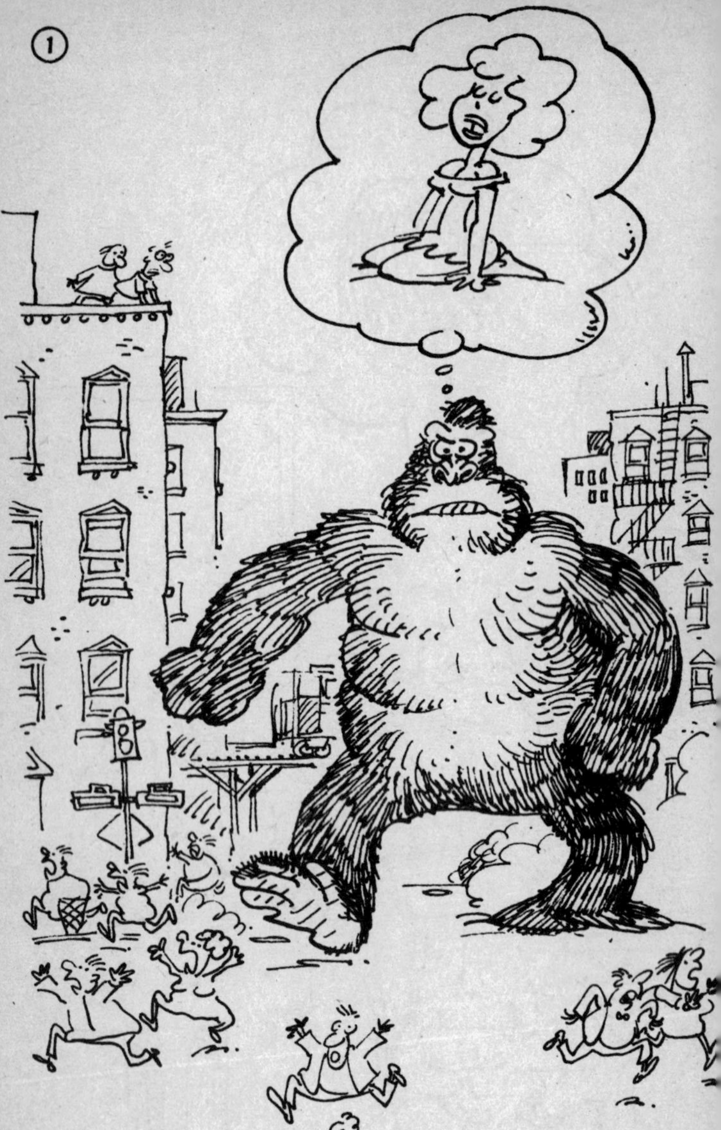

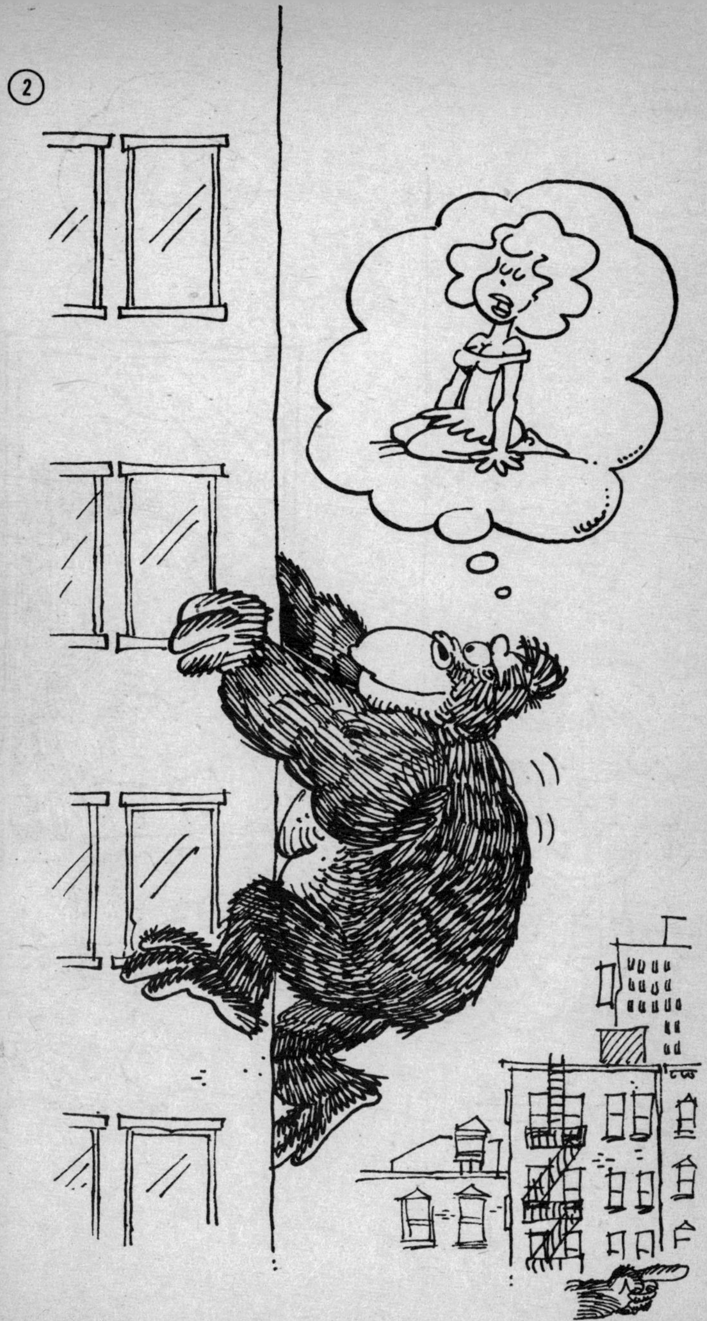
2

③

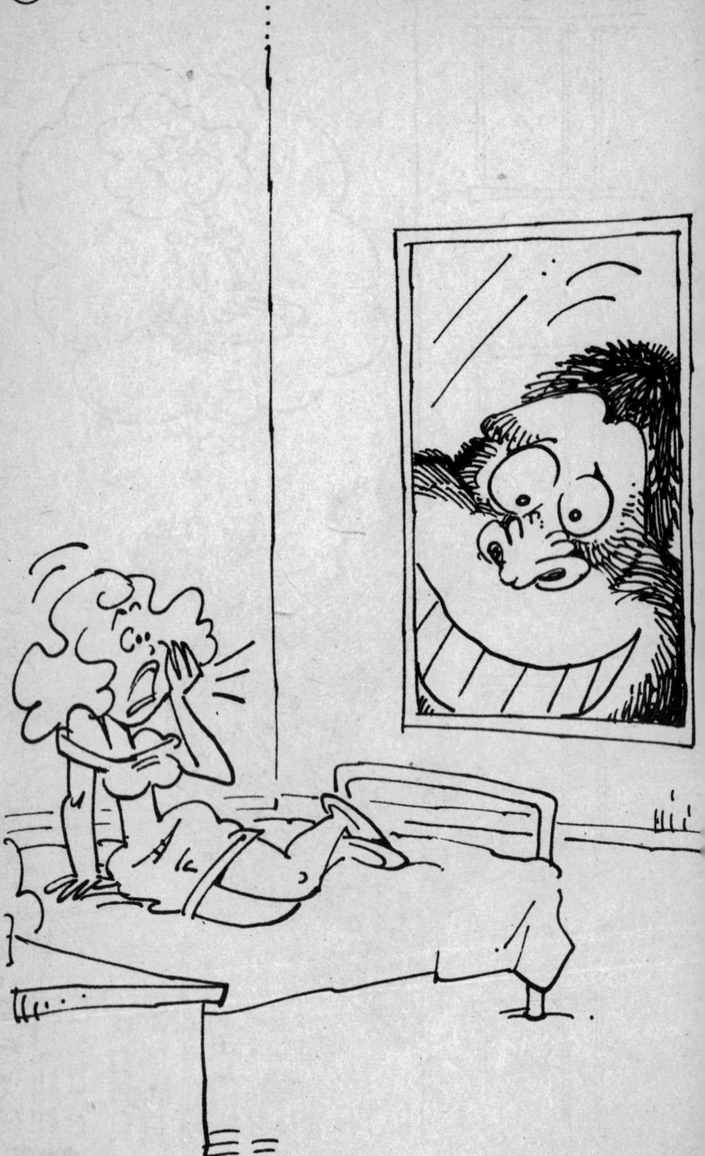

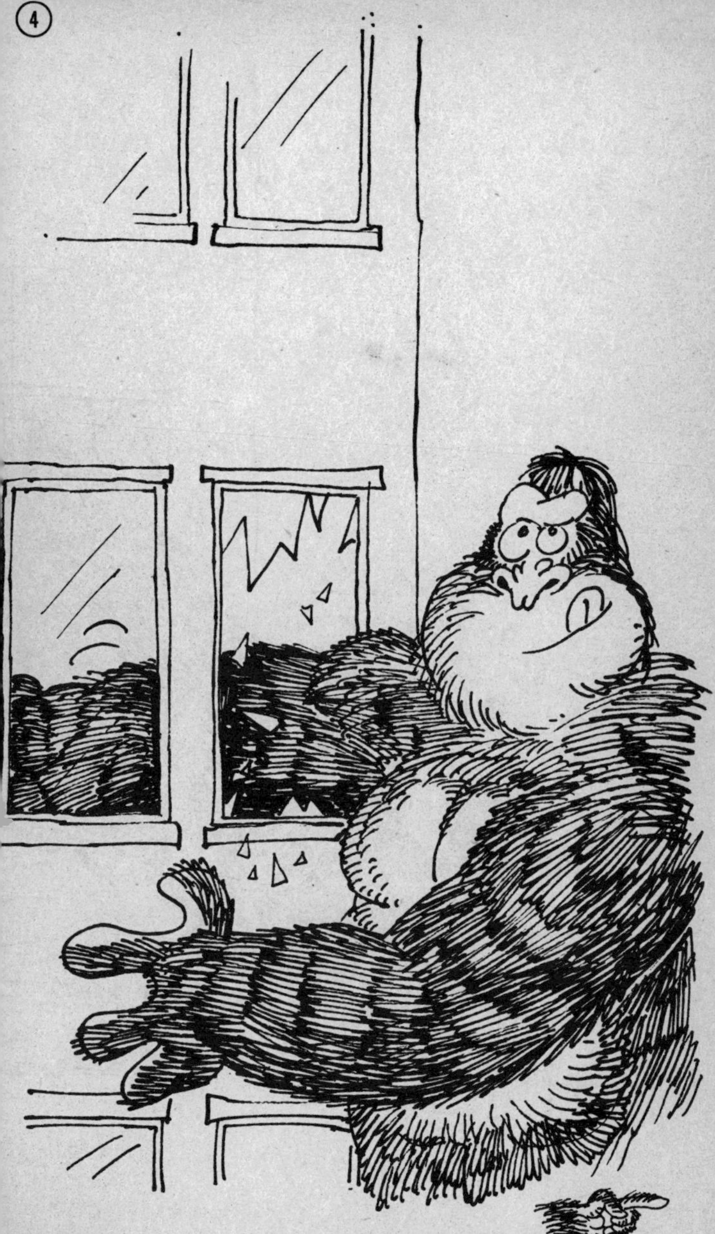
4

5

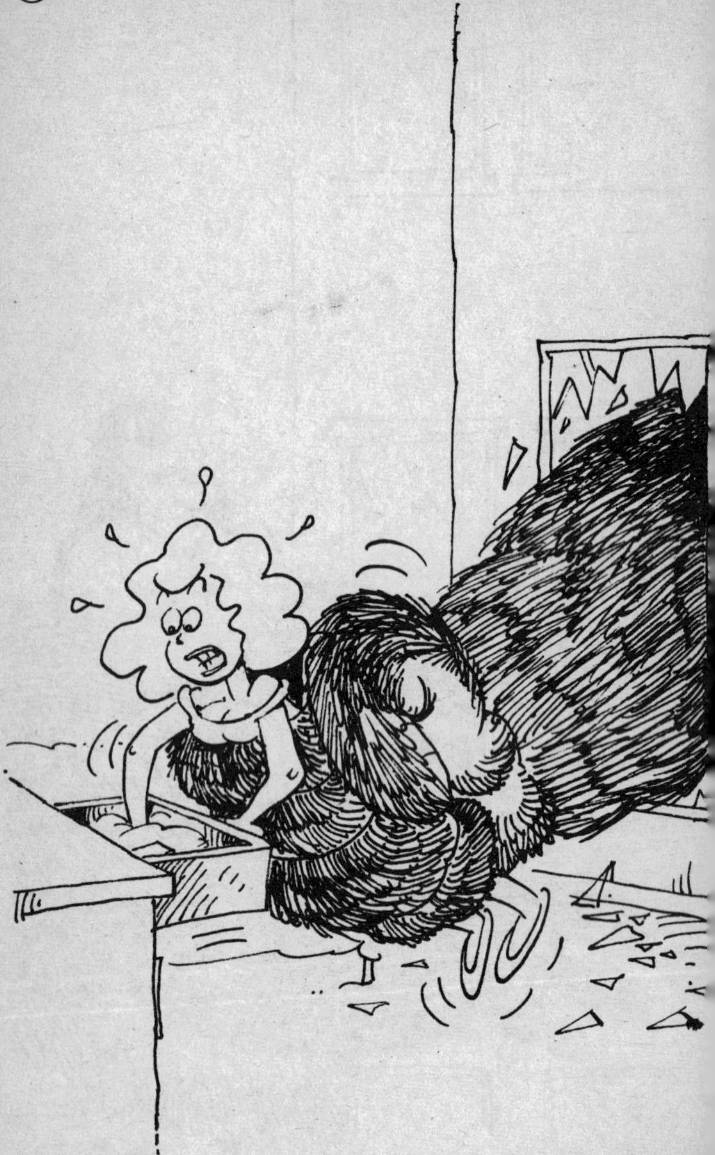

6

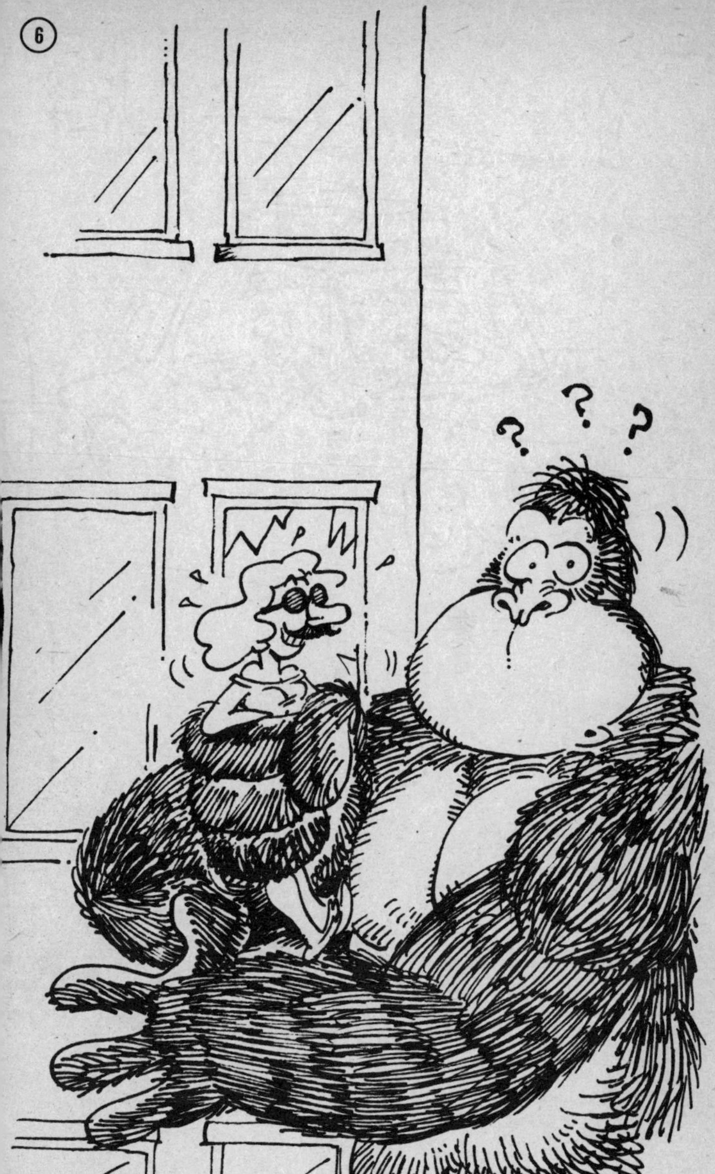

1

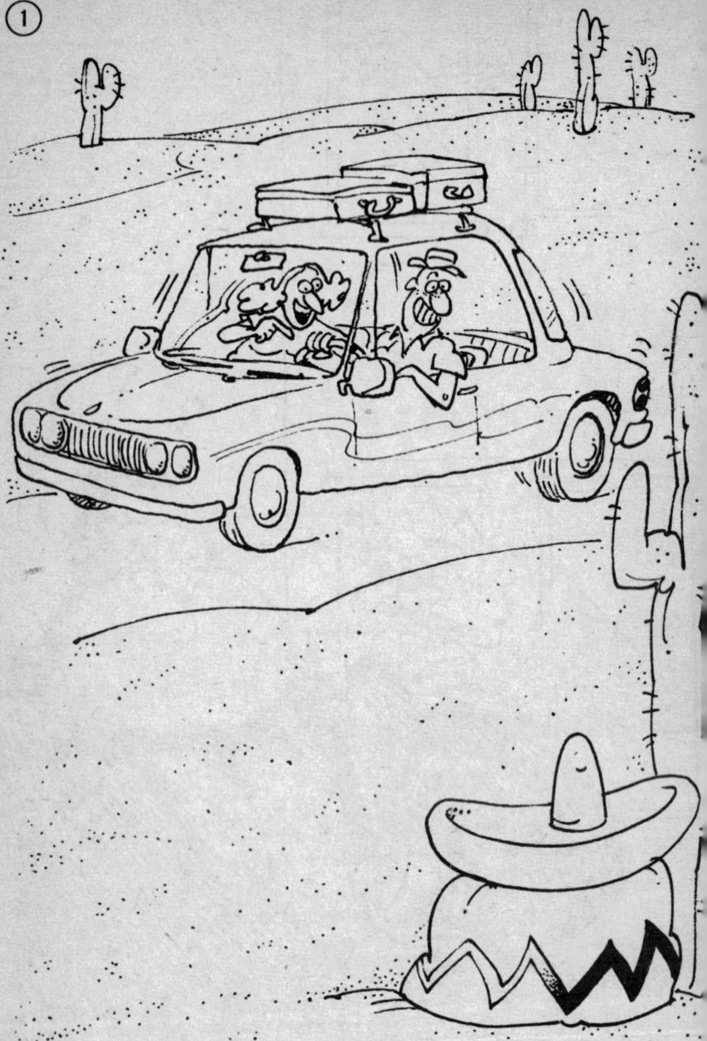

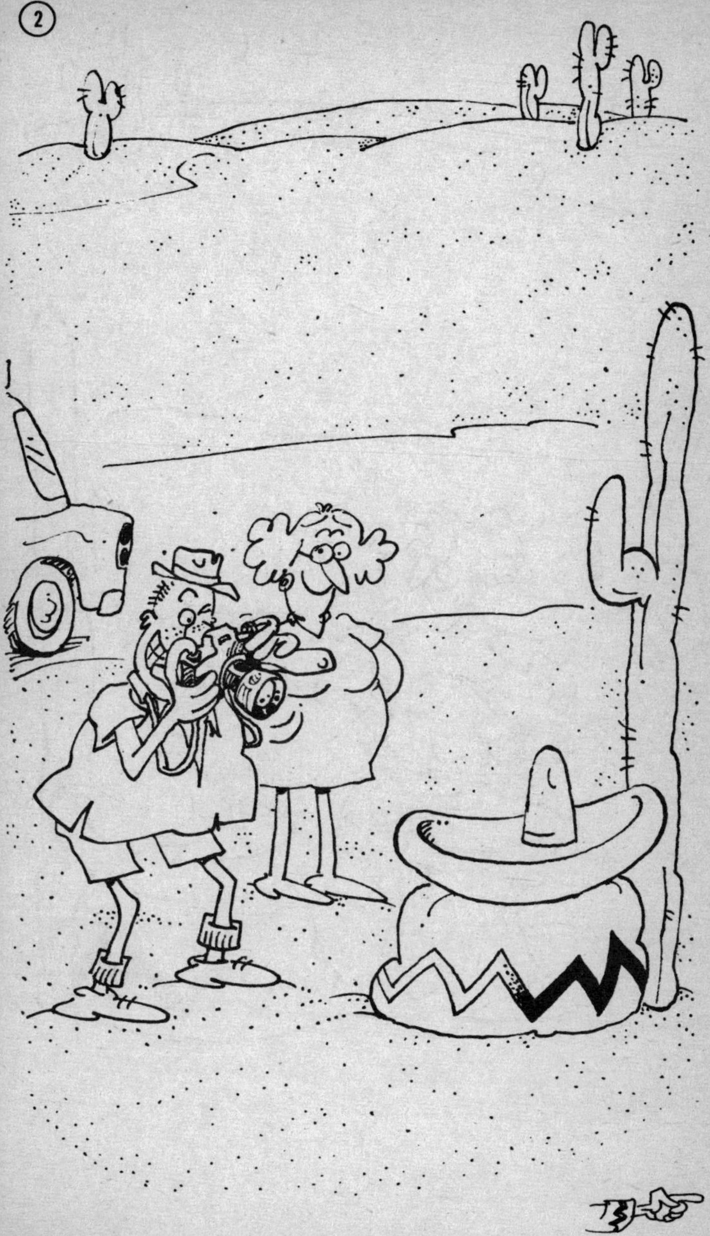
2

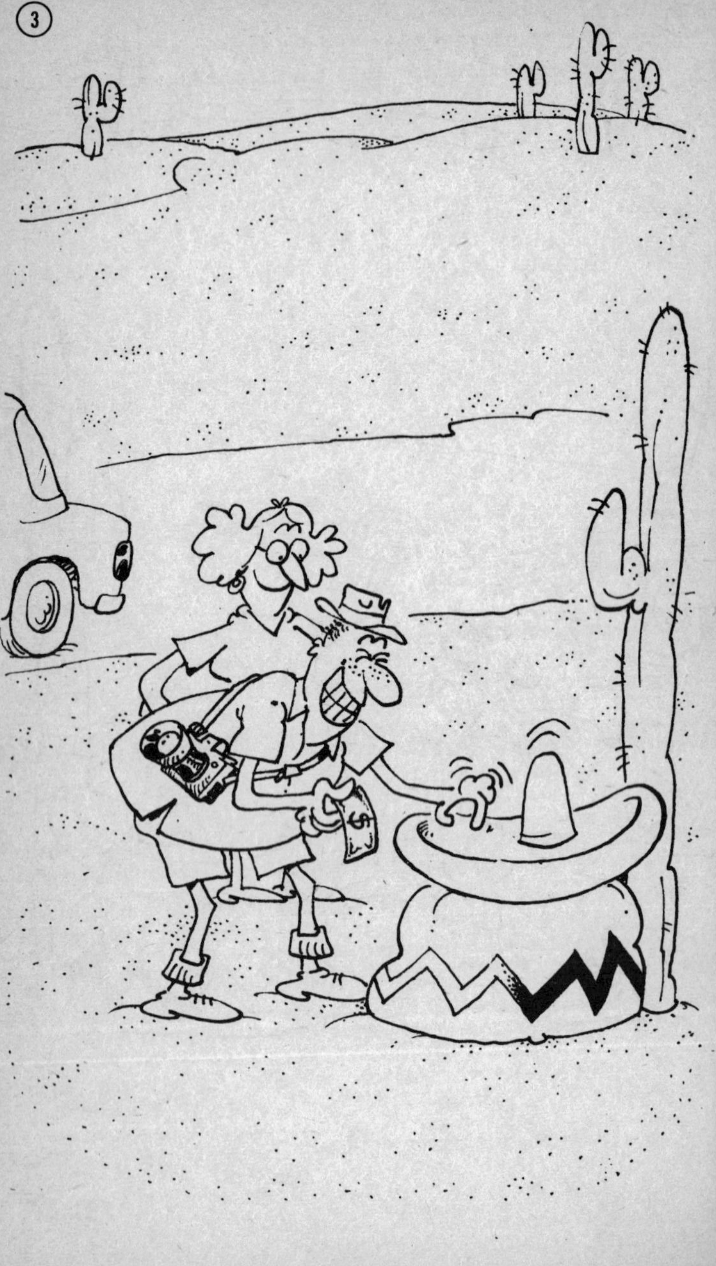
3

4

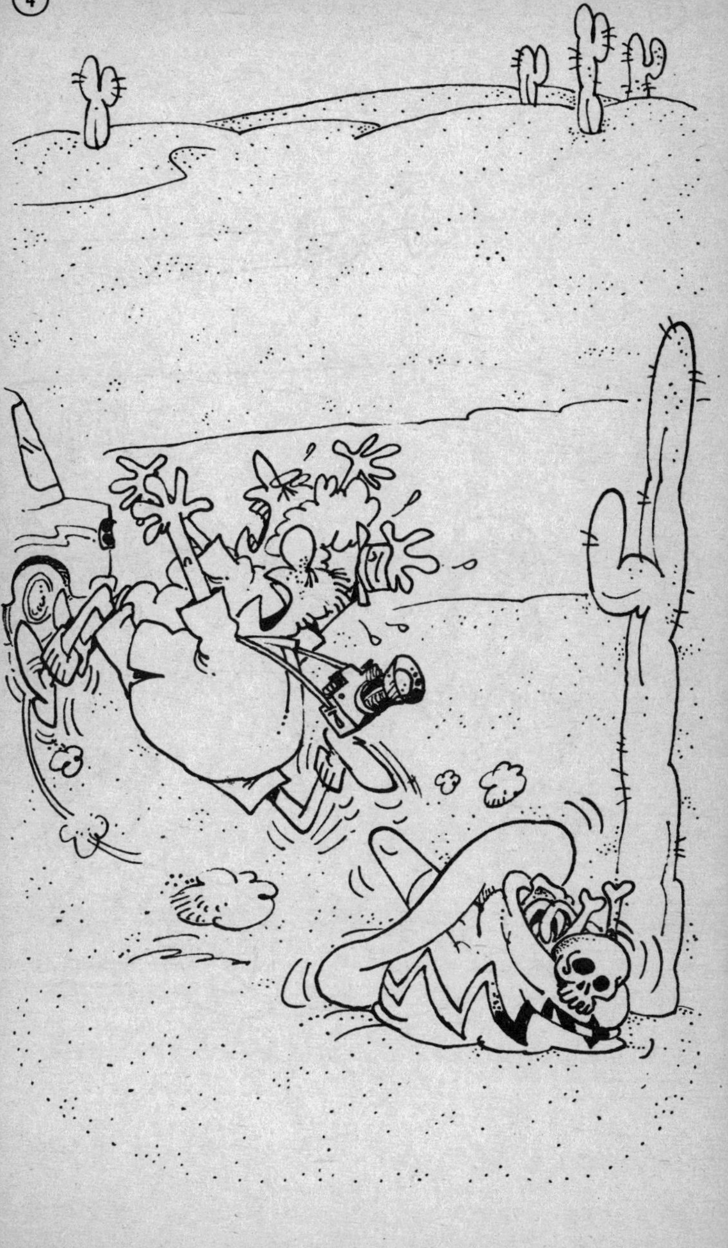

(1)

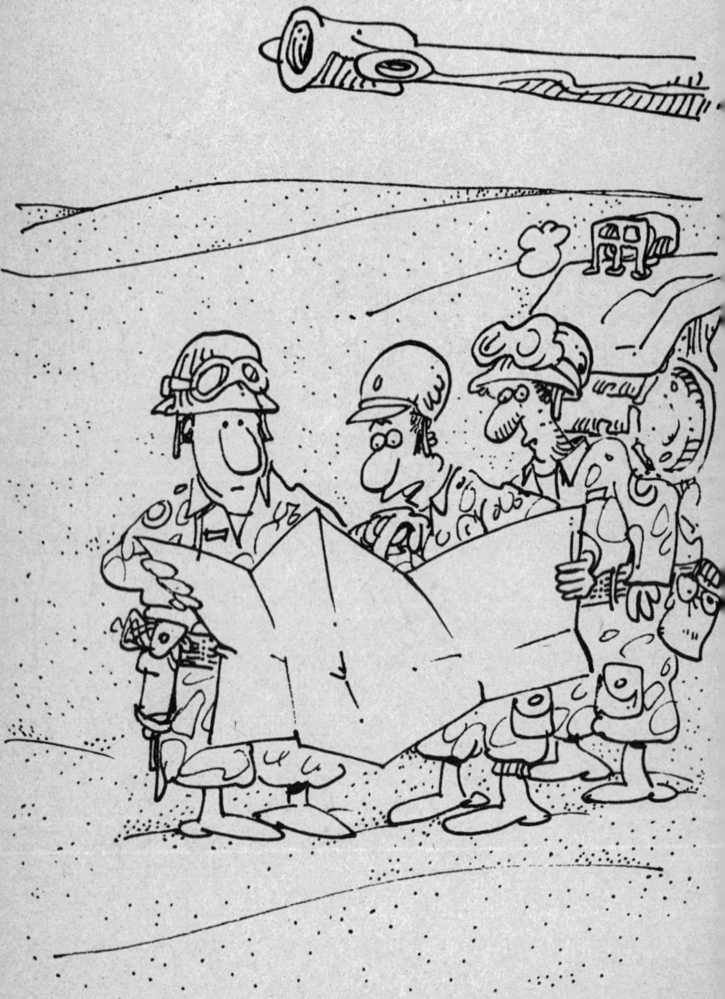

2

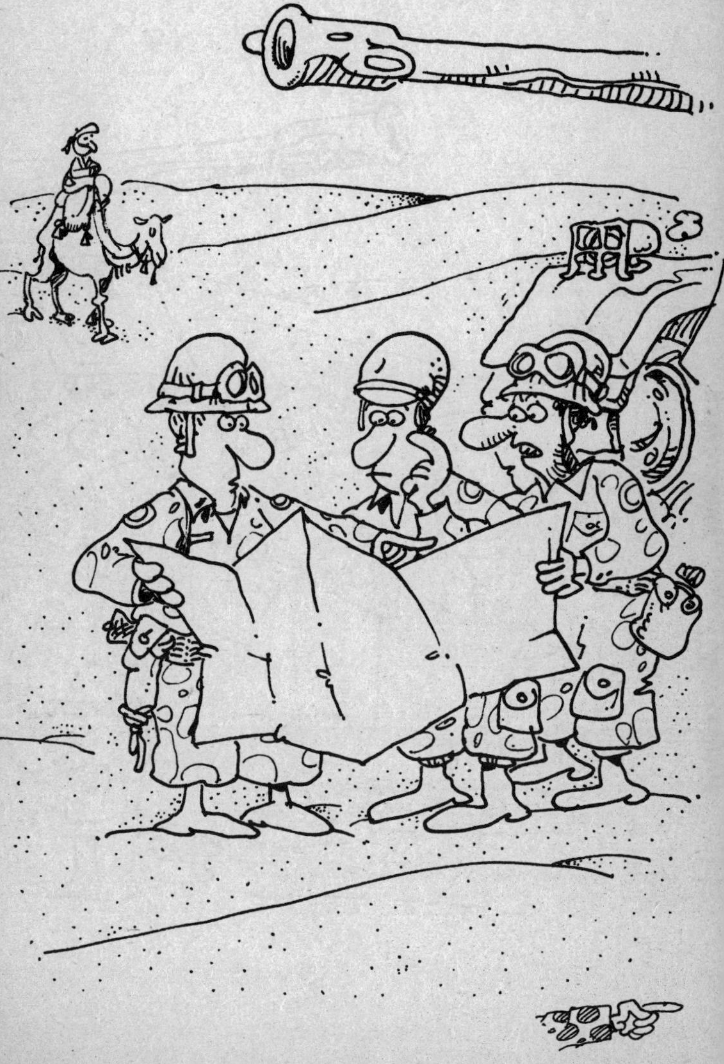

3

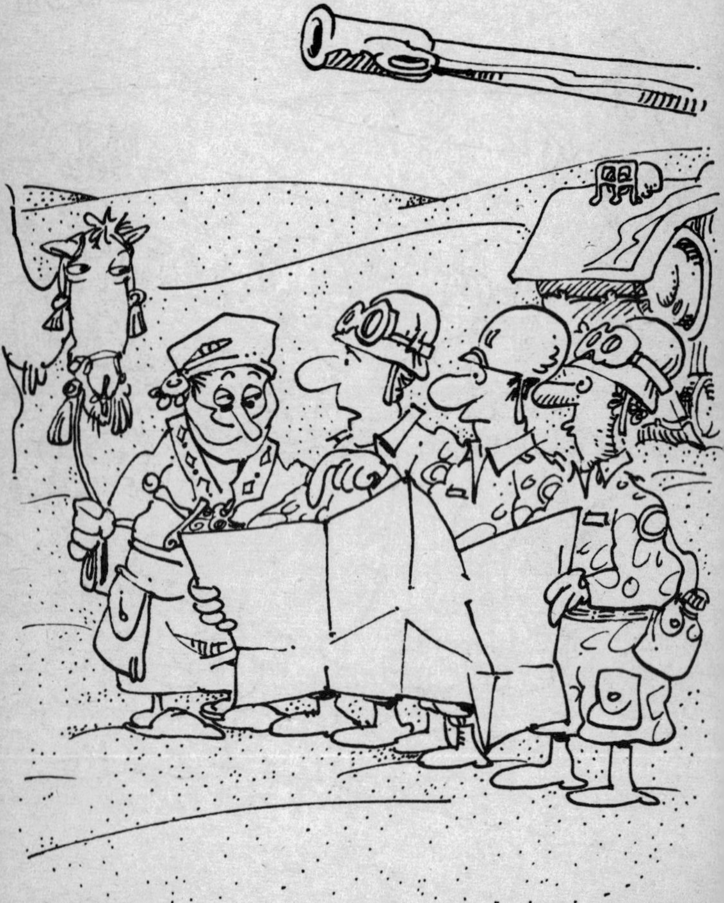

4

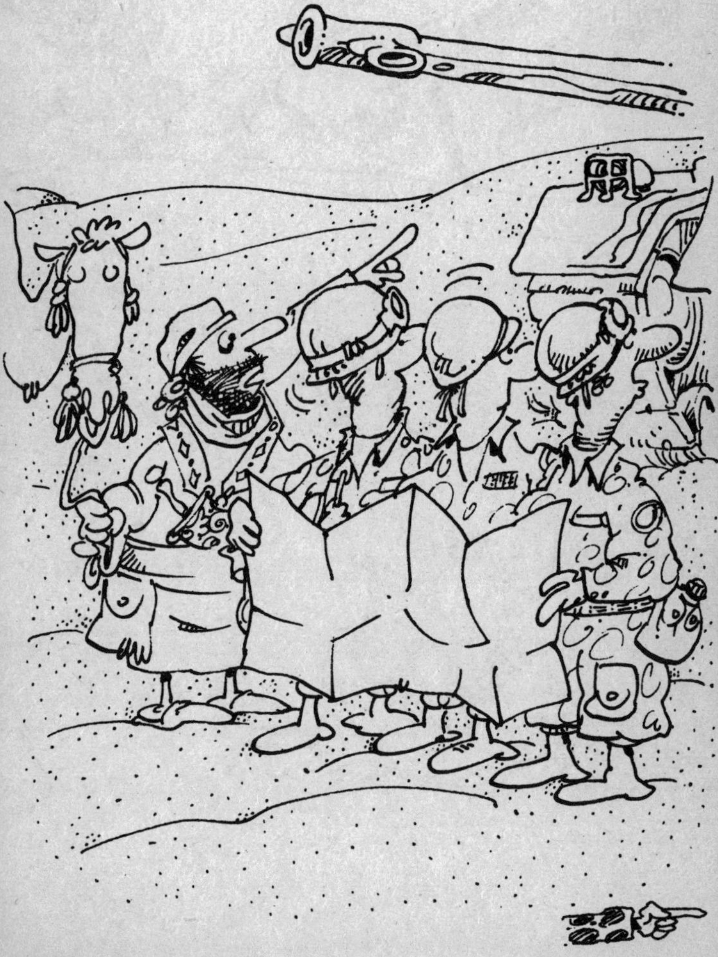

5

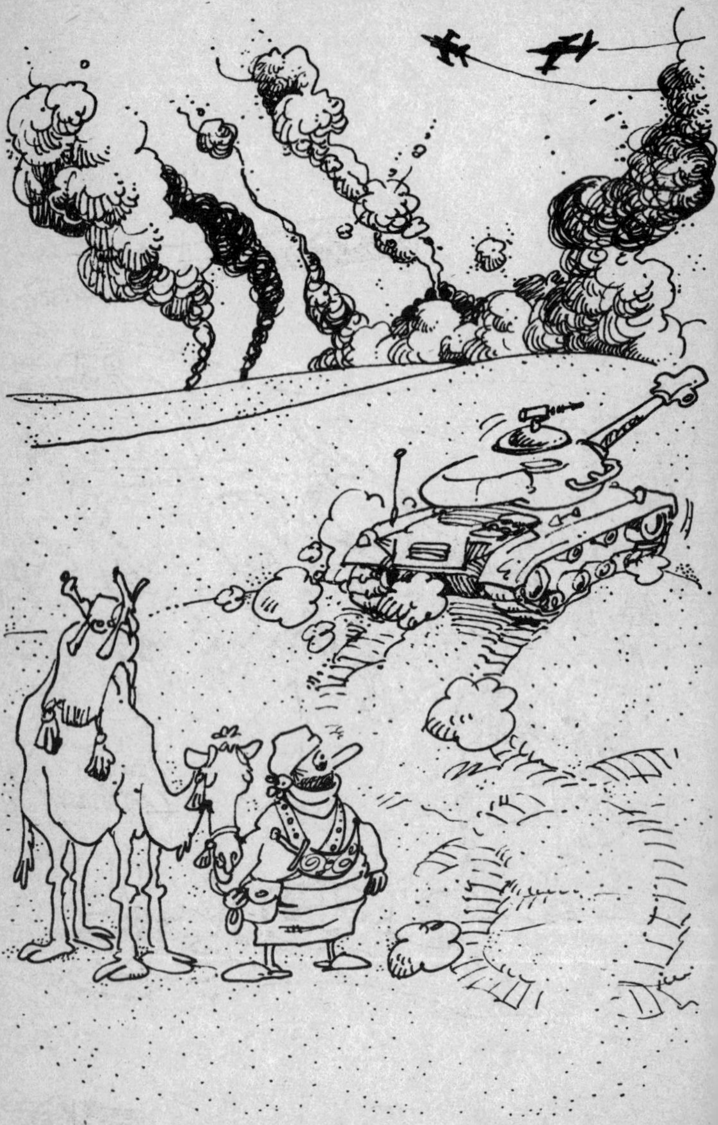

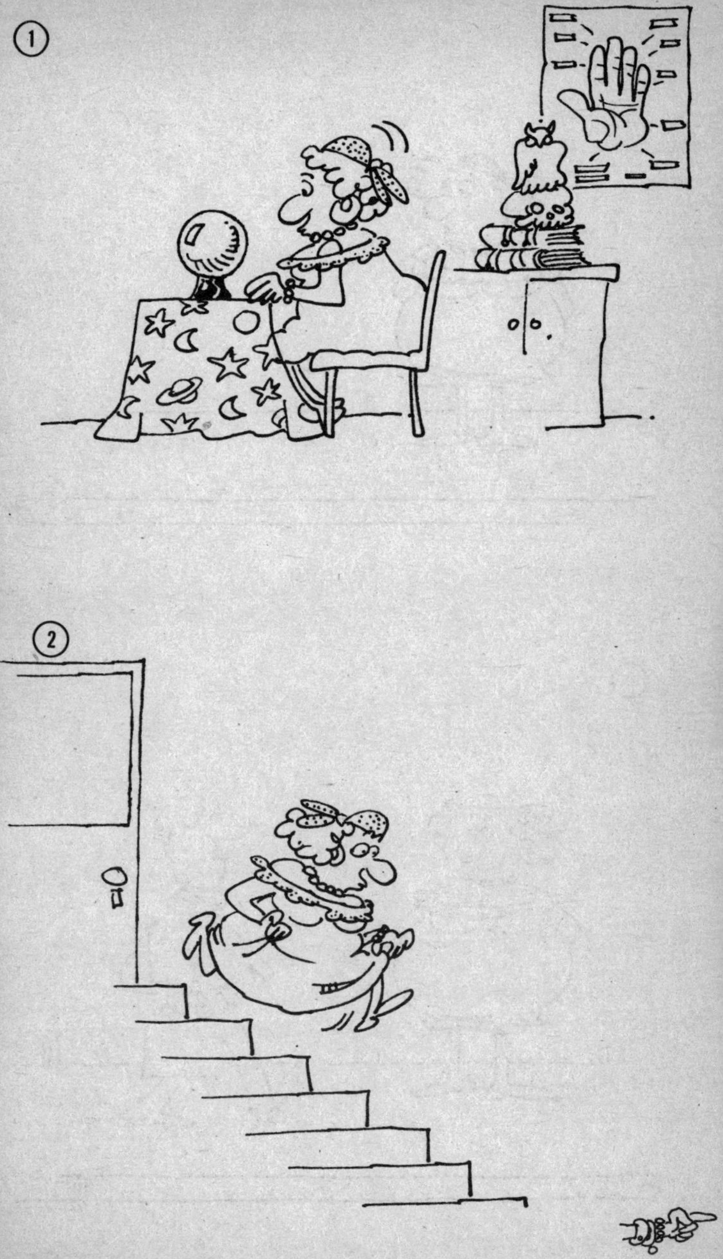

3

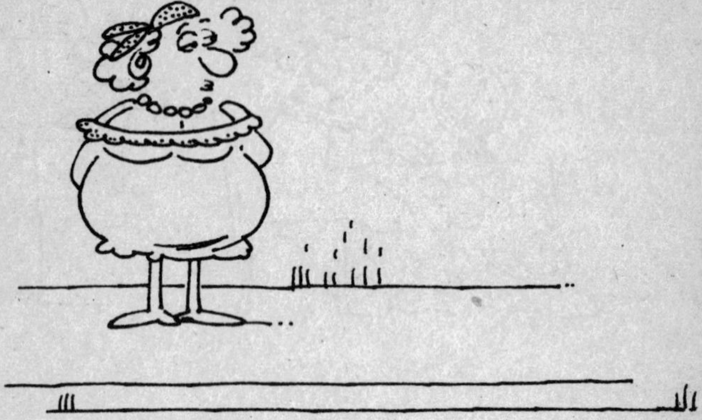

4

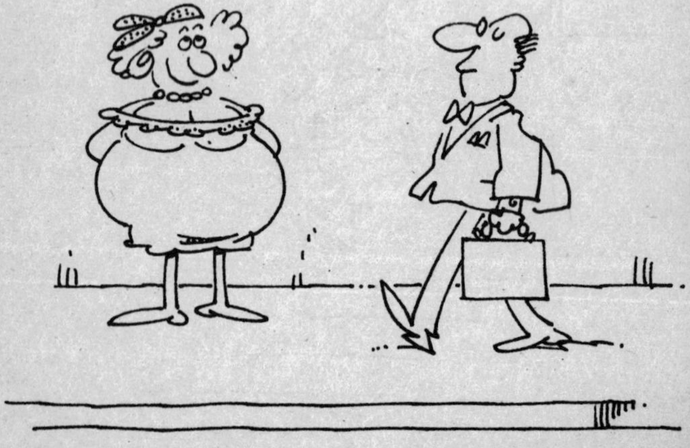

5

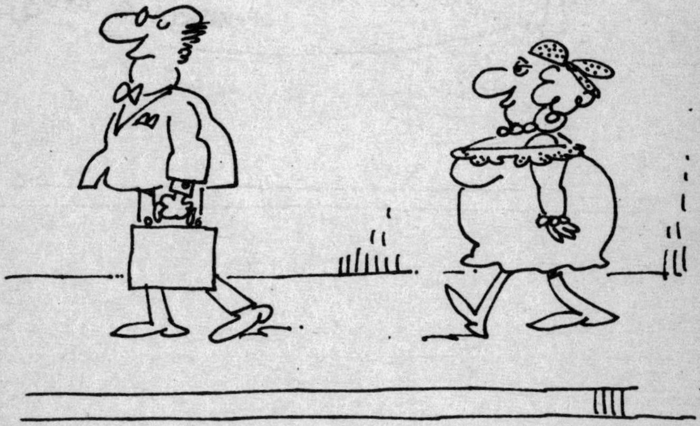

6

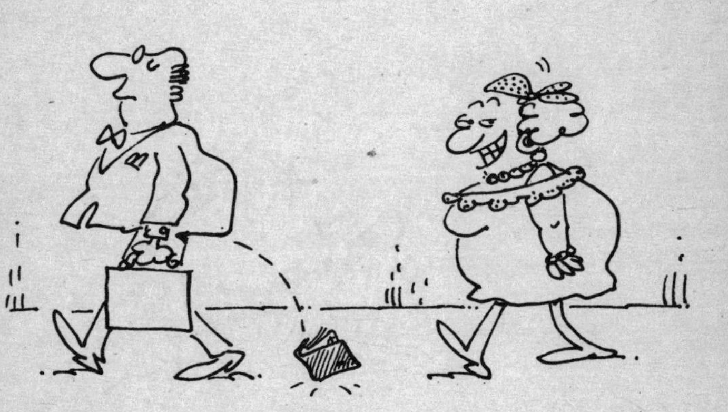

(1)

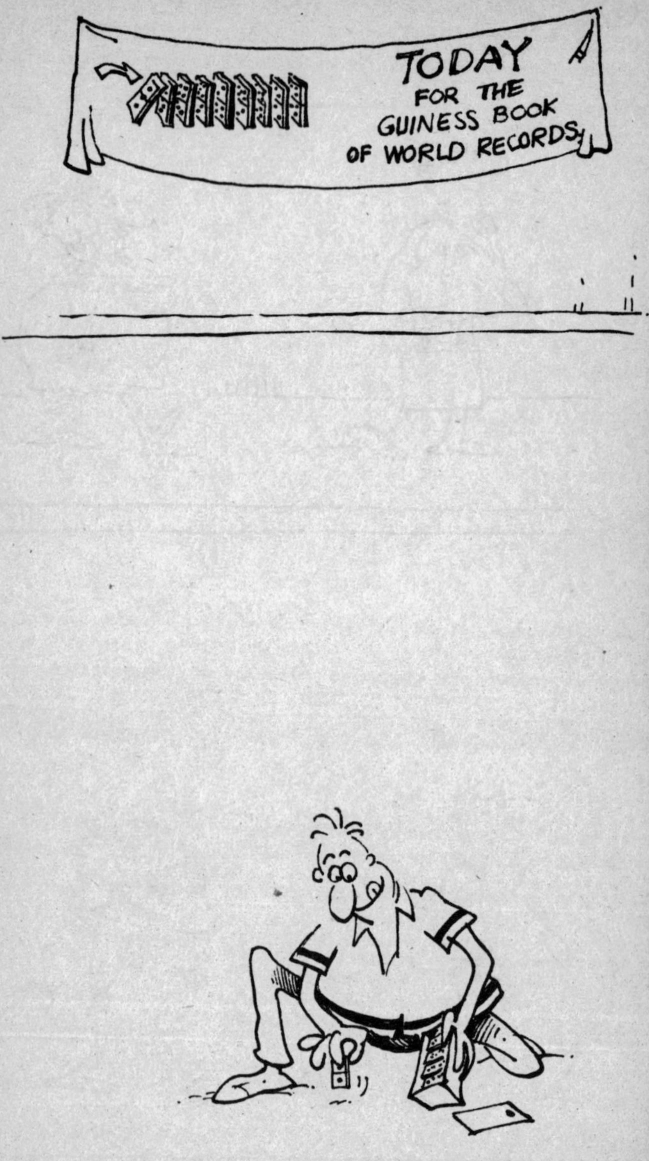
TODAY
FOR THE
GUINESS BOOK
OF WORLD RECORDS

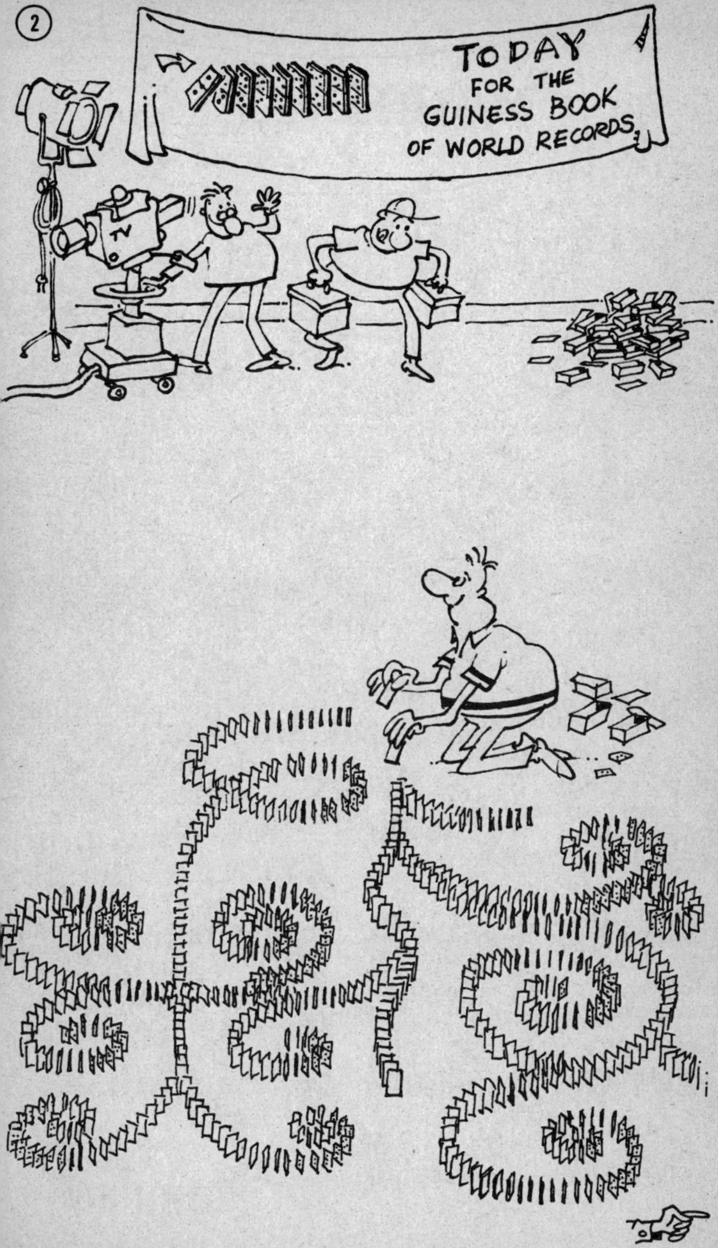
2
TODAY
FOR THE
GUINESS BOOK
OF WORLD RECORDS
TV

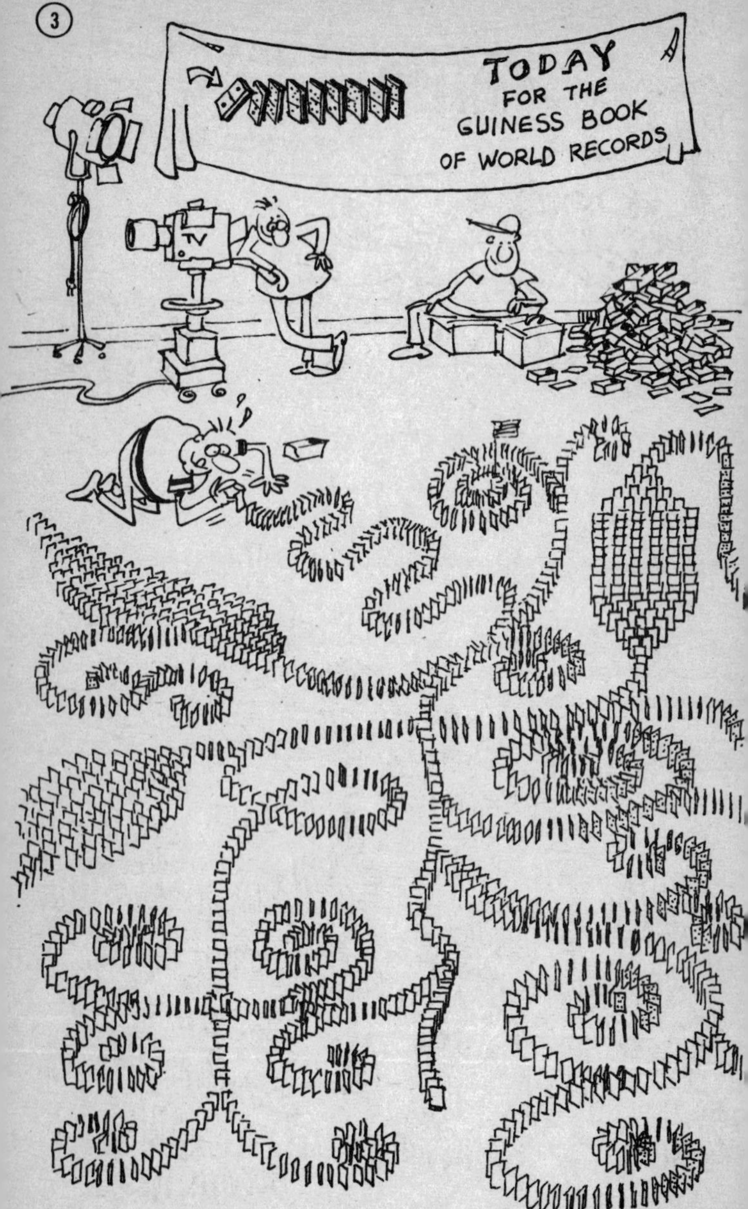
3
TODAY
FOR THE
GUINESS BOOK
OF WORLD RECORDS
TV

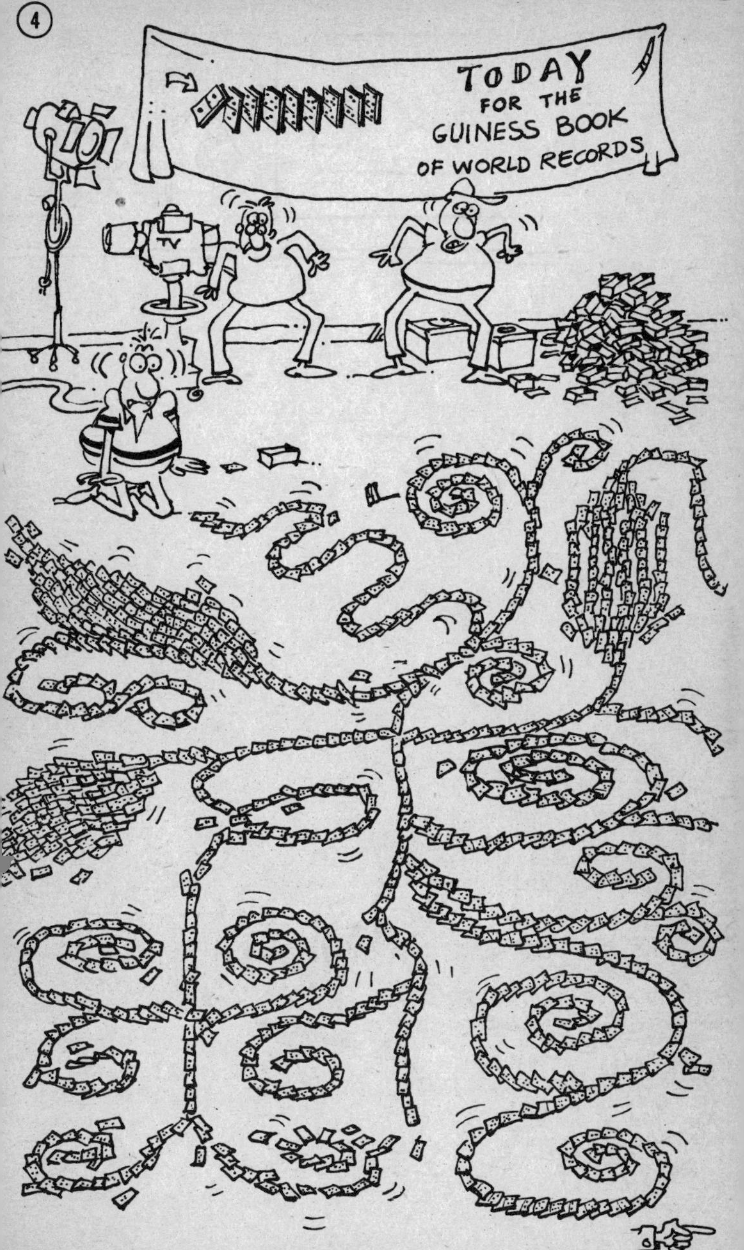
④
TODAY
FOR THE
GUINESS BOOK
OF WORLD RECORDS
TV

5

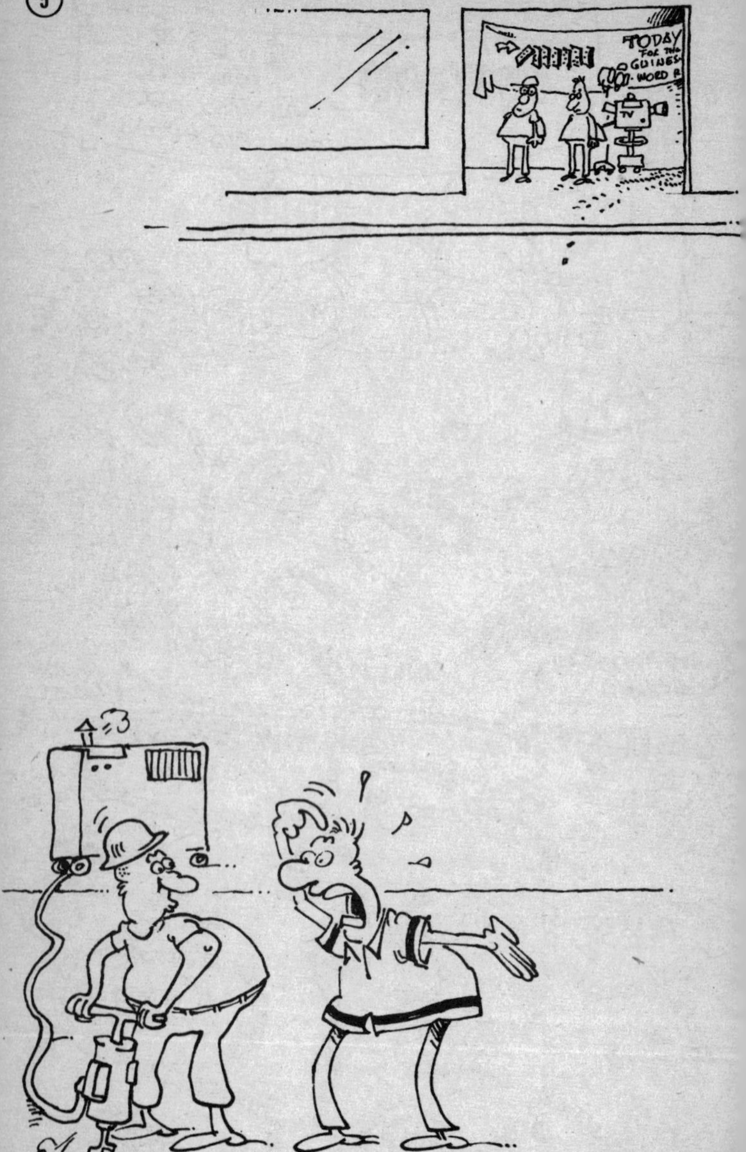

TODAY

①

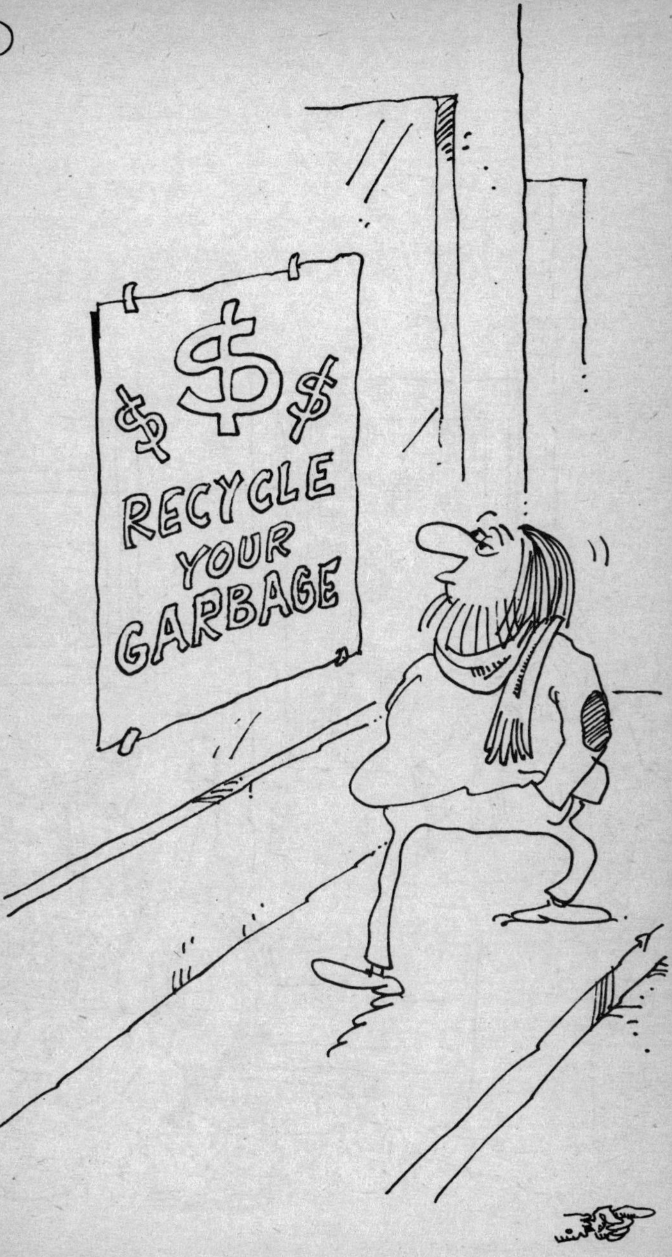
$ $ $
RECYCLE
YOUR
GARBAGE

(2)

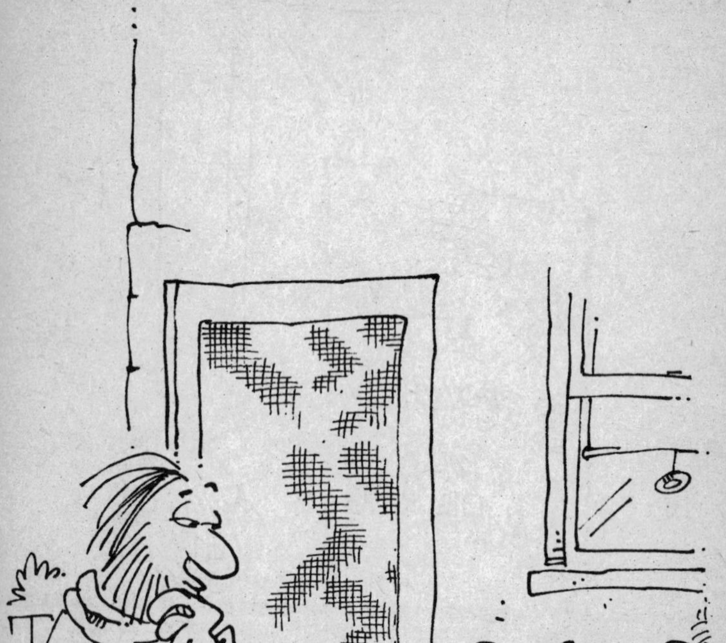
GROO

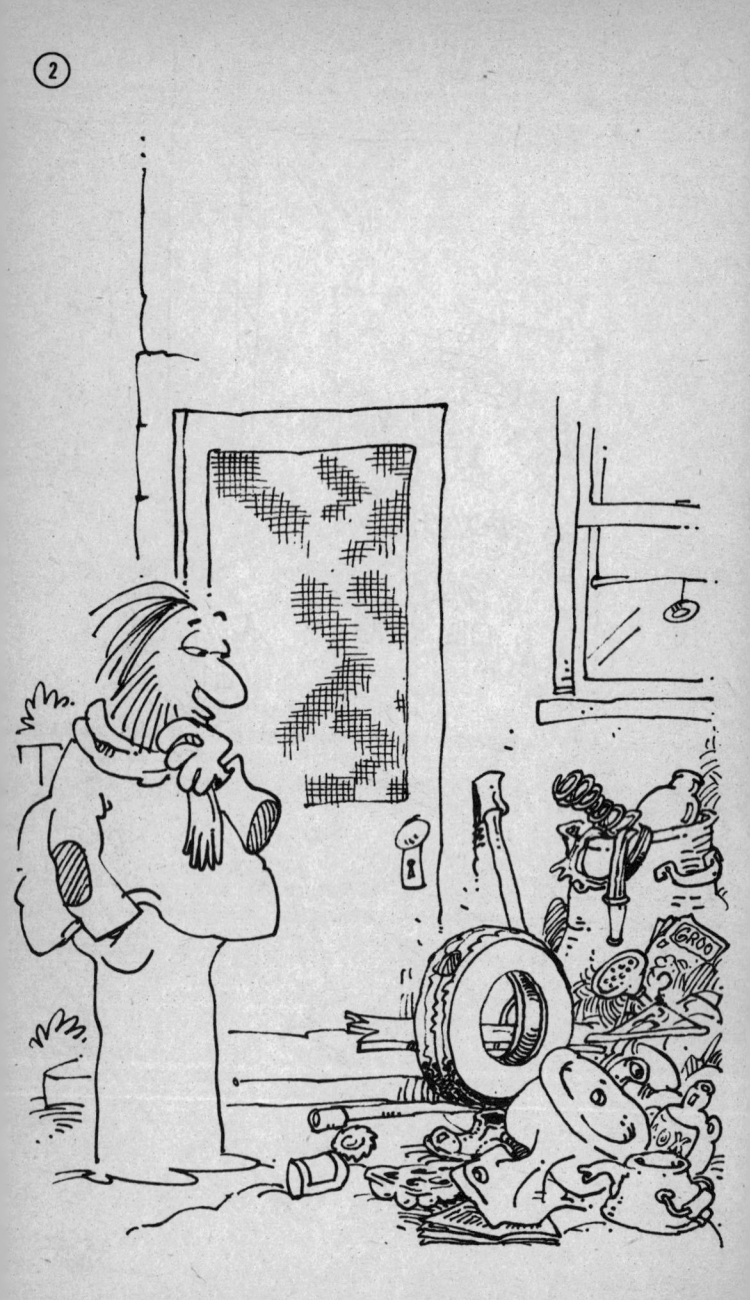

3

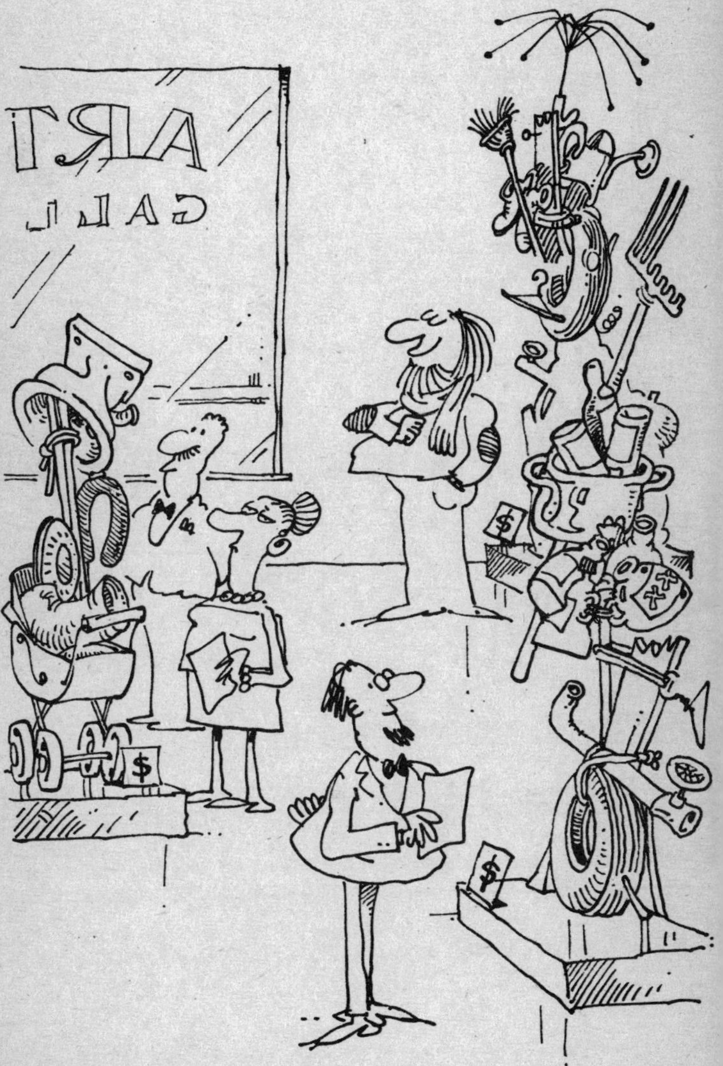
ART
GALL

(1)

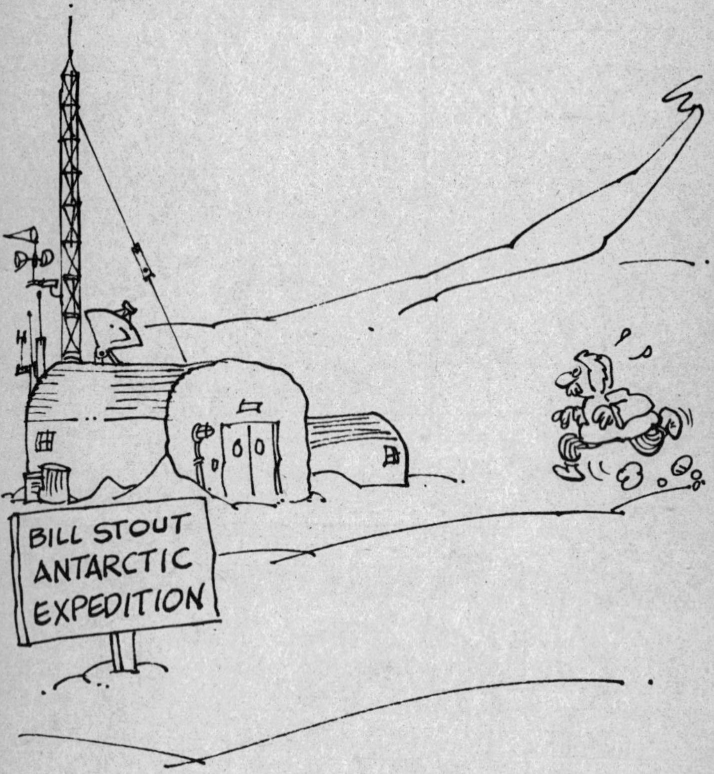
BILL STOUT
ANTARCTIC
EXPEDITION

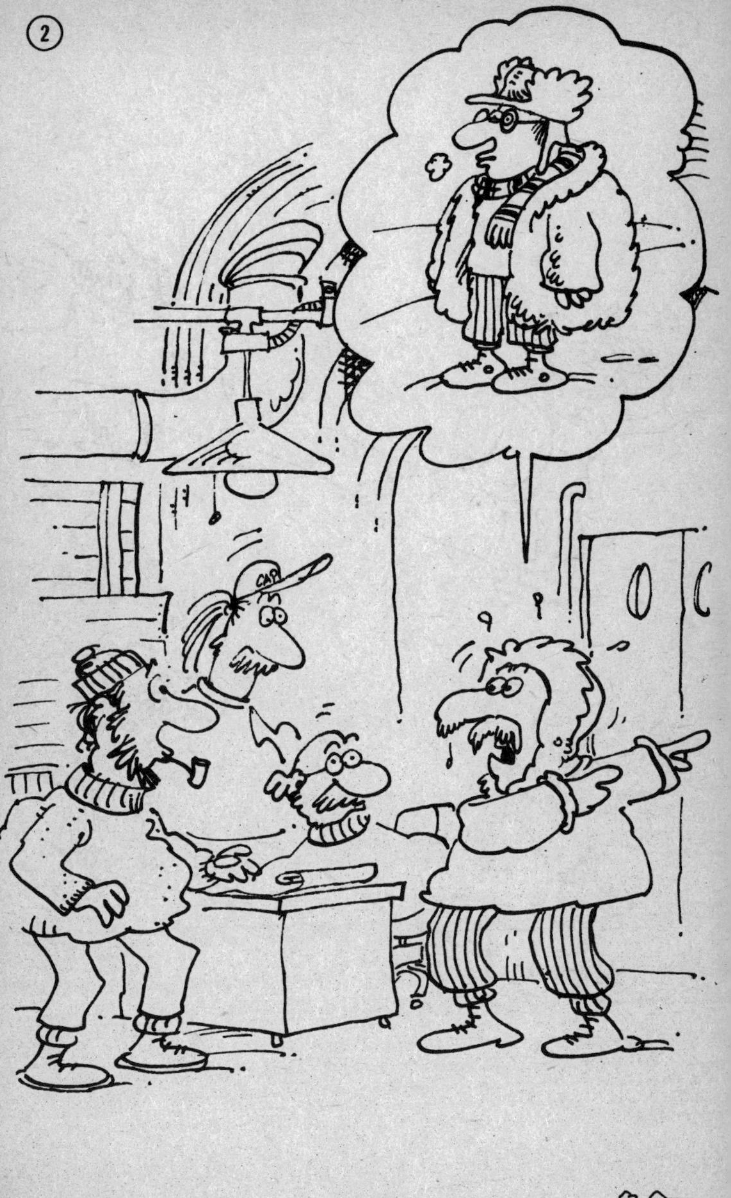
2
CAP

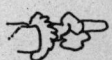

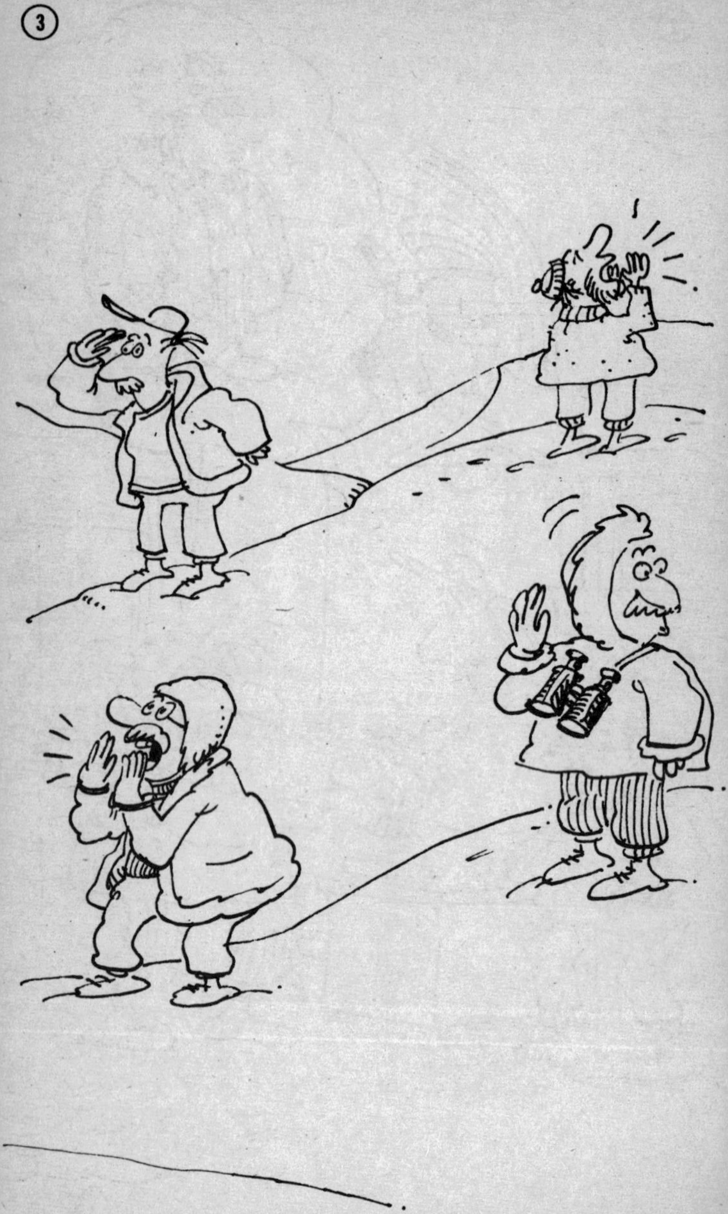
3

4

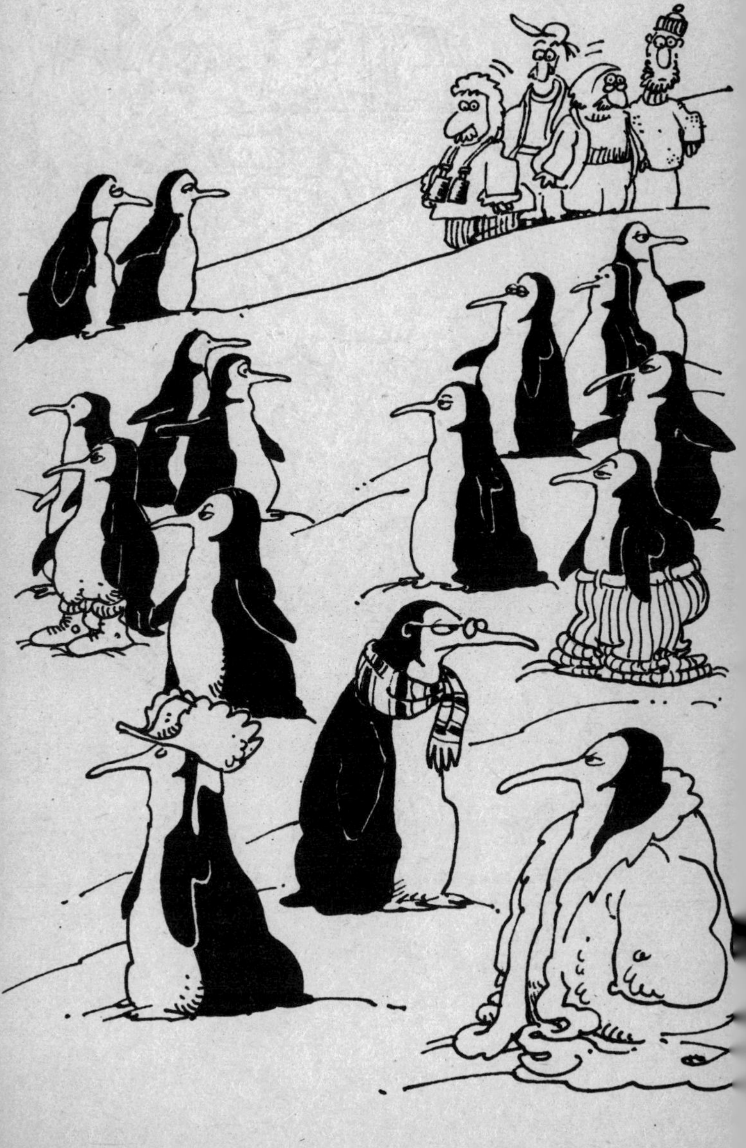

②

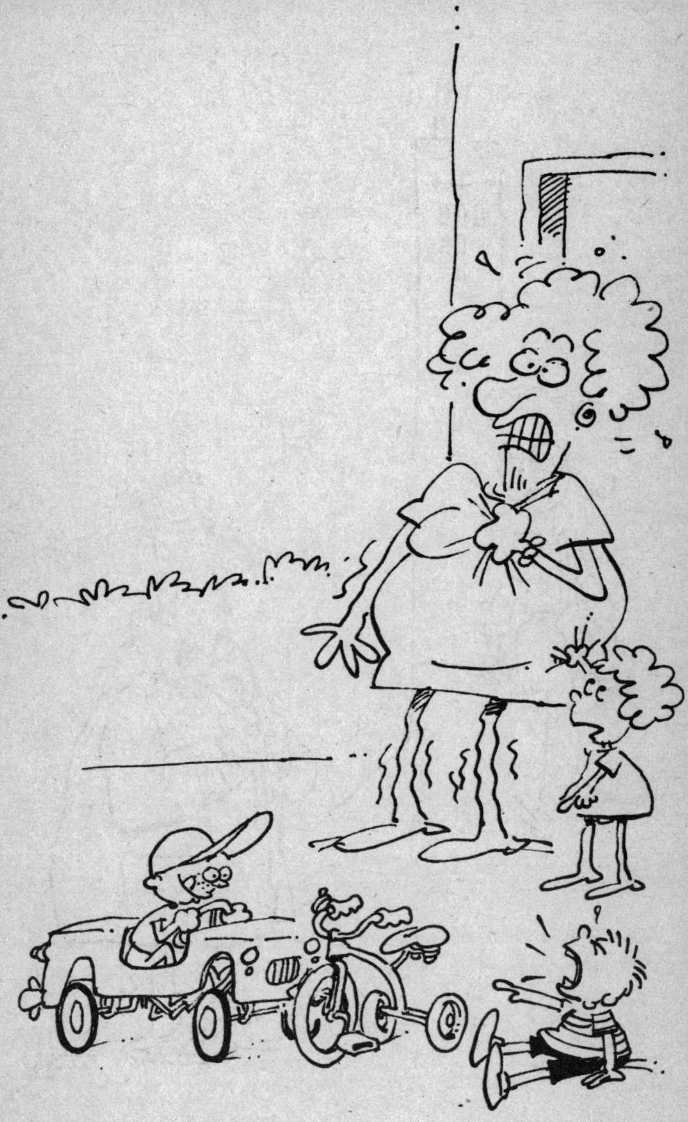

(1)

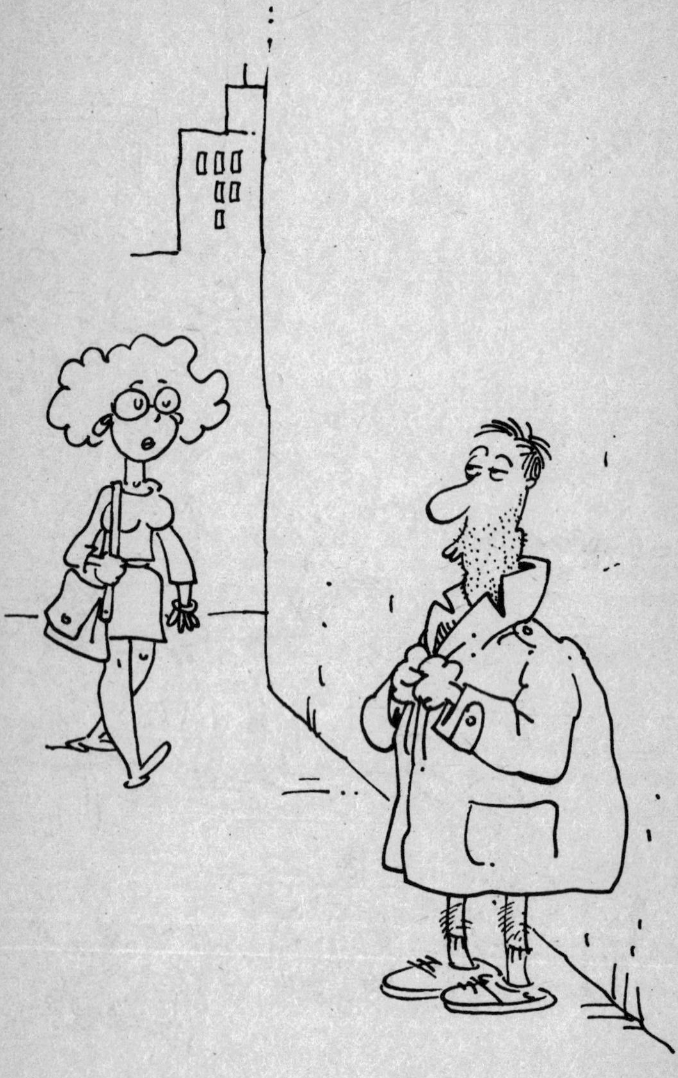

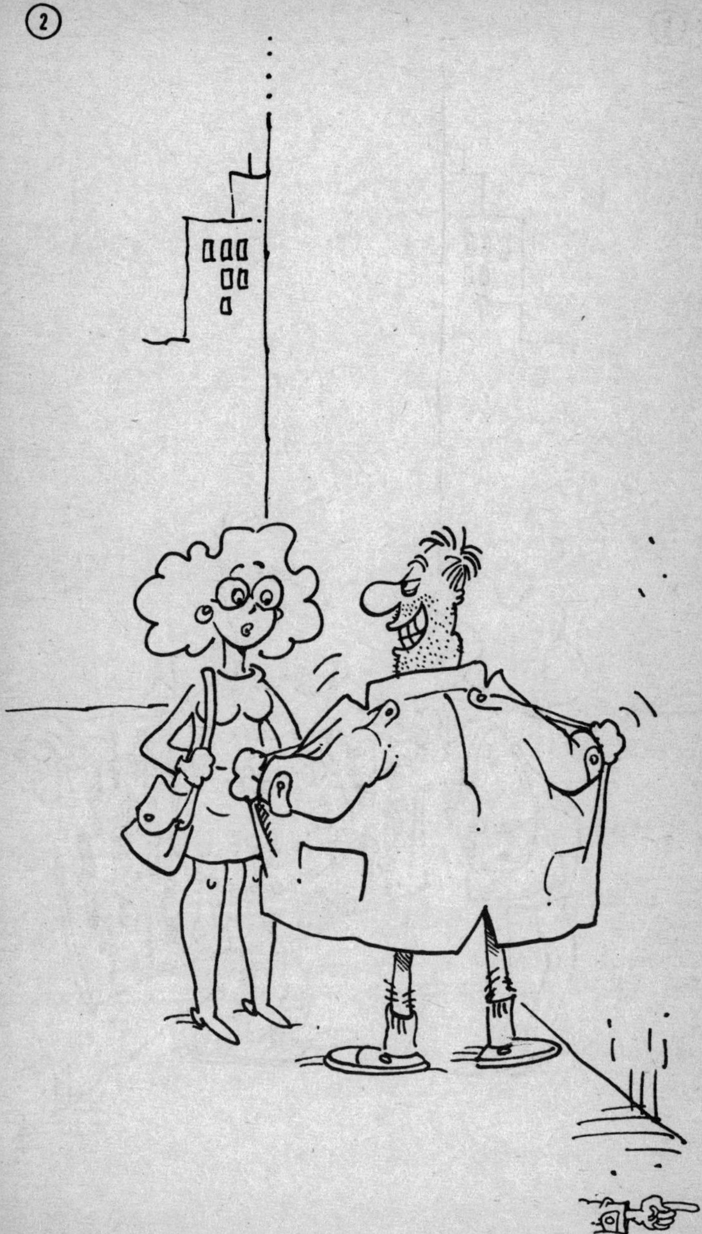

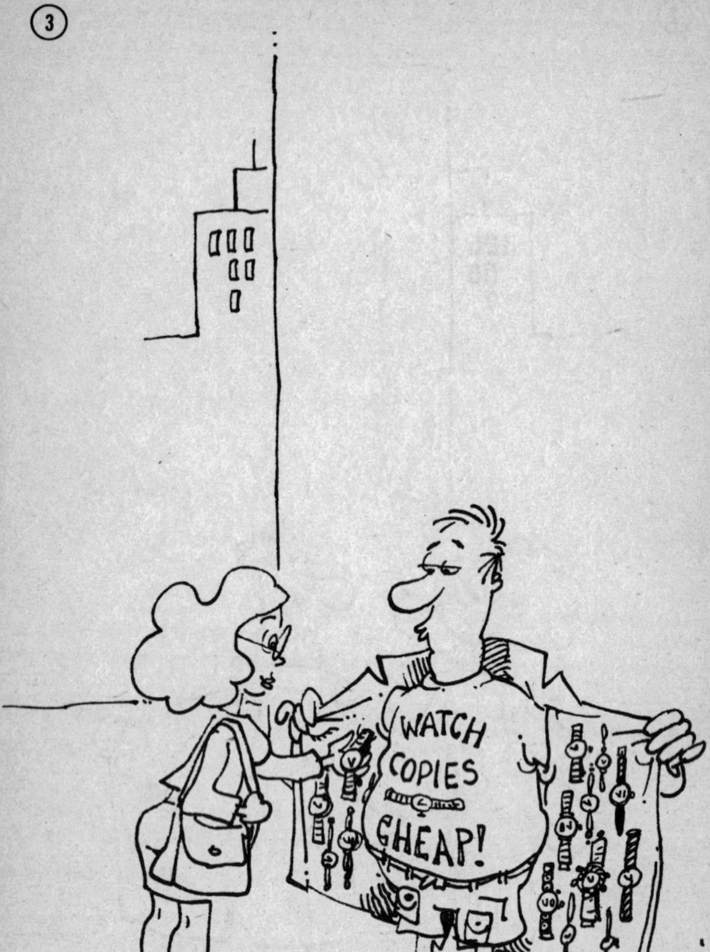
WATCH
COPIES
CHEAP!

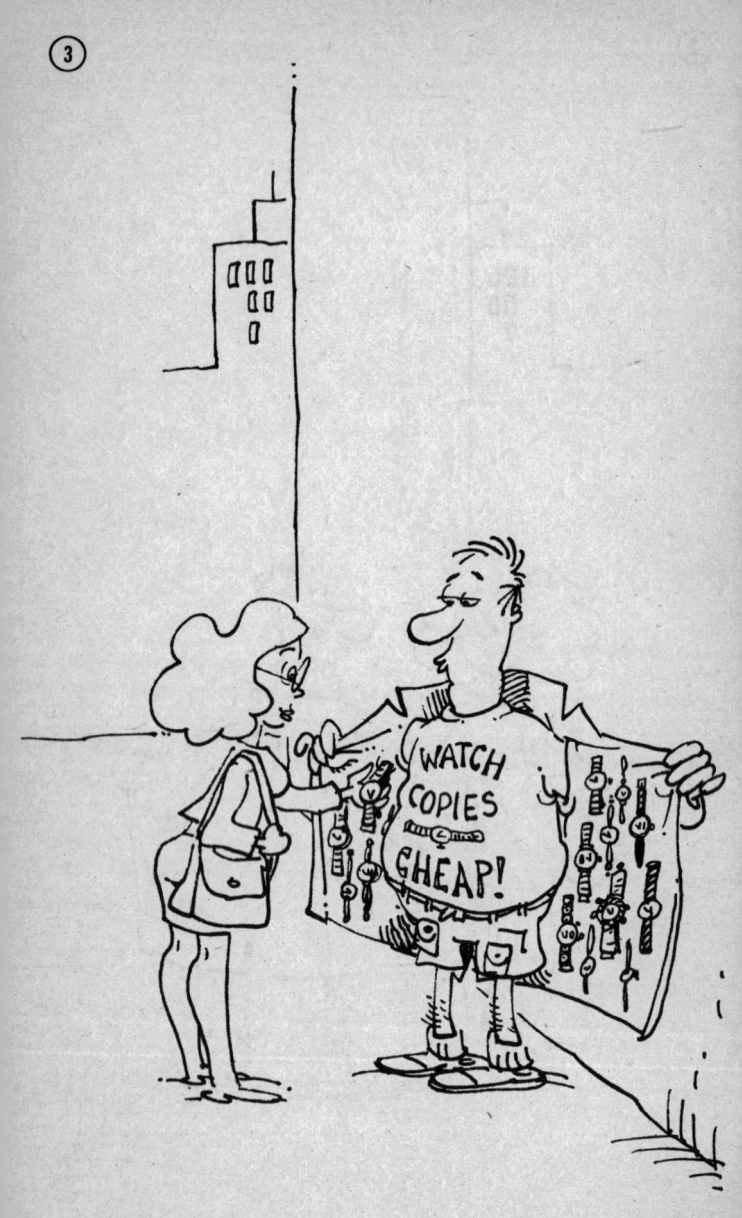

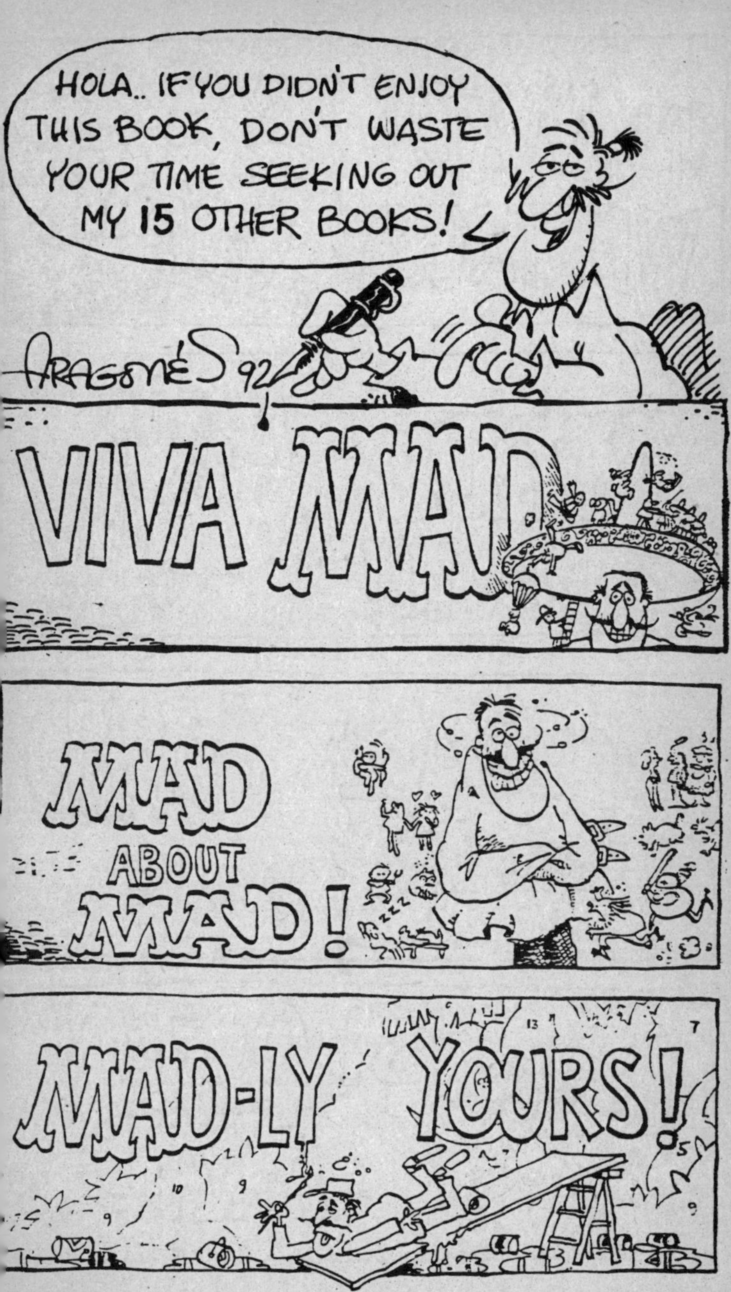

HOLA.. IF YOU DIDN'T ENJOY THIS BOOK, DON'T WASTE YOUR TIME SEEKING OUT MY 15 OTHER BOOKS!
ARAGONÉS '92
VIVA MAD
MAD ABOUT MAD!
MAD-LY YOURS!

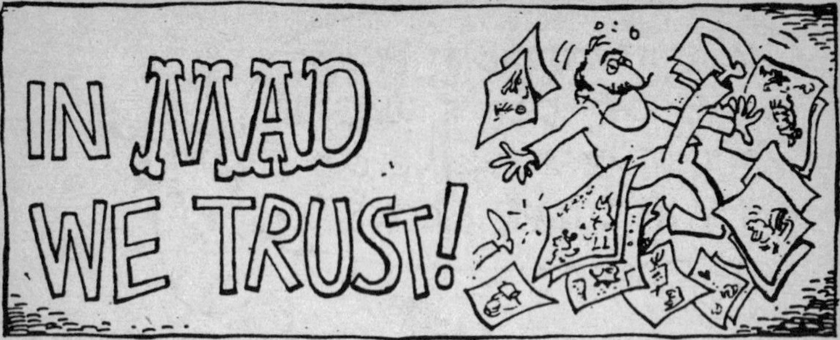
IN MAD WE TRUST!

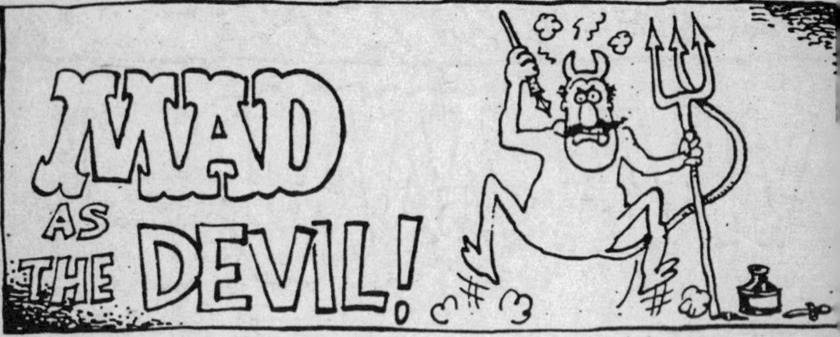
MAD AS THE DEVIL!

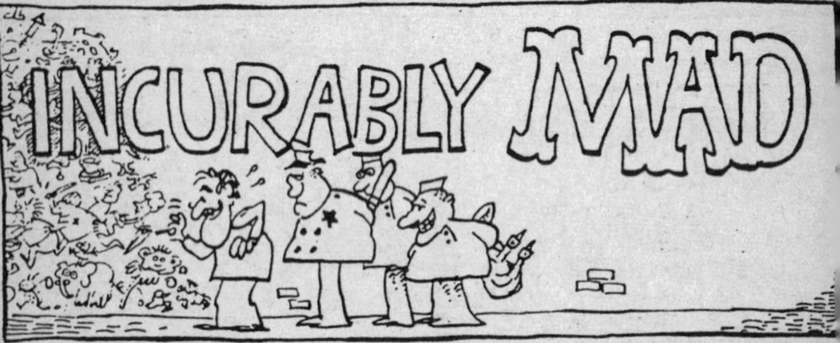
INCURABLY MAD

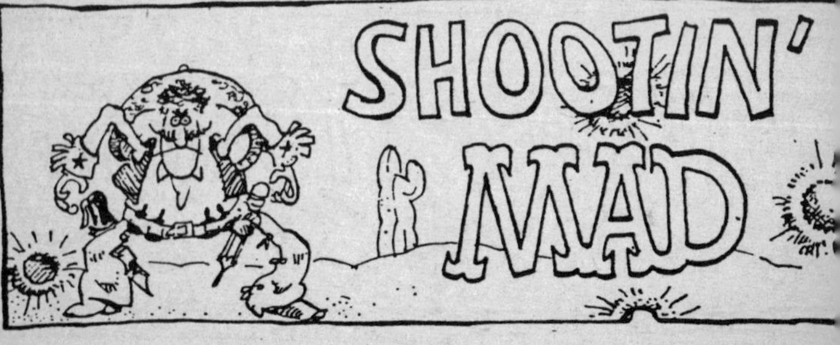
SHOOTIN' MAD

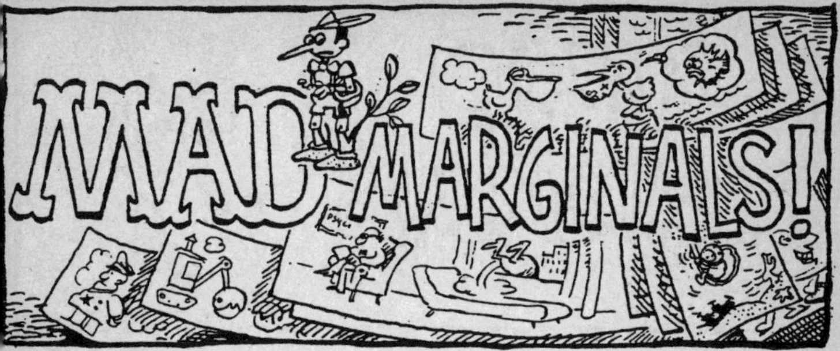
MAD MARGINALS!

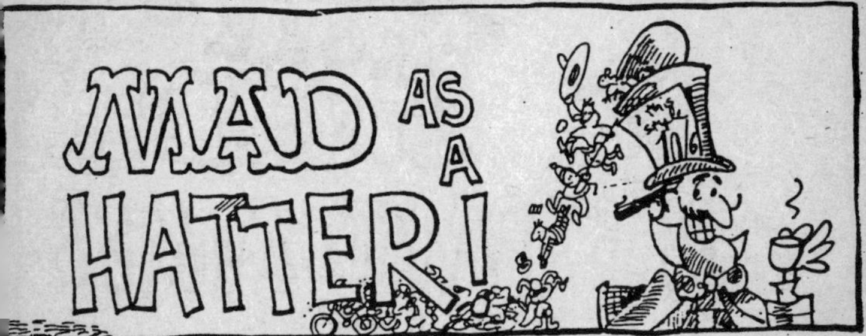
MAD AS A HATTER!

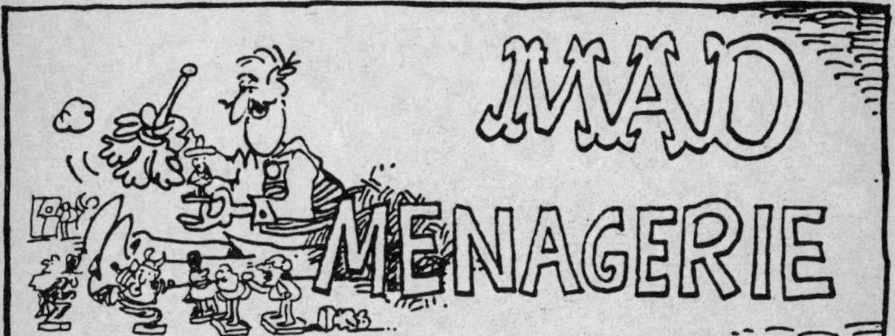
MAD MENAGERIE

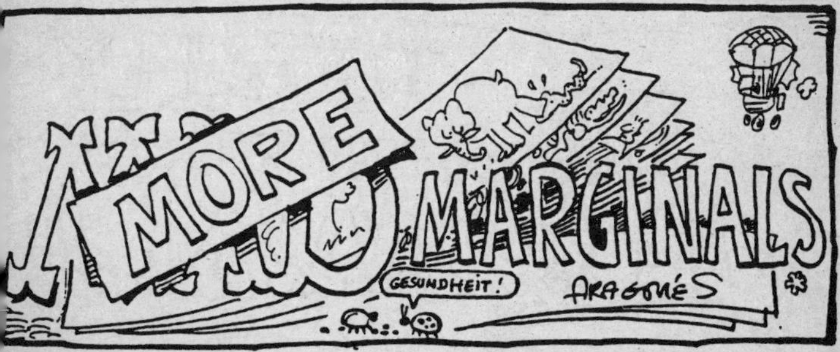
MORE MAD MARGINALS
GESUNDHEIT!
ARAGONÉS

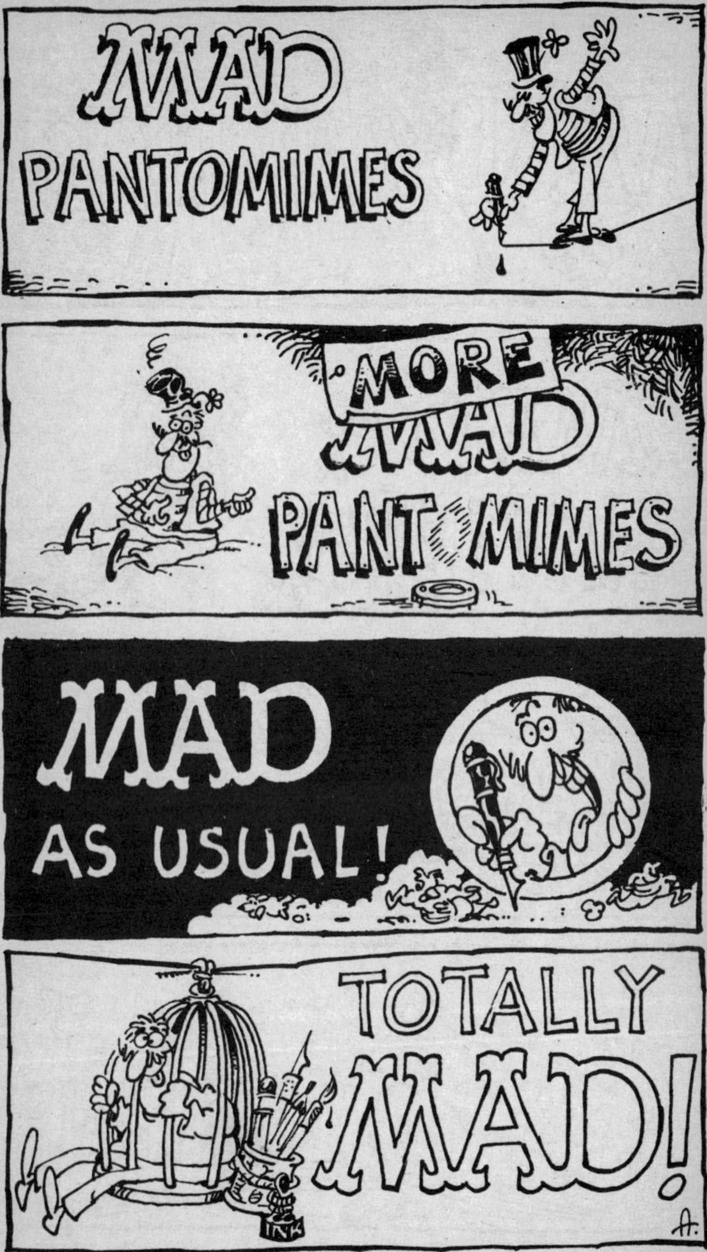
MAD PANTOMIMES
MORE MAD PANTOMIMES
MAD AS USUAL!
TOTALLY MAD!
INK